Frommer's®

8/08

P9-DIZ-211

Provence & the Riviera

day BY **day**™

1st Edition

by Anna Brooke

WILEY

Wiley Publishing, Inc.

Contents

Published by:

Wiley Publishing, Inc.

111 River St.
Hoboken, NJ 07030-5774

ISBN: 978-0-470-14604-0
Editor: Maureen Clarke
Production Editor: Katie Robinson
Photo Editor: Richard Fox
Cartographer: Guy Ruggiero
Production by Wiley Indianapolis Composition Services

For information on our other products and services or to obtain technical
support, please contact our Customer Care Department within the U.S.
at 800/762-2974, outside the U.S. at 317/572-3993 or fax 317/572-4002.

Wiley also publishes its books in a variety of electronic formats. Some
content that appears in print may not be available in electronic formats.

Manufactured in China

5   4   3   2   1

A Note from the Publisher

Organizing your time. That's what this guide is all about.

Other guides give you long lists of things to see and do and then expect you to fit the pieces together. The Day by Day guides are different. These guides tell you the best of everything, and then they show you how to see it *in the smartest, most time-efficient way*. Our authors have designed detailed itineraries organized by time, neighborhood, or special interest. And each tour comes with a bulleted map that takes you from stop to stop.

Hoping for a fresh picnic lunch amid lavender fields or a meander through a medieval perched village with staggering views of the Provençal landscape? How about swimming along the Côte d'Azur, and then drying off in the sun, in a cove between the white cliffs of the Calanques? Or rolling the dice, elbow to elbow with billionaires, in the Monte Carlo casino? Whatever your interests or schedule, the Day by Days give you the smartest routes to follow. We take you to the top attractions, hotels, and restaurants. We help you access those special moments that locals get to experience—those "finds" that turn tourists into travelers.

The Day by Days are your top choice if you're looking for one complete guide for all your travel needs. The best hotels and restaurants for every budget, the greatest shopping values, the wildest nightlife—it's all here.

Why should you trust our judgment? Because our authors personally visit each place they write about. They're an independent lot who say what they think and would never include places they wouldn't recommend to their friends. They're also open to suggestions from readers. If you'd like to contact them, please send your comments my way at mspring@wiley.com, and I'll pass them on.

Enjoy your Day by Day guide—the most helpful travel companion you can buy. And have the trip of a lifetime.

Warm regards,

Michael Spring
Publisher
Frommer's Travel Guides

About the Author

British-born **Anna Brooke** began her love affair with France on a camping trip to Brittany at age 13. After gaining an honors degree in French and European studies, she moved to Paris in 2000 and has spent the last 7 years becoming a full-fledged bohemian, juggling life between freelance travel writing (*MTV France, Time Out Paris,* Alastair Sawdays, and Dorling & Kindersley), TV presenting and voiceovers (Discovery Channel and Trivop TV), and acting (3 years singing in a cabaret, short movies, and ads). She is currently writing a one-woman show and dreaming of hosting her own travel program. Any offers kindly welcome; contact her at annaebrooke@yahoo.fr.

Acknowledgments

From the bottom of my heart I would like to thank Maureen Clarke for being such a wonderful editor; Anne Bracconi, Claire Serizay, and Andrea Stemler for their precious help in Provence; the regional PACA, Riviera and Monaco Tourist Offices for their priceless contributions; and Pascal Chind and my fabulous family for their love and support.

Dedication

In loving memory of Peggy and William Postans and Sally and Arthur Brooke.

An Additional Note

Please be advised that travel information is subject to change at any time—and this is especially true of prices. We therefore suggest that you write or call ahead for confirmation when making your travel plans. The authors, editors, and publisher cannot be held responsible for the experiences of readers while traveling. Your safety is important to us, however, so we encourage you to stay alert and be aware of your surroundings.

Star Ratings, Icons & Abbreviations

Every hotel, restaurant, and attraction listing in this guide has been ranked for quality, value, service, amenities, and special features using a **star-rating system.** Hotels, restaurants, attractions, shopping, and nightlife are rated on a scale of zero stars (recommended) to three stars (exceptional). In addition to the star-rating system, we also use a **kids** icon to point out the best bets for families. Within each tour, we recommend cafes, bars, or restaurants where you can take a break. Each of these stops appears in a shaded box marked with a coffee-cup-shaped bullet ☕.

The following **abbreviations** are used for credit cards:

AE	American Express	DISC	Discover	V	Visa
DC	Diners Club	MC	MasterCard		

Frommers.com

Now that you have this guidebook to help you plan a great trip, visit our website at **www.frommers.com** for additional travel information on more than
3,600 destinations. We update features regularly to give you instant access
to the most current trip-planning information available. At Frommers.com,
you'll find scoops on the best airfares, lodging rates, and car rental bargains.
You can even book your travel online through our reliable travel booking
partners. Other popular features include:

A Note on Prices

In the "Take a Break" and "Best Bets" sections of this book, we have used a
system of dollar signs to show a range of costs for 1 night in a hotel (the
price of a double-occupancy room) or the cost of an entree at a restaurant.
Use the following table to decipher the dollar signs:

Cost	Hotels	Restaurants
$	under $100	under $10
$$	$100–$200	$10–$20
$$$	$200–$300	$20–$30
$$$$	$300–$400	$30–$40
$$$$$	over $400	over $40

An Invitation to the Reader

In researching this book, we discovered many wonderful places—hotels,
restaurants, shops, and more. We're sure you'll find others. Please tell us
about them, so we can share the information with your fellow travelers in
upcoming editions. If you were disappointed with a recommendation, we'd
love to know that, too. Please write to:

Frommer's Provence & the Riviera Day by Day, 1st Edition
Wiley Publishing, Inc. • 111 River St. • Hoboken, NJ 07030-5774

20 Favorite
Moments

20 Favorite **Moments**

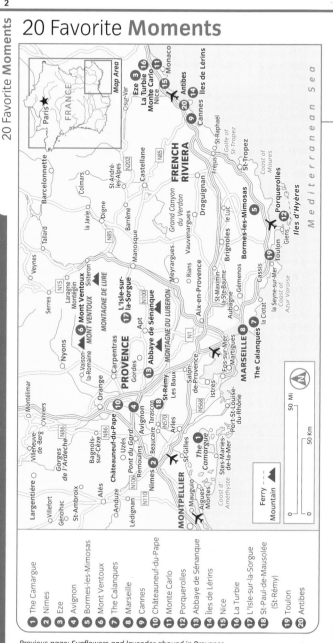

Previous page: Sunflowers and lavender abound in Provence.

From Provence's plush fields of lavender, Roman ruins, sun-drenched olive groves, sloping vineyards, and medieval villages; to the glamorous resorts, glitterati-clad beaches, gastronomic restaurants, and clear seas of the Côte d'Azur, this region has inspired generations of artists and continues to compel visitors from all over the world today. Here are 20 of my own favorite experiences in the South of France.

1 Riding the white horses of the Camargue like a cowboy. The desolate marshy flatlands of the Rhône Delta are home to pink flamingos, bulls, and white horses ridden by salty French cowboys called *gardians.* Saddle up at Le Sambuc, where you'll discover a world of rare birds, salt lagoons, and sweeping panoramas unreachable by car. See p 79.

2 Visiting the Roman Arena in Nimes, a marvel of ancient civil engineering. Even if you've seen Roman Arles, you'll be bowled over by the grand fortitude of Nimes' 1st century amphitheater, built to stage bloodthirsty gladiatorial battles and chariot racing. *See p 175.*

3 Indulging in a gastronomic meal at a Provençal *table d'hôte.* When you're dining at Michelin-starred Château Eza, in the chocolate-box village of Eze, perched 429m (467 yds.) above the Mediterranean, life doesn't get much better. *See p 35.*

4 Ambling through the animated streets of Avignon at night. Pretty by day but even more striking by night, the former papal city comes into its own on a summer evening. Well-off cafe patrons flood the

French cowboys (gardians) of the seaside Camargue region.

La Route du Mimosas.

streets, and the air rings with lively conversation, lending even medieval alleyways a contemporary sophistication. *See p 12.*

⑤ Discovering your favorite perched village. My vote goes to Bormes-les-Mimosas, with its cobbled streets lined with fragrant mimosa bushes. Come between January and March, when the whole town is awash with yellow flowers, and sweet scent fills the air. *See p 63.*

⑥ Posing for a photograph at the summit of Mont Ventoux. Whether you attempt the steep 5-hour hike, struggle up on a bike, or (sensibly) drive 1,912m (2,084 yds.) to the top, the nor'easter that gusts over this dazzling white limestone cap will give you the ultimate windswept look. *See p 76.*

⑦ Bathing in the Calanques. Explore the hidden splendor of creeks and beaches snuggled between the jagged, white cliffs between Marseille and Cassis. En-*Vau*, the prettiest Calanque, is known for its sandy beach and needle-like rock formations. *See p 153.*

⑧ Eating bouillabaisse in Marseille's Miramar. As the light shimmers off the old port, grab a table on Miramar's sunny terrace, order a crisp white wine, and wait for the bouillabaisse to arrive. This rich, ancient traditional recipe—made from many kinds of impeccably fresh fish, saffron, and orange zest—is reason alone to visit Marseille. *See p 156.*

Abbaye de Sénanque in summer, engulfed by lavender.

Nice's pre-Lenten carnival.

9 Star-spotting at the Martinez in Cannes. Come here during the film festival and you'll be hobnobbing with showbiz biggies and the Botoxed set. A reservation in the room next door to Leo DiCaprio can't be guaranteed, but if you're lucky enough to get in, a memorable night is surefire. *See p 142.*

10 Tasting Châteauneuf-du-Pape wine. In the green vineyard-studded hills around Châteauneuf-du-Pape grow France's most famous product. When you're driving around the Vaucluse, don't hesitate to pop into one of the many châteaux whose Côte du Rhône wines are among the best in the country. *See p. 84.*

11 Raising the stakes at the casino in Monte Carlo. You may not even mind *losing* money at this beautiful palace on the Riviera. Play blackjack in the opulent Salons Privés, roulette in the Belle Epoque Salons Européens, or sip champagne beneath the risqué frescos on the ceiling of the Rose Bar. *See p 161.*

12 Eating a picnic lunch on Porquerolles, the most paradisiacal of the Hyères islands, is a must for nature lovers, who will adore the expanses of pine forests, olive groves, vineyards, and glorious beaches. *See p 57 and 67.*

13 Visiting the Abbaye de Sénanque in bloom is possibly the most clichéd summer activity in Provence. But that doesn't make the seas of lavender surrounding the 12th-century Cistercian monastery any less breathtaking, especially when approached from Gordes. *See p 88.*

14 Sunbathing on the St-Honorat Beaches. When bawdy mobs and jet-set frivolities get to be too much, take a boat from Cannes to the Îles de Lérins, a scenic islet owned by Cistercian monks whose peaceful outcrops and beaches are a perfect antidote to crowd fever. *See p 68.*

15 Attending Nice's annual carnival—the most colorful festival in the South of France. What began in the Middle Ages as a masked pre-Lenten street party has turned into an explosive weeklong extravaganza with giant puppets, over-sized head-masks, flowers, and bright costumes. After the parades, heavy partying ensues (late Feb–Mar). *See p 167.*

16 Basking in the glory of Rome in the bougainvillea-scented village of La Turbie, the gigantic *trophée des Alpes* was erected to celebrate Emperor Augustus's victory against the Ligurians in 13 B.C. It used to mark the frontier between Italy and Gaul, and it still affords triumphant views over Cap Ferrat and Eze. *See p 104.*

17 Sifting through antiques in L'Isle-sur-la-Sorgue. Whether you covet an original Louis XIV chair, or seek a 1920s reproduction of an 18th-century bed, or just fancy perusing other people's junk in search of hidden treasure, pretty L'Isle-sur-la-Sorgue, with its crystalline river and old waterwheels, is a paradise for antique lovers of every stripe. *See p 87.*

18 Experiencing the haunting tranquility of the St-Paul-de-Mausolée monastery, where Vincent van Gogh committed himself, after lopping off his ear in Arles. The

Local olives for sale at Antibe's covered market.

tormented artist whiled away many an hour, silently painting the medieval cloisters and monastery gardens. A series of illustrated panels show his works on the sites where he painted them. For fans, it is a moving experience. *See p 182.*

19 Marveling at France's military prowess in Toulon. Whether you're a Navy aficionado or not, the incongruous sight of anti-submarine and anti-missile frigates, minesweepers, and the occasional nuclear submarine docked in the town center will not fail to impress. *See p 91.*

20 Filling up at Antibes' Provençal market. Colorful, bustling, and bursting at the seams with delicious produce, charcuterie, and cheeses, Antibes' covered market makes a plum spot to stock a picnic basket. *See p 101.* ●

Antiques shopping in L'Isle-sur-la-Sorgue.

1 Strategies for Seeing the Region

Strategies for Seeing the Region

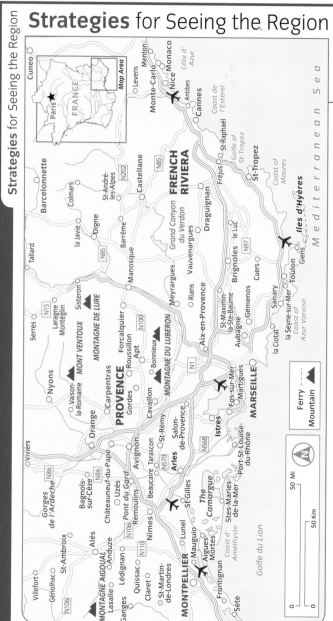

Previous page: Lavender field in summer.

Provence and the Riviera are regions to experience rather than "see"; life moves more slowly in the south of France, and hasty sightseeing cuts against the grain of daily life. With so many compelling small towns, villages, and rural landscapes, you'll be tempted to visit them all, but if you rush you'll miss the essence of the place. Here are strategies to help you enrich your time and travels.

Rule #1: Allow for down time

Don't cram your days full of activities. Build in plenty of time to unwind; to stop and smell the lavender; to eat long, hearty lunches; to slowly savor the wine and admire the views. These humble experiences could well become the pinnacle of your trip if you don't sully them by rushing. To make the most of your time, decide what you want to do most that day, then plan your other activities in the same area.

Rule #2: Take distances into account

Provence and the Riviera are as easy to traverse as a small U.S. state. Under normal conditions, you can drive between many of the region's most popular stops in less than an hour. In traffic, however, it's another story. Certain destinations—particularly those away from the *autoroute* (highway)—can take much longer to reach during peak periods. If you're visiting popular spots in summer, around school vacations, or on public holidays, tack at least 30 minutes onto estimated drive times (even longer on the Côte d'Azur). As a general rule, roads are well maintained and sign-posted, but carry a detailed road map. See p 201 for crucial driving tips in France.

Rule #3: Time your visit right

If it's your life-long dream to see lavender fields, don't visit in spring; lavender blooms in July and August. Skip summer, however, if you want to experience the region at its most authentic—minus hoards of tourists. Opt for March and April or September and October instead, when the weather is warm, but tourists are back at work. February can also be lovely on the Riviera, when Menton's Lemon festival, Bormes-les-Mimosas's mimosa festival, and Nice's carnival brighten the streets. Work out in advance what you want to see and do, then choose the season accordingly. See p 196 for a calendar of events.

A quayside coffee break in Marseille.

Rule #4: Decide whether to hotel-hop or stay in one place

Some of the region's most popular stops are near one another. By choosing a base for several days and exploring the surrounding area on day trips, you'll save time checking in and out of rooms, packing and unpacking. Avignon, St-Rémy, Les Baux, Nîmes, and Arles are so close you'd do best to bed down in just one town, reserving your energy for hotel changes on the longer hauls. On the Côte d'Azur, Nice is a fine station from which to explore Monaco, Menton, and the coastal villages around Cagnes, St-Paul-de-Vence, and Biot.

Rule #5: Plan trips around lunch

If you're driving from town to town, it's best to arrive before lunch. Most restaurants serve from noon to 2 or 2:30pm sharp, and many shops close at noon for the midday meal. If you don't want to follow such a strict schedule, pack your own food and follow your heart's desire to a picnic spot under the Provençal sun.

Rule #6: Plot your point of entry and means of transport there

Provence has small airports in Marseille, Nîmes, and Nice, but none receive flights from the U.S. or Canada. If you must fly to the region, you will inevitably take off from Paris at either the Charles de Gaulle or Orly airports. Planes are a time-effective means of transport for Nice and the Riviera: Nice's airport is practically in the town center and receives daily flights from Paris and other European cities. The quickest and most cost-effective way to access Provence from Paris, however, is on France's legendary high-speed TGV trains. Avignon takes just 2 hours, Aix-en-Provence 2½, and Marseille a little under 3. You can rent cars at all the region's airports and train stations (see p 201 for a list of agencies). If you drive from Paris, the main *autoroutes* into the region are the A6, A7, and A8. From Paris, you should allow at least 6 hours to reach Avignon, 8 for Marseille, and up to 10 for Nice. ●

A cyclist near the village of Suzette.

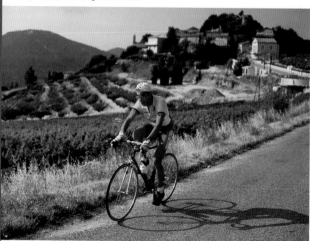

Provence in **Three Days**

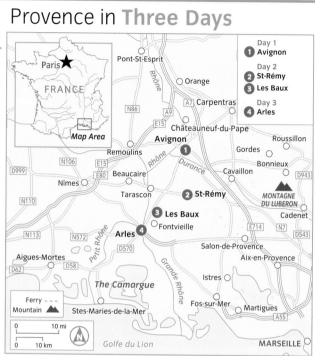

Day 1
1 Avignon

Day 2
2 St-Rémy
3 Les Baux

Day 3
4 Arles

From the seaside salt flats of the Camargue to the *village perches* spilling down the rocky plateaux of the Lubéron, Provence's landscapes are so varied you don't have to travel far for a dramatic change of scenery and atmosphere. The region's varied yet compact scale is a blessing if you have just 3 days to explore it. This tour covers four requisite stops: Avignon, Provence's elegant cultural capital; the chocolate-box town of St-Remy and the nearby cloisters where Vincent van Gogh convalesced during his final years; the gravity-defying Les Baux; and Arles, with its Roman vestiges, bull-fights, and other strong Provençal traditions with a Spanish twist.
START: **Avignon. Trip length 41km/25.5 miles (82km/51-mile loop).**

Travel Tip

For hotels, restaurants, and detailed information on sights in these towns, see chapter 6: Avignon p 128; St-Rémy p 180; Arles p 122.

1 **Avignon.** Contained within medieval ramparts, Avignon is easy to explore on foot. Most sites surround the **Place de l'Horloge,** named after the 15th-century clock that dominates the square. From

Previous page: The port of Cassis.

there, it's easy to reach the fortress-like **Palais des Papes (pope's palace).** This Gothic castle was built as the headquarters of Christendom when the papacy fled to Avignon—officially from 1309 until 1376, followed by the reign of two antipopes that lasted until 1417. Equally emblematic is Avignon's half-fallen 12th-century **Pont St-Bénézet** (Pont d'Avignon), just outside the city walls. Art enthusiasts should flock to the nearby 12th-century **Musée du Petit Palais,** with its fine medieval paintings and Roman and Gothic sculpture; the **Musée Calvet** (a beautifully restored fine arts museum); or to the **Musée Anglade,** with an eclectic collection of furniture and fauvist canvases. The **Musée Lapidaire** is an archaeological museum in a stunning 17th-century Jesuit church. And the **Collection Lambert** holds an extensive avant-garde and Conceptual art collection.

If culture is not your prime concern, consider some retail therapy on **rue des Teinturiers, rue de la République, rue des Marchands,** and **rue St-Agricol.** Or head for the glorious **Les Halles Centrales** covered market on Place Pie (no phone; Tue–Sun 6am–1:30pm).

The whole city becomes a stage in July, during the world-famous **Festival d'Avignon.** Unless you want to see theater, however, it's best to avoid the crowds at this time.

After a meal and a wondrous night of roaming through Avignon's floodlit streets and monuments, bed down and then head out early to St-Rémy. ⏱ *1 day. Avignon tourist board, 41 cours Jean Jaures. ☎ 04-32-74-32-74. www.ot-avignon.fr. For more on Avignon, see p 128 in chapter 6.*

From Avignon, take the N570 (ave de Tarascon), then continue on the D570n. Cross the Pont de Rognonas bridge and, at the next island, turn left onto the D571 to St-Rémy (via Châteaurenard and Eyragues). Distance: 21km (13 miles).

2 St-Rémy. Arrive in this affluent, quintessentially Provençal town as early as possible on your second day. The **Café des Arts,** 30 bd Victor-Hugo (no phone; 7:30am Mon–Sat, Sun 8am) serves excellent coffee and croissants. If you arrive early on Wednesday or Saturday, stroll around the buzzing street markets. In the morning, you can visit the 14th-century **Collégiale St-Martin** (collegiate church), walk past **Nostradamus's birthplace** on rue

Dining al fresco at night in Avignon.

Hoche, wander around the stunning 18th-century **Hôtel Estrine,** with its van Gogh–themed displays, marvel at the 16th-century galleried courtyard of the **Musée des Alpilles,** or opt for the fragrant displays at the **Musée des Arômes et des Parfums.**

After lunch, either continue exploring St-Rémy or detour to the nearby Gallo-Roman ruins at **Glanum** (just outside the town center on the D5) or the **St-Paul-de-Mausolée** monastery, where van Gogh convalesced and painted during the final year of his life (north of Glanum on the D5). In any case, head off to Les Baux by mid-afternoon. ⏱ ½ day. *St-Remy tourist board, pl Jean Jaurès.* ☎ *04-90-92-05-22. www.saintremy-de-provence.com. For more on St-Remy, see p 180 in chapter 6.*

From St-Rémy take the D5 for 6km (4 miles), then turn right onto the D27 to Les Baux. Distance: 10km (6 miles).

❸ **Les Baux.** After checking into your hotel in Les Baux (see box), wander through the center of this medieval engineering marvel, teetering on a steep, bare-bauxite ridge. Les Baux is small, so even if you arrive in the late afternoon, you'll have time to see the former **Hôtel de Ville** (city hall and 16th-century chapel), the 12th-century **Eglise**

St-Vincent (church), the former 16th-century **Temple Protestant,** the present city hall in the **Hôtel de Manville,** and **Place St-Vincent,** which affords panoramas over the Fontaine valley, the Alpilles, and the Val d'Enfer (Hell's Valley). If you can bear the crowds, don't miss sunset here.

The following morning, rise early and head for **rue du Trencat,** carved from bedrock. At the end of the street, visit the **Musée d'Histoire des Baux** (open 9am), which affords access to Les Baux's ruined citadel and shambled houses, a hauntingly beautiful sight. If you suffer from vertigo or feel shaky on your feet, beware of the steep steps that lead to the keep and dungeon. The views from here are magnificent, but go gingerly; the climb can be dangerous. Then head for Arles. ⏱ ½ day. *Les Baux tourist office, rue Porte Mage.* ☎ *04-90-54-34-39. www. lesbauxdeprovence.com. For detailed information on Les Baux, see p 35, chapter 3, and p 109, chapter 5.*

Tip

If you can't find lodgings in Les Baux, try Arles, only 20km (12 miles) away. On your second day, you could skip Glanum or the St-Paul-de-Mausolée monastery in the afternoon, and head straight to Les

The ruins of Les Baux.

Arles' annual feria.

Baux. You will have enough time to explore the whole village before driving to Arles for the night.

From Les Baux, take the D27 then the D78f. After 3km (2 miles), take the D17 (via Fontvieille). At the island, take the D570n to Arles. Distance: 10km (6 miles).

4 Arles. Either you arrived in Arles the night before or you're checking into your hotel. Either way, prepare for a jam-packed day. Before you visit Arles' Roman vestiges, the **Musée d'Arles Antique is** the best way to grasp how Arles would have looked in ancient times. From here, make sure you tour the 1st-century *arènes* (Roman arenas), once the site of bloody gladiatorial battles, and now the region's leading bullfight venue. Other requisite ancient stops include the **Thermes de Constantin** (Roman baths), the **Théâtre Antique** (Roman theater), **les Alycamps** (graveyard), and the two columns on **Place du Forum.** Whether you stay in the **Hôtel d'Arlantan** or not, pop into the lobby to see Roman ruins exposed under a glass floor.

Art fans must visit the **Espace van Gogh,** one of the former Provençal hospitals that sheltered the artist and became the subject of his paintings, the **Fondation van Gogh** tribute museum, and the **Musée Réattu.**

As you wander through the streets, make a detour to the lovely Romanesque **Eglise St-Trophime** (church) and cloisters, and the **Hôtel de Ville** (city hall).

Arlesians have a strong sense of identity—Provençal with a Catalan twist. The **Musée d'Arlatan** is a folklore museum devoted to Arles' costumes and traditions as well as the Provençal language.

During the Easter *feria*, revelers descend on Arles, often in traditional dress, restaurants stir up enormous pans of paella, bulls fight in the Roman arena, and a spirit of bacchanalia prevails. It's fun, but you won't leave with an accurate sense of Arles. ⏱ *1 day. Arles tourist office, esplanade Charles de Gaulle/bd Craponne.* ☎ *04-90-18-41-20. www.tourisme.ville-arles.fr. For detailed information on Arles, see p 122 in chapter 6.*

To return to Avignon after this whirlwind tour, take the D570n from Arles. After 32km (20 miles), cross the Pont de Rognonas bridge and continue on the N570 to Avignon.

Provence & the Riviera **One Week**

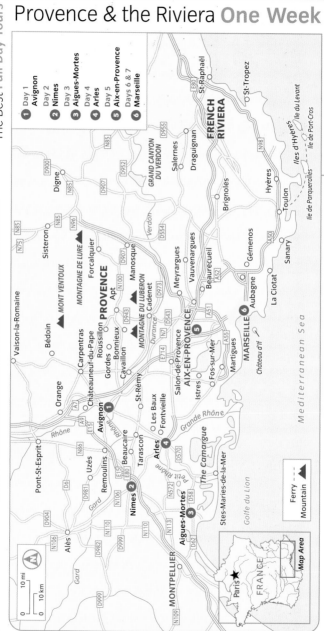

1. Day 1
   Avignon
2. Day 2
   Nîmes
3. Day 3
   Aigues-Mortes
4. Day 4
   Arles
5. Day 5
   Aix-en-Provence
6. Days 6 & 7
   Marseille

Ferry ---
Mountain ▲

With a full 7 days, you can dip down to the Mediterranean coast and still have time to explore the diverse inland regions of Provence. This trip begins in Avignon and takes you into the Roman heart of Nîmes, with its ancient amphitheater; Aigues-Mortes, ensconced by ramparts and salt marshes; Arles, known for its Roman vestiges and bullfights; chi-chi Aix-en-Provence, birthplace of Paul Cézanne and former capital of the region; and gritty, exotic Marseille, where you will spend 2 days exploring the city and surrounding coastal attractions, with a chance to wind down over a glass of wine and some fine seafood. For a more leisurely rhythm, you could take 10 days to cover this route. START: **Avignon. Trip length 253km/ 157 miles (350km/217-mile loop).**

Travel Tip

For hotels, restaurants, and detailed information on sights in these towns, see chapter 6: Avignon p 128; Nîmes p 174; Arles p 122; Aix-en-Provence p 114; Marseille p 144.

1 Avignon. At one time Avignon was the capital of both Provence and Christendom. Today it is one of France's most important cultural centers with a world-renowned theatre festival. It is also celebrated for its sumptuous town houses, medieval streets, and the centuries-old children's song (Sur le Pont d' Avignon), inspired by its tumble-down medieval bridge. Try to arrive

the night before, or in the early morning, to make the most of your day, before wining and dining in one of the city's great restaurants. After a night in a hotel, head for Nîmes first thing the following morning. ⏱ *1 day. For a 1-day itinerary, see bullet* **1**, *"Provence in Three Days," above. For detailed information on Avignon, see p 128 in chapter 6.*

Travel Tip

Unless your hotel has a private car park, it's nearly impossible to find space inside Avignon's ramparts. Park in one of the paid lots around the perimeter or ask your concierge where to park.

The 2,000 year-old Pont du Garde, near Nîmes.

Exit Avignon via la Porte de l'Oulle and join the N100. After 20km (12 miles) join the A9 and follow signs to Nimes, exiting the highway at junction 25. Distance: 50km (31 miles).

2 Nimes. Although it's technically outside Provence, in the Langue-doc region, Nimes is essentially Provençal. Feed your belly on food specialties such as *brandade de morue* (see below), almond biscuits called *croquants,* and marinated olives; and your mind on its numer-ous attractions. Check into a hotel, then prepare yourself for one busy day during which you can see high-lights like: the **Ampitheatre Roman**—a two-storied vestige more complete than the Colosseum in Rome; the miraculously con-served **Maison Carré** (Roman temple); the **Carré de l'Art,** a modern architectural take on the Maison Carré that houses the contemporary art museum; the stunning **Jardin de la Fontaine** gardens, lined with trees and more Roman and pre-Roman ruins; and the **Castellum,** a Roman water tower.

If you'd rather spend time in museums, head for: The **Musée des Beaux Arts,** which show-cases 17th- to 20th-century painting and sculpture; the **Musée des Cultures Taurines,** devoted to *tauromachy* (bull fighting); and the **Musée du Vieux Nimes,** which recounts the city's history. 🕐 *1 day. Nimes tourist office, 6 r Auguste.* ☎ *04-66-58-38-00. www.ot-nimes.fr. For detailed information on Nimes, see p 174 in chapter 6.*

Take a Break

☕ **Brandade Raymond.** Don't leave town without sampling *bran-dade de morue*—a cod and potato purée that is one of the region's best dishes when it's prepared correctly. The most authentic *brandade* comes from Raymond, where you can buy it in a tin to take home. *34 rue Nationale.* ☎ *04-66-67-20-47. $$.*

Leave Nimes early for Aigues-Mortes, and follow signs for the A9 toward Montpellier. Leave the A9 at junction 26 and follow

Aigues-Mortes.

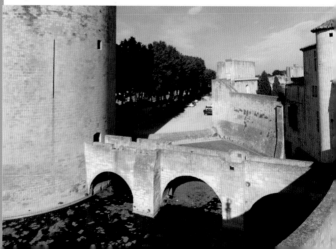

Culture Fix in Aix

As the region's former capital, Aix-en-Provence has a wealth of good museaums. The **Musée Granet** covers European painting from the 16th to the 20th centuries; **Musée du Vieil Aix** looks at *Aixois* traditions; the **Fondation Vasarely** sparks international interest with its avant-garde art and modern buildings; the **Musée d'Histoire Naturelle** is a fossil lovers' paradise; and the **Musée des Tapisseries** houses rare tapestries. If you're interested in Cézanne, you can visit his **atelier,** left as it was when he died. Finally, for an indulgent treat, you could opt for a pampering session in the **Thermes Sextius** spa, built on the site of Roman baths. See Aix-en-Provence, p 114.

signs to Aigues-Mortes (via N313, N113 and D979). Distance: 42km (26 miles).

③ Aigues-Mortes. This medieval, grid-patterned settlement is spellbinding in the way its ancient battlements and defense towers rise sharply from the melancholy, salty flatlands of the Camargue. Aigues-Mortes is tiny and easy to cover on foot. Much of its charm comes from narrow streets teeming with art galleries, cafes, and craft shops. Once you check into your hotel, however, you may want to take the good 2-hour tour run by the tourist office (Place St-Louis; ☎ 04-66-53-73-00). It will give you an overview of what to see and do.

As you wander around, look out for the beautiful baroque **Chapelle des Pénitents Blancs,** the 17th-century **Chapelle des Pénitents Gris,** and the **Eglise Notre-Dame-des-Sablons**—a Gothic church once used as a salt warehouse. The ramparts encircle the entire town, but they're accessible from Place Anatole France **(Porte de la Gardette).** You can enter

the **Tour de Constance**—a humongous, circular keep, once used as a prison. Also look out for the grisly **Tour des Bourguignons,** a 15th-century tower used to house the salted bodies of dead Bourguignon soldiers during the Hundred Years War.

If you have time in the afternoon, jump into the car and head 3km (2 miles) south (along the D979) to the **Salins du Midi,** a working salt farm that teaches visitors about local salt production. You could also opt for a relaxing **boat tour** along the La-Grau-du-Roi canal.
🕐 *1 day. Aigues Mortes tourist office, pl St Louis.* ☎ *04-66-53-73-00. www.ot-aiguesmortes.fr. For detailed information on Aigues-Mortes, see p 108.*

From Aigues-Mortes take the D979 and join the D46 (right at the island). At the second island join the D58; then, after 13km (8 miles), join the D38c, followed by the D570. After 24km (15 miles) join the N11 and follow signs to Arles. Distance: 46km (29 miles).

Baths in Aix-en-Provence.

④ Arles. Day 4 takes you to Arles. For detailed suggestions on how to make the most of Arles in 1 day, see p 15 in The Best of Provence in Three Days, above. ⏰ *1 day. For detailed information on Arles, see p 122 in chapter 6.*

Leaving Arles, follow the N113 for 19km (12 miles). Near St-Martin-de-Crau join the A54 and follow signs to Aix. They will take you onto the A7 (Aeroport de Marignane) and the A8 (exit junction 31). Distance: 80km (50 miles).

⑤ Aix-en-Provence. This chic spa town encompasses the best of Provence: gorgeous 17th- and 18th-century town houses, medieval streets, bustling markets, fine food, thronging cafes, Roman baths, and former artist residents (Cézanne and Zola) whose legacies have helped to shape France today. Once you've checked into your hotel, you can easily spend the day wandering through the streets. The **Cours**

Mirabeau is the main drag, dotted with fountains; **rue Gaston-de-Saporta** is littered with shops; and the **Mazarin** quarter is the peaceful, grid-patterned district of Aix's former bourgeoisie. ⏰ *1 day.*
Aix-en-Provence tourist office, 2 pl Gén de Gaulle. ☎ *04-42-16-11-61. www.aixenprovencetourism.com. For detailed information on Aix-en-Provence, see p 114 in chapter 6.*

From Aix join the A8 highway, then follow signs to Marseille (via A51 and A7). Distance: 35km (22 miles).

⑥ Marseille. We recommend spending at least 2 days in France's fascinating oldest town. Granted it has all the undesirable trappings of any big city—crowds, commerce, crime, and car fumes—along with its monuments, restaurants, bars, cafes, and markets. Marseille's nerve center is its ancient port, crackling with energy and change. Fishing and pleasure boats are crammed in rows like pretty sardines, and characters come and go from all over the world, chiefly Europe and Africa. Stroll through the traditional **Panier** district to visit the intriguing **Vieille Charité,** which houses two excellent museums. For far-reaching vistas across the town and coastline, climb up to Marseille's emblematic **Notre-Dame-de-la-Garde** basilica. Other noteworthy religious buildings are the **Cathédrale de la Major** and the **Abbaye St-Victor.** The **Vieux port,** protected by two old forts (**St-Jean,** with its Mediterranean civilization museum, and **Fort St-Nicolas**) is the hub of town and the setting of a wonderful morning fish market. Art lovers could visit the **Musée Cantini** (post-War art and fauvism), the **Musée Grobet-Labadie**

(rare paintings and furniture), and the **Musée de la Faïence** (ceramics). Shoppers can get their kicks on the **Cours Julien, rue St-Ferréol, rue Sainte,** and **rue de la Tour.** To learn about Marseille's history, head for the **Musée d'Histoire de Marseille,** the **Musée des Docks Romains,** and the **Maison Diamantée.** To see Marseille's splendid Belle Époque architecture stroll up the Canebière towards the richly decorated **Palais Longchamp.** For a dose of modernity, head out of the center to Le Corbusier's **Cité Radieuse.**

On day 2, we recommend exploring Marseille's coastline. If you don't mind sharing sand with droves of sunbathers, the **Prado Beaches** foot the bill nicely. Boats frequently leave the Vieux Port for excursions to the **Château d'If** island fortress and Marseille's wild **Frioul** islands. **Les Calanques,** the stretch of picturesque rocky creeks between Marseille and Cassis, are truly hypnotic. North of town, **l'Estaque** is the fishing port prized by many Impressionist and Fauvist painters. 🕐 *2 days. Marseille*

Fresh lunch on a beach in the Calanques.

tourist office, 4 La Canebière. ☎ *04-91-13-89-00. www.marseille-tourisme.com. For detailed information on Marseille, see p 144 in chapter 6.*

To return to Avignon, take the A7 (toward Aix), and exit at junction 24 to join the N7.

Vallon des Auffes, a tiny fishing port tucked behind a bridge in Marseille.

Provence & the Riviera Two Weeks

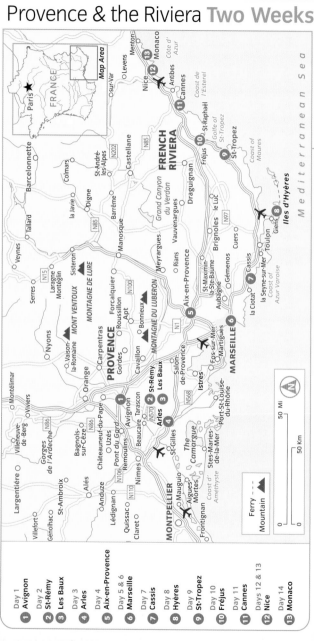

Day 1
1 Avignon

Day 2
2 St-Rémy

3 Les Baux

Day 3
4 Arles

Day 4
5 Aix-en-Provence

Days 5 & 6
6 Marseille

Day 7
7 Cassis

Day 8
8 Hyères

Day 9
9 St-Tropez

Day 10
10 Fréjus

Day 11
11 Cannes

Days 12 & 13
12 Nice

Day 14
13 Monaco

Ferry - - - -
Mountain ▲

This tour combines destinations covered in both the 3-day and weeklong tours. You'll spend your first week in Provence, before continuing along France's sunshine coast through the pretty port of Cassis, Hyères and its offshore islands, glamorous St-Tropez, quaint Fréjus, star-studded Cannes, and buzzing Nice, to the principality of Monaco. If you wish to return to Avignon, tack an extra day onto your tour to allow ample driving time and give yourself the chance to visit any places you might have missed. START: **Avignon.** **Trip length: 428km (266 miles) (plus 270km/168 miles back from Monaco to Avignon).**

Travel Tip

For hotels, restaurants, and detailed information on sights in these towns, see chapter 6: Avignon, p 128; St-Rémy, p 180; Arles, p 122; Aix-en-Provence, p 114; Marseille, p 144; Cannes, p 136; Nice, p 164; Monte Carlo, p 158.

1 **Avignon.** Celebrated for its quality theater, architecture, and history, Avignon is your first port of call. Arrive the night before, or early in the morning, to make the most of your day. For a 1-day itinerary, see bullet **1** of the 3-day tour. ⏱ *1 day.* *For detailed information on Arles, see p 122 in chapter 6.*

From Avignon, take the N570 (ave de Tarascon), then continue on the D570n. Cross the Pont de Rognonas bridge and, at the next island, turn left onto the D571 to St-Rémy (via Châteaurenard and Eyragues). Distance: 21km (13 miles).

2 **St-Rémy.** Get to St-Rémy as early as possible, so you can squeeze in a maximum number of sights in the morning, before heading off to the village of Les Baux in the afternoon. If you would rather concentrate on just one town, spend the day and night in St-Rémy, and make time to visit the Roman

vestiges in nearby **Glanum,** or see the beautiful **St-Paul-de-Mausolée** asylum, where Vincent van Gogh convalesced after lopping off his ear. For a ½-day itinerary, see bullet **2** of Provence in Three Days. ⏱ *½ day. For detailed information on St-Remy, see p 180 in chapter 6.*

From St-Rémy take the D5. After 6km (4 miles), turn right onto the D27 to Les Baux. Distance: 10km (6 miles).

3 **Les Baux.** Famous for its wines, olive oil, ruins, and panoramic views, Les Baux makes for a memorable visit. If you want to treat yourself to some luxury, try the **L'Oustau de Baumanière** (see p 36) hotel and restaurant; it costs a pretty packet, but boy does it impress. For a ½-day itinerary, see bullet **1** in "The Best of Provence in

The streets of St-Rémy.

Three Days." ⏱ ½ day. *For detailed information on Les Baux, see p 109.*

From Les Baux, take the D27 then the D78f. After 3km (2 miles), take the D17 (via Fontvieille). At the island, take the D570n to Arles. Distance: 10km (6 miles).

④ Arles. If you arrive early in the morning, you can easily cover both Roman and medieval Arles in 1 jam-packed day, plus photograph several sites that inspired van Gogh. For a 1-day itinerary, see bullet ④ in Provence in Three Days. ⏱ *1 day. For detailed information on Arles, see p 122 in chapter 6.*

Leaving Arles follow the N113 for 19km (12 miles). Near St-Martin-de-Crau join the A54 and follow signs to Aix. They will take you onto the A7 (Aeroport de Marignane) and the A8 (exit junction 31). Distance: 80km (50 miles).

⑤ Aix-en-Provence. Refined and beautiful Aix competes with Marseille as the unofficial capital of Provence. Make up your own mind by getting here early enough to soak up as much of it as possible. For a 1-day itinerary, see bullet ⑤ in Provence in One Week. ⏱ *1 day. For detailed information on Aix-en-Provence, see p 114 in chapter 6.*

From Aix, join the A8 highway, then follow signs to Marseille (via A51 and A7). Distance: 35km (21 miles).

⑥ Marseille. Because there is so much to see and do here, schedule at least a 2-night stopover. Your first day could be spent exploring the city itself, leaving the second day free to visit Marseille's wild and somewhat romantic off-shore island of **If** (with its François I military stronghold), and the **Frioul isles**—a haven for birdlife and flora. For a 2-day itinerary, see bullet ⑥ of the Best of Provence in One Week. ⏱ *2 days. For detailed information on Marseille, see p 144 in chapter 6.*

From Marseille, join the A50 and follow signs for La Valentine. Leave the highway at junction 8 and continue on the D559a to Cassis. Distance: 31km (19 miles).

⑦ Cassis. This small and attractive fishing resort lies in a bay dominated by the massive **Cap Canaille** cliff, famous for the way in which its rocky façade changes color throughout

A day's work in Cassis.

the day, according to the weather and sunlight. This is a place in which to relax. Sit in one of the cafes on the **port** and watch the world go by. Meander in and out of the narrow streets lined with boutiques, or work on your tan on one of three beaches. If you can't sit still, the tourist office can organize guided walks over the surrounding **Calanques** cliffs, or you could opt to see them by boat. Just before sunset, one of the most memorable things you can do is drive up the nearby **Route des Crêtes** (21km/13 miles long) for sweeping panoramas over the coastline, when the orange and purple light reflects off the tranquil sea. Spend the night in Cassis and leave for Hyères in the morning. ⏱ *1 day. Cassis tourist office, quai des Moulins.* ☎ *08-92-25-98-92. www.ot-cassis.com. For detailed information on Cassis, see p 111.*

Exit Cassis on the D559 and take the A50 (dir Toulon-Centre). Once in Toulon, follow signs to Hyères on the A57, which eventually becomes the A570. Distance: 63km (39 miles).

8 Hyères. Famous for its palm trees and mild climate, this winter resort has been popular since the 19th century. The main town is split into medieval Hyères and 19th-century Hyères, and you can cover it in 3 to 4 hours. Early in the morning, head for the old town. You'll need to be fit to walk around: Streets are uneven, narrow, and often steep. **Place Massillon** has a daily market, near the **Tour St-Blaise** (a 12th-c. tower linked to the Templar Knights), and **Place St-Paul,** by the **Collégiale St-Paul** (12th- and 17th-century) affords some fine views. On one of the highest points, you'll find the **Villa Noailles,** famous for extravagant parties

The cliffs of Hyères.

thrown by artists such as Picasso and Dalí in the 1920s. Back in the new town, don't miss the faded but beautiful **Godillot District,** with its Belle Epoque hotels and villas—testimony to Hyères' popularity among aristocrats.

After lunch, leave the center along the D97 to the tip of Hyères at la **Tour Fondue,** where boats embark for the **Île de Porquerolles**—a magnificent island ideal for cycling and a great place to spend the afternoon (see chapter 3 for detailed information). After your excursion, enjoy dinner back in the main town and get a good night's rest. ⏱ *1 day. Hyères tourist office, av Ambroise Thomas.* ☎ *04-94-01-84-50. www.hyeres-tourisme.com. For detailed information on Hyères, see p 92 in chapter 5.*

Leave Hyères along the ave de Rottweil. At the crossroads, take the Route de Nice to the D12. After 2.5km (1½ miles), join the N98 (via La Londe-les-Maures and Cagolin). After 40km (25 miles), join the D98a at Gassin to St-Tropez. Distance: 50km (31 miles).

⑨ St-Tropez. St-Tropez's glamour is infamous, but this sexy image betrays the port town's humble alter ego as a fishing village. Spend the morning wandering around the center, through the **port,** its tiny **fish market,** and around the former fisherman's quarters, the **Ponche district.** Don't miss the **Château Suffran** (remains of the former St-Tropez Seigneurs' castle) on Place de l'Hôtel de Ville, or the views along the coastline from the **Môle Jean Reveille** jetty, or from the lofty heights of the **Citadelle** ramparts. One of the best spots for coffee or a meal is **Place des Lices**—a tree-shaded square prized by *boules* players and market-goers alike. If you have a sweet tooth, this is a fine spot for a nibble on St-Tropez's specialty cake, *la tarte Tropézienne,* sold by a bakery of the same name on the square.

Two wonderful museums are worth exploring: the **Musée de l'Annonciade,** with its fantastic modern art collection, and the **Musée des Papillons**—an old-world Provençal house entirely given over to butterflies. If the weather's fine, don't forget your bathing suit. St-Tropez has several beaches for all tastes. Spend the night here, then get up bright and early for Fréjus. 🕐 *1 day. St-Tropez tourist office, Quai Jean Jaurès.* ☎ *08-92-68-48-28. www.ot-saint-tropez.com. For detailed information on St-Tropez, see p 186 in chapter 6 and p 44 in chapter 3.*

From St-Tropez, take the D98 to Sainte-Maxime, then join (on the

The docks of St-Tropez.

right) the N98 to Fréjus. Distance: 36km (22 miles).

⑩ Fréjus. Although it's renowned as a beach town, the shore is not Fréjus's main attraction, even if it does reel in bathers by the dozen. Once you've checked into your hotel, spend a leisurely day wandering the old town, crammed with charming cafes and boutiques. Fréjus is also known for its **Roman amphitheatre** and **aqueduct,** on the outskirts of town. Another fine historical site is the **Groupe Episcopal** with its **baptistery, cathedral,** and **cloisters.** If you're traveling with kids, you could spend the afternoon at Fréjus's **Parc Zoölogique** (zoo) or at **Aqualand** waterpark. Sleep here and head off the next morning to Cannes. 🕐 *1 day. Fréjus tourist office, 325 r Jean Jaurès.* ☎ *04-94-51-83-83. www.frejus.fr. For detailed information on Fréjus, see chapters 3 and 5.*

Leave Fréjus on the D37 then join the A8 to Cannes, exiting at junction 41. Distance: 38km (24 miles).

⓫ **Cannes.** Thanks to its world-famous film festival, Cannes attracts the rich and famous like bees to honey. There are three parts to the city: **La Croisette** is where you'll find flashy shops, restaurants, beaches, and hotels, as well as the **Palais des Festivals,** with its famous red carpet and surrounding **Allée des Stars.** The old town of **Le Suquet** is where you'll see authentic Cannes, with its Forville market and Musée de la Castre (ethnic and 19th-c. art museum) complete with a 12th-century watch tower and adjacent 17th-century church (Notre-Dame de l'Esperence). **Les Îles des Lérins** are Cannes' peaceful offshore islands, one of which is cared for by Cistercian monks. Get here early then choose the Cannes you'd prefer to see. After a night on the tiles, drive to Nice. 🕐 *1 day. Cannes tourist office, Bureau Palais des Festivals La Croisette.* ☎ *04-92-99-84-22. www.palaisdesfestivals.com. For detailed information on Cannes, see p 136 in chapter 6 and p 68 in chapter 4.*

La Croisette in Cannes.

A carnival clown in Nice.

Leave Cannes along the D6285 and head for the A8 twd. Nice and Nice-Centre. Distance: 33km (20.5 miles).

⓬ **Nice.** We recommend spending 2 days in Nice. On the first day, use your morning to visit **Vieux Nice.** Here you'll breathe the scents of Nice's street food and see the vibrant *Cours Saleya* market, the baroque *Chapelle de la Miséricorde,* the *Chapelle de l'Annonciation* dedicated to Ste-Rita, the eerie **Palais Lascaris,** and the **Cathédrale de Sainte Réparte.** After lunch and a stroll along the **Promenade des Anglais,** jump on the **Grand Tour** bus, which will give you an excellent commentated overview of the whole city, allowing you to decide which areas to revisit the next day. One ideal destination for Day 2 is **Cimiez,** where you can see Roman remains in the **Musée d'Archéologie** and marvel at the **Matisse** museum. Other fantastic museums include: **Musée National Message Biblique Marc Chagall,** the **Musée d'Art**

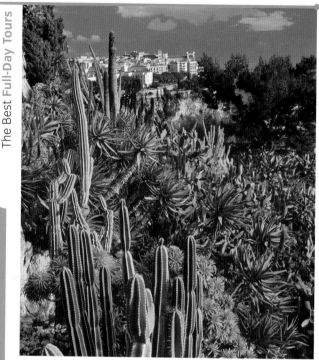

Monte Carlo's Jardin Exotique, overlooking the Côte d'Azur.

Contemporain (modern art), **Musée des Arts Asiatiques** (Asian arts), the **Musée des Beaux-Arts** (fine arts), and **Musée International d'Art Naïf Anatole-Jakovsky** (Naïve Art). Sleep here then head for Monaco. ⏱ *2 days. Nice tourist office, 5 promenade des Anglais.* ☎ *08-92-70-74-07. www.nice tourisme.biz. For detailed information on Nice, see p 164 in chapter 6, p 103 in chapter 5, and p 32 in chapter 3.*

From Nice, rejoin the A8 and follow signs to Monaco. Distance: 21km (13 miles).

⑬ **Monaco.** The principality of Monaco impresses visitors with its cleanliness and friendliness. Check into your hotel, then head straight for the **royal palace** and its museums, on "the Rock." At 11:55am, make sure you are outside to witness the changing of the guard. From here, the fabulous aquarium in the **Musée Océanographique** or the sea views from the **Jardin Exotique** make for a good visit, followed by a commentated tour around town on the **Azur Express Tourist train.** Once you have gawked at the stylish bodies thronging the beaches along **Ave Princesse Grace,** head for a flutter in the world-famous **casino** in Monte Carlo. ⏱ *1 day. Monaco tourist office, 2 a bd Moulins.* ☎ *04-93-75-87-67. www.visit monaco.com. For detailed information on Monaco, see p 158 in chapter 6 and p 98 in chapter 5.* ●

Provence for **Gourmands**

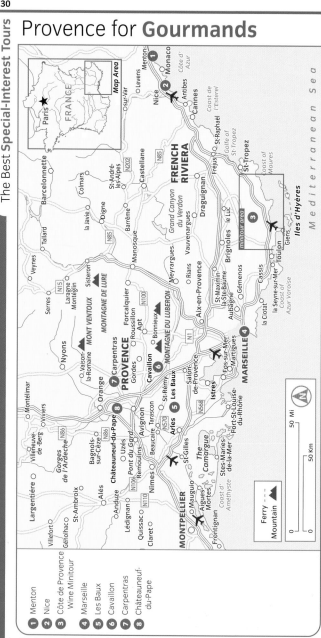

1 Menton
2 Nice
3 Côte de Provence Wine Minitour
4 Marseille
5 Les Baux
6 Cavaillon
7 Carpentras
8 Châteauneuf-du-Pape

Previous page: A vineyard near the village of Châteauneuf-du-Pape.

Fertile soil baked in sunshine, sprinkled with just the right amount of rain along a lengthy coast: Provence's climate has all the right ingredients for glorious harvests of wine grapes, olives, tomatoes, eggplants, zucchinis, peppers, garlic, fresh herbs, truffles, melons, lemons, and more. And locals know what to do with the goods. Centuries-old culinary traditions influence every *Provençal* kitchen, where age-old specialties and contemporary creations are based on some of the world's finest olive oils and produce picked that very morning. You're never more than an hour from the Mediterranean in this region, so fresh seafood takes pride of place on most tables. To top it off, fine local wine—Côtes du Rhône, including Châteauneuf-du-Pape, and crisp Côte de Provence rosés—fuels lively chatter and makes dining here an indelibly memorable experience.

START: **Menton (30km/19 miles East of Nice). Trip length: 7 days.**

Travel Tip

For recommended hotels, see chapter 6: Nice p 164 and Marseille p 144.

1 Menton. Wedged between the sea and an amphitheater of mountains, between Monaco and Italy, Menton is blessed with the mildest weather on the Riviera. Its microclimate has made it a center for citrus-fruit cultivation since the 1500s. During the annual **Fête du Citron** (Lemon Festival), from mid-February to early March, the town becomes a roiling mass of vivid yellow, as locals decorate floats, windows, streets, and themselves with lemons. *Tarte au citron,* France's delicious, biscuit-based tart with lemon cream, is a Menton specialty; ★★ **La Cigale's** heavenly versions, at 27 av Carnot (☎ 04-93-35-74-66), are the best in town. In August, foodies flock to La **Fête des Les Bazaïs,** on the quai Henry Bennett, for a giant cauldron of bean, meat, and vegetable soup. The festival dates from the Middle Ages, when Menton's plague-ravaged

Menton during its annual Lemon Festival.

The owner of Chez Thérèsa with fresh-baked socca, a Niçoise specialty.

villagers cooked an immense stew to show barbaric invaders that they had enough resources to withstand a siege. Another sweet specialty is the *Fougasse Mentonnaise*, a doughy cake flavored with orange flower and coated with sugar and aniseed. For something savory, look out for *stockfish*—dried fish cooked in garlic, onion, parsley, potatoes, and white wine, and then flambéed in cognac. *Menton tourist office, 8 av Boyer 06500.* ☎ *04-92-41-76-76. www.menton.fr.*

From Menton, drive west onto the A8. Turn off at junction 55 and follow signs to Nice.

❷ **Nice.** Nice thrived as an Italian protectorate until 1814, and the boot's imprint on Niçoise cooking remains distinct. As in Italy, many traditional dishes begin with superb olive oil. *Socca* is a thin-crusted, pizza-like bread, made from chickpea flour and olive oil; a delicious variant is *pissaladière*—*socca* topped with anchovies and caramelized onions. Both are sold at **Chez Thérèsa** (in the boutique and on the market stall in the Cours Saleya, see p 165) and **Chez René Socca,** 2 rue Miralheti

(☎ 04-93-92-05-73), which doubles as a wine bar.

The restaurant-shop **Oliviera** (see Nice, p 173) sells what may be the Mediterranean's best oils. Passionate owner Nadim can tell the story of every oil he sells and readily conducts blind taste tests.

Other Niçoise specialties include the giant sandwich called *pan-bag-nat*—bread dipped in olive oil and filled with tuna, eggs, and salad—once the prized meal of fishermen. *Salade Niçoise* is Nice's most exported dish. The traditional version is a toss, however, rather than an arrangement, of salad leaves, tuna, eggs, anchovies, tomatoes, cucumber, onion, black olives, and garlic. *Omelette de poutine* is a delicious local omelet made with parsley, olive oil, fresh lemon juice, and *poutines*—baby sardines caught over a 30-day period in February and March. Another local delicacy is *beignets de fleurs de courgette*—batter-coated zucchini flowers, deep-fried and served in a tomato sauce. *Soupe au pistou* is a hearty bean, tomato, and zucchini broth, flavored to taste with garlic, olive oil, and basil pesto.

As you wander the old town, look out for bakeries selling **tourte aux blettes**—a sugar-coated pie made with cabbage *(blette)*, raisins, and pine nuts. A savory variant swaps the sweet ingredients for rice and parmesan cheese.

Many traditional Niçoise menus offer delicious round zucchinis, tomatoes, or onions stuffed with pork mince called **petit farcis**—a name shared by the best cooking school in Nice, **Petits Farcis.** Cordon Bleu–trained chef Rosa Jackson (see p 173) taught this writer how to cook sea bass the right way, with fresh Provençal herbs bought during an early morning saunter that day around the bustling **Cours Saleya** food markets. *For more information on Nice, see chapter 6 p 164.*

From Nice, head west on the A8. Turn off at junction 36 (St-Tropez/ Ste Maxime) and take the N555, the N7, then the D10 (Les Arcs) to Taradeau. Distance: 80km (50 miles).

③ Côte de Provence Wine Minitour. Amid steep hills and sea views, the **Var** region is the land of rosé wine *par excellence*. This mini-tour takes you into the diverse, dra-matic landscape of the Haut Pays (inlands), where gravelly, well-drained soils; generous sunshine; and winter showers yield some of France's best rosés. All these wineries are *premier cru*. For minitour, see p. 34.

From Hyères join the A570 and follow signs to Toulon (via A57). Enter, then leave Toulon on the A50 and follow signs to Marseille. Distance: 85km (53 miles).

④ Marseille. Fresh fruits of the sea define Marseillaise cuisine— most notably bouillabaisse, a fish stew as old as the city itself (from 600 B.C.). It's now expensive when prepared properly, but fishermen have been concocting it for cen-turies to make use of the least desir-able portion of their catch. From the words *bouillir* (to boil) and *baisse* (to turn down the heat), genuine bouil-labaisse is traditionally two dishes: a saffron-tinted broth, with orange zest and fennel seeds, followed by a variety of fish poached in the base. Servers present the fish first, to demonstrate its impeccable fresh-ness, then ladle more soup over it,

Traditional bouillabaisse in Marseille.

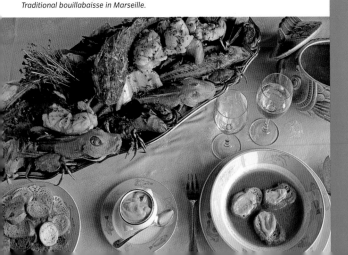

Côte de Provence **Wine Minitour**

3A Château de Selle (Taradeau)

3B Château de St-Martin (Taradeau)

3C Château Roubine (Lorgues)

3D Jas d'Esclans (La Motte-en-Provence)

3E Château de Bregançon (Bormes-les-Mimosas)

3F Château de Mauvanne (Hyères)

An 18th-century bastide once owned by the Counts of Provence, **3A the Château de Selle** in Taradeau, rd 73 (☎ 04-94-47-57-57; www.domaines-ott.com), now makes world-famous rosés, blending cabernet-sauvignon, grenache, and cinsaux grapes. For crisper rosé, visit nearby **3B Chateau de St-Martin,** rte des Arcs (☎ 04-94-99-76-76; www.chateaudesaintmartin.com). This vineyard has a ruined 2nd-century B.C. Roman villa and a Gallo-Roman grape press on-site.

Take the D10 for 8km (5 miles) to Lorgues. **3C Chateau Roubine's** vines, route de vin RD 562 (☎ 04-94-85-94-94; www.chateauroubine.com), yield light fruity wines yet date to Roman times. In 1307, the Knights Templar donated the site to the Order of St Jean. It's now owned by former fencing champion Philippe Riboud.

From Lorgues, go back to the N7 in Les Arcs. Take the D555 and veer right on the D91 to La Motte. Stop briefly at the **3D** Jas d'Esclans for

award-winning organic wines, route de Callas La Motte en Provence (☎ 04-98-10-29-29; www.jasdesclans.com).

West along the coast (60km/37 miles on the N98 then take the D559 at La Garrigue), the **3E Château de Bregançon,** 639 rt de Léoube, Bormes-les-Mimosas (☎ 04-94-64-80-73; www.chateaudebregancon.fr), is a 17th-century château on 350 hectares (864 acres) of vines. The rosé is peachy-hued, from cinsault, syrah, and grenache grapes.

From Bormes, take the D559 to La Garrigue and join the N98, then (via Londe-les-Maures) join the D10 to Hyères (20km/12 miles). **3F** Château de Mauvanne, 2805 route de Nice, Hyères (☎ 04-94-66-40-25; www.mauvanne.com), has been making wine since the 1600s. Current owner Bassim Rahal produces some of the region's best rosés. *⏱ 2 days. Most wineries are open Mon–Sat 10am–noon, 2–6pm; call for details.*

Table with a View

For a gastronomic escapade just 15 minutes from Nice (east on D6007), serious foodies should head for the perched village of Eze. At the summit of its steep, narrow, medieval streets (wear comfortable shoes), you'll reach Château Eza—in an old castle with Michelin-starred food, impeccable service, and views over jagged cliffs and the Côte d'Azur. Specialties include foie gras with fig and beetroot purée. Reservations required. *Rue de la Pise, Eze Village.* ☎ *04-93-41-12-24. www. chateaueza.com. Menus 39–95€. AE, MC, V. Open daily noon–2pm, 7:30–9pm.*

served with *une rouille* (a sauce of red chilies, garlic, olive oil, egg yolk, and cayenne). **Miramar** (see p 156) on the Vieux port is an excellent place to try it and learn to prepare it.

Other specialties to seek out in Marseille are **poupeton**—a soufflé made with the fish left over from bouillabaisse; **alibofis**—lightly battered sweet breads; and **oursinade,** a platter of sea urchins freshly caught from the ocean. Just behind the Cours d'Estienne d'Orves, **La Trilogie des Cépages,** 35 rue de la Paix Marcel Paul (☎ 04-91-33-96-03; www.trilogiedescepages.

com), combines inventive, regional cooking with wine tasting lessons. They present a new wine every third Thursday of the month. *For detailed information on Marseille, see chapter 6, p 144.*

Take the A7 from Marseille and after 49km (30 miles) join the A54. Exit at junction 13 and follow signs to Les Baux. Distance: 87km (54 miles).

⑤ Les Baux. Too picturesque for its own good, Les Baux (see p 109) balances on the edge of the Alpilles mountains. Sometimes it seems as though tourists may push it over

Grapes awaiting harvest.

Olives from the region surrounding Les Baux.

the brink, yet it produces some of the most flavorful olive oils in the region. The oil's rich golden color has earned it the name *huile d'or* (golden oil); purist chefs swear that only oils from Les Baux can impart traditional Provençal flavor. **Terre des Huiles,** Grand-rue (☎ 04-90-54-37-62), sells a wide selection.

A Provençal olive grower.

Les Baux is also a classified wine growing region. Reds and rosés dominate, but a few whites slip through. Ask the tourist office (☎ 04-90-54-34-39) about wine tours or try the **Château Romanin** outside the village. Its cellar is in an eerie troglodyte cathedral, 13210 St-Rémy (☎ 04-90-92-45-87; www.romanin.fr).

If you can splurge, the culinary highlight of your trip could be **L'Oustau de Baumanière** (☎ 04-90-54-33-07; www.oustaude baumaniere.com). At this luxury hotel and restaurant in the heart of the village, chef Jean-André Charial concocts wonders such as lobster with confit of peaches and fresh almonds. *Les Baux de Provence tourist office, rue Porte Mage. ☎ 04-90-54-34-39. www.lesbauxde provence.com.*

From Les Baux, take the D27 for 2km (1¼ miles), then join the D5 (left) for 8km (5 miles). At St-Rémy, take the D99a, the D99 for 12km, and follow signs to Cavaillon.

6 Cavaillon. There's one reason not to miss this pretty but otherwise ordinary town: cantaloupe melons. The Cavaillon region has been cultivating them for at least 5 centuries—possibly longer, from when Avignon was the official papal residency. Writer Alexander Dumas loved them so much, he donated all 194 of his published works to the town in exchange for a life annuity of 12 melons a year. Each July, during the 4-day melon festival, the whole town goes cantaloupe: A pyramid of melons dominates the marketplace, artists paint and sell melon-themed works, and mini-bus excursions take visitors to local melon farms.

Don't leave town without stopping at **Auberge de Cheval Blanc,** 84460 Cheval Blanc (☎ 04-32-50-18-55; www.auberge-de-cheval blanc.com; menus 23–47€. AE, MC, V. Dinner Thurs–Sun; lunch Mon, Thurs–Sun). Talented chef Hervé Perasse prepares dishes such as turbot roasted in vanilla in a beautiful dining room, near Cavaillon. *Cavaillon tourist board, 79 pl François Tourel.* ☎ *04-90-71-32-01. www. cavaillon-luberon.fr.*

Exit Cavaillon and take the D938. After 10km (6 miles), turn left onto the D31, then 12km (7 miles) later onto the D49 to Carpentras. Total distance: 30km (19 miles).

7 Carpentras. This archetypal Provençal town hosts an exceptional Friday market along its tree-lined outer boulevards. Carpentras is particularly famous for its truffle market, which supplies France with more than half its black diamonds between November and March. Hard fruit-sweets called *berlingots* are another specialty. They come in every color under the sun at **Confiserie du Mont-Ventoux,**

Black diamonds from the Carpentras truffle market.

288 ave N.D. de Santé (☎ 04-90-63-05-25). In the morning, you can watch as they're made. *Carpentras tourist board, pl Aristide Briand.* ☎ *04-90-63-00-78. www.carpentras-ventoux.com.*

Exit Carpentras and take the D942. After 3km (2 miles), join the D31, then after 1km (⅔ miles), turn right onto the D87. After 7km (4 miles), join the D16. Enter Bédarrides, exit via the N7, and turn immediately right onto D66, then follow the D17 to Châteauneuf-du-Pape. Distance: 23km (14 miles).

8 Châteauneuf-du-Pape. This small, scenic town produces heavy red Côtes du Rhone wines, first planted by the 14th-century Avignon popes, now famous the world over. For more information, see p 84 in chapter 5. *Châteauneuf-du-Pape tourist office, pl Portail.* ☎ *04-90-83-50-34.*

Provence for **Art Lovers**

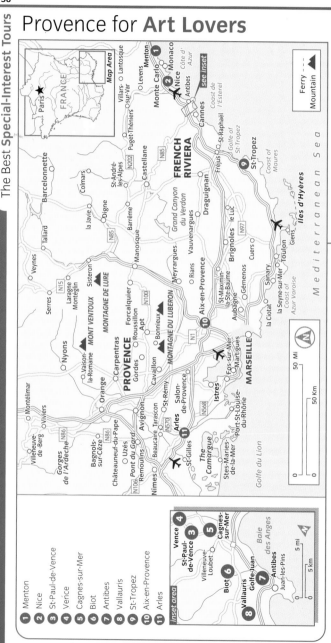

Map Area

FRANCE

★ Paris

see inset

Ferry ---
Mountain ▲

Mediterranean Sea

1 Menton
2 Nice
3 St-Paul-de-Vence
4 Vence
5 Cagnes-sur-Mer
6 Biot
7 Antibes
8 Vallauris
9 St-Tropez
10 Aix-en-Provence
11 Arles

1 Menton
2 Monaco
Monte Carlo
Nice
Antibes
Cannes
Côte d'Azur
Côte de l'Esterel
Villars-sur-Var
Lantosque
Levens
Puget-Théniers
St-Raphael
Golfe de St-Tropez
9 St-Tropez
Côte de Maures
Fréjus

FRENCH RIVIERA

N85
Barcelonnette
Colmars
St-André-les-Alpes
Castellane
Grand Canyon du Verdon
Draguignan
Barrême
Digne
la Javie
N85
Veynes
Talard
Manosque
Meyrargues
Rians
Vauvenargues
Brignoles
le Luc
N97
Cuers
Iles d'Hyères
Toulon
Giens
la Seyne-sur-Mer
Sanary
Gémenos
Aubagne
la Ciotat
Coast of Azur Varoise
St-Maximin-la-Ste-Baume
10 Aix-en-Provence

MONTAGNE DE LURE
Sisteron
Laragne Montéglin
Serres
N15
Nyons
MONT VENTOUX
Forcalquier
N100
Roussillon
Apt
Bonnieux
Gordes
MONTAGNE DU LUBERON
Cavaillon
N1
Carpentras
PROVENCE
Orange
Vaison-la-Romaine
Montélimar
Viviers
Villeneuve-de-Berg
N86
Gorges de l'Ardèche
N104
Bagnols-sur-Cèze
Uzès
Châteauneuf-du-Pape
Pont du Gard
Remoulins
N86
Avignon
St-Rémy
Salon-de-Provence
N568
Istres
Fos-sur-Mer
Martigues
MARSEILLE
Beaucaire
Tarascon
N570
11 Arles
St-Gilles
Nîmes
Port-St-Louis-du-Rhône
Golfe du Lion
The Camargue
Stes-Maries-de-la-Mer

Mediterranean Sea

N

0 ___ 50 Mi
0 ___ 50 Km

Inset area

4 Vence
3 St-Paul-de-Vence
5 Cagnes-sur-Mer
6 Biot
7 Antibes
8 Vallauris
Golfe-Juan
Villeneuve-Loubet
Juan-les-Pins
Baie des Anges

0 ___ 5 mi
0 ___ 5 km

Like moths to a flame, artists have gravitated toward Provence's vivid sunlight and vibrant landscape for centuries. Long before the rise of Impressionism for which Provence is most famous, the medieval Schools of Avignon and Nice were influential as well. Sculptor Pierre Puget (1620–94) was deemed Provence's answer to Michelangelo, and Provence's varied scenery inspired Grassois painter Jean-Honoré Fragonard's (1732–1806) romantic rococo style. Impressionists Claude Monet and Auguste Renoir eased the world into Modernism with their treatment of light, and Raoul Dufy, Pierre Bonnard, and Paul Signac carried the torch decades later. Both Paul Cézanne, a native Aixois, and Vincent van Gogh endlessly depicted sun-kissed Provençal landscapes. Pablo Picasso and Henri Matisse both settled here, and Jean Cocteau spent much of his life on the Côte d'Azur, creating his own museum in Menton, the start of our tour. START: **Menton (30km/19 miles east of Nice). Trip Length: 7–10 days.**

Travel Tip

For hotels and restaurants, see chapter 6: Nice p 164; St-Tropez p 186; Aix-en-Provence p 114; Arles p 122.

❶ **Menton.** Parisian born artist, dramatist, and surrealist filmmaker Jean Cocteau (1889–1963) was a big fan of Menton and left the town two important legacies: his sublime murals in the **Salle des Mariages,** Mairie de Menton, Place Ardoino (☎ 04-92-10-50-00), in Menton's City Hall, including the famous *Noce Imaginaire*; and the **Musée Jean Cocteau,** Bastion du Vieux Port (☎ 04-93-57-72-30; Wed–Mon 10am–noon, 2–6pm). The building Cocteau chose was a ruined 17th-century fort on the port. He oversaw all the restoration work, designing the floor mosaics on the ground level, the window mosaics on the first floor, and the wrought-iron window decorations of his *zoomorphes.* He donated his tapestries, set designs, and drawings as well, but then he died before his museum opened in 1967. The **Musée des Beaux Arts** is set in the sumptuous 17th-century **Palais Carnolès** (former residence of Monaco's princes), a work of art in its own right. Its eclectic collections include primitive Italian works (12th–15th c.), Flemish and Dutch paintings from the 17th and 18th century, and Greek icons. The citrus groves surrounding the museum include some 400 lemon, lime, grapefruit, and kumquat trees, 3 ave de la Madone (☎ 04-93-35-49-71; Wed–Mon 10am–noon, 2–6pm). The town's fabulous **Palais de l'Europe,** Galerie d'Art Contemporain, 8 ave Boyer (☎ 04-92-41-76-66; Wed–Mon 10am–noon, 2–6pm), a former casino built in 1909, overlooks the stunning Biovès gardens. *Menton tourist office, 8 av Boyer 06500.* ☎ *04-92-41-76-76. www.menton.fr.*

A replica of Rodin's The Kiss in Nice's Musée des Beaux Arts.

From Menton, drive west onto the A8. Turn off at junction 55 and follow signs to Nice.

2 Nice. The fifth biggest city in France attracted several 19th- and 20th-century artists, including Henri Matisse, who loved Nice's "crystalline, limpid" light. He lived at several addresses from 1917 until his death in Cimiez in 1954. Before he died, he bequeathed the city a vast collection of paintings, sculptures, drawings, engravings, paper cutouts, and illustrated books. His iconic *Nu Bleu IV* (Blue Nude IV) and locally inspired *Tempête à Nice* (Nice in Storm) are here. Photographs show Matisse at work on the murals in the **Chapelle du Rosaire** in Vence (see p 41).

Russian-born **Marc Chagall** (1887–1985) lived in St-Paul-de-Vence, but his museum, the **Musée National Message Biblique Marc Chagall** (see p 168), is in Nice. He bequeathed the town paintings as well as sculptures, a mosaic, and three huge stained-glass windows. Chagall ordered the glass set amid cold-toned flora such as olive,

pine, and oak trees. Le Corbusier's disciple André Hermant designed the building. It's one of the world's most important Chagall collections.

Fauvist painter Raoul Dufy made revolutionary use of light and color in Nice, choosing the town as the background and inspiration for his works. A small but fine selection of paintings hangs on the walls of the **Musée des Beaux Arts** (see p 169). One of the best contemporary art museums outside Paris is Nice's **MAMAC** (Musée d'Art Moderne et d'Art Contemporain), which presents French and American avant-garde art from the 1960s onward. (Both American Pop Art and French New Realism were very present on the Riviera, drawing inspiration from daily life. American Pop artists such as Andy Warhol appropriated objects from mass culture, while the work of the New Realists derived from manipulations of those same objects, often breaking them or putting them under glass.) The building is a tetrapod arch surrounded by four square, windowless towers, connected by glass footbridges, with panoramic terrace

MAMAC, the Museum of Modern and Contemporary Art in Nice.

views. *For detailed information on Nice, see chapter 6, p 164.*

Exit Nice on the A8 toward Cagnes. Exit at junction 48 and follow signs for Vence/Cagnes-sur-Mer. Join the D2 as soon as possible (Route de Serres) to St-Paul. Distance: 20km (12 miles).

❸ St-Paul-de-Vence. This fortified medieval settlement—presiding over the Vence countryside amid orange and olive trees—is one of the most visited *villages perchés* in France. It was rediscovered by painters such as Amedeo Modigliani, Pierre Bonnard, Chaim Soutine, and Paul Signac in the 1920s. Since then, hundreds of artists have followed suit, along with serious art dealers whose boutiques and galleries flank the narrow, often teeming cobblestone streets. No art buff should miss the **Fondation Maeght** (☎ 04-93-32-81-63; www.maeght.com; daily 10am–7pm July–Sept; 10am–12:30pm, 2:30–6pm Oct–June). On a pine hill north of town, it's in a pink and white structure that epitomizes Mediterranean avant-garde architecture, designed by José Luis Sert. Marguerite and Aimé Maeght were art dealers in Cannes who hobnobbed with Chagall, Matisse, and Joan Miró. The couple's private collections form the basis of the museum. An Alexander Calder *stabile* rises from the lawn like a futuristic monster. In the courtyard, marble statues by Miró and mosaics by Chagall form a surrealistic garden. A labyrinth displays yet more sculpture and ceramics by Miró, and a chapel has spectacular stained glass signed by Georges Braque and Raoul Ubac. The foundation also exhibits works by a younger generation of artists. At the village entrance, the **Auberge de la Colombe d'Or** (☎ 04-93-32-80-02; www.la-colombe-dor.com; doubles from 230€; mains 15€–40€; AE, MC, V; closed

Fondation Maeght in St-Paul-de-Vence.

Nov–mid-Dec) is a chic, historic restaurant serving gourmet fare alongside original paintings by former artist patrons, including Picasso and Matisse. It also doubles as a plush hotel with a Miró mobile statue overlooking the pool. *St-Paul-de-Vence tourist office, 2 r Grande.* ☎ *04-93-32-86-95. www.saint-pauldevence.com.*

Drive 4km (2½ miles) north along the D2.

❹ Vence. This resort town's historic core is charming enough, but don't miss the **Chapelle du Rosaire** (or Chapelle Matisse) on its outer edges, at 466 av Henri Matisse (☎ 04-93-58-03-26; admission 2.50€, 1€ reduced; Mon, Wed, Sat 2–5:30pm, Tue, Thurs 10–11:30am, 2–5:30pm; closed Nov). Matisse designed it as a gift to the Dominican nuns who cared for him during the last years of his life. He called the chapel his "masterpiece, despite all its imperfections." It is his complete and final work—arguably the most exquisite piece of 20th-century art on the Riviera. The interior is made from Carrara marble and other reflective white materials, dazzling when dappled with colorful

The Matisse Chapel on the outskirts of Vence.

reflections from the stained-glass windows. *Vence tourist office, 8 pl Grand Jardin.* ☎ *04-93-58-06-38. www.vence.fr.*

Take the D236 from Vence and, after 2km (1 mile), join the D36 to Cagnes. Distance: 10km (6 miles).

⑤ Cagnes-sur-Mer. Renoir deemed the perched old town of Cagnes-sur-Mer (see p 42) "the place where I want to paint until the last day of my life." He got his wish in 1919, when he died in his family home, Les Collettes—today's **Musée Renoir,** 19 chemin des Collettes (☎ 04-93-20-61-07; admission 3€, 1.50€ reduced; May–Sept Wed–Mon 10am–noon, 2–6pm; Oct–Apr Wed–Mon 10am–12pm, 2–5pm)—leaving a still life behind to dry. Les Collettes' house and olive groves have been restored to look as they did when Renoir lived here. Although crippled by arthritis, he began experimenting with sculpture in Cagnes, and the museum has 20 portrait busts and portrait medallions that constitute the largest collection of Renoir sculpture in the world. You can explore the drawing room and dining room on your own before going up to the artist's

bedroom. In his atelier are his wheelchair, easel, and brushes. *Cagnes tourist office, Place du Dr Maurel 06800.* ☎ *04-92-02-85-05. www.cagnes-tourisme.com.*

Leave Cagnes and take the D341 (bd J.F. Kennedy) for 45km (28 miles) and turn right onto D6098, followed by the D241 and D6007. After 3km (2 miles), join the D4 to Biot. Distance: 10km (6 miles).

⑥ Biot. Famous for its bubble-flecked glass known as *verre rustique,* Biot has also been known for its pottery since ancient times, when local merchants began exporting local earthenware jars to Phoenicia. It's also where Fernand Léger painted until the day he died. A magnificent collection of his work is on display at the **Musée Nationale Fernand-Léger,** Chemin du Val-de-Pome (☎ 04-92-91-50-30; www.musee-fernandleger. fr; admission 4€; July–Sept Wed–Mon 10:30am–6pm; Oct–June Wed–Mon 10am–12:30pm and 2–5:30pm), a striking stone-and-marble building enhanced by Léger's mosaic-and-ceramic mural facade. The collection includes paintings, ceramics, tapestries, and sculptures showing the artist's development from 1905 until his death. His paintings abound with cranes, acrobats, scaffolding, railroad signals, buxom nudes, casings, and crankshafts. *Biot tourist office, rue St-Sébastien.* ☎ *04-93-65-78-00. www.biot.fr.*

From Biot, take the D704 (route d'Antibes) and follow signposts. Distance: 6km (4 miles).

7 Antibes. This unpretentious port town with a bustling covered market is home to the Château Grimaldi, once the palace of the Grimaldi princes of Antibes, who ruled from 1385 to 1608. Nowadays, the castle shelters the world-class **Musée Picasso,** Place du Mariejol (☎ 04-92-90-54-20; June–Sept Tues–Sun 10am–6pm; Oct–May Tues–Sun 10am–12pm, 2–6pm), which is closed for renovations until mid-2008. When Picasso came to town after the war, he stayed in a small hotel at Golfe-Juan until the museum director at Antibes invited him to work and live at the museum. He spent the year 1946 painting here, and, upon his departure, donated all the work he'd created: paintings, ceramics, drawings, lithographs, oils on paper, sculptures, and tapestries. In addition, a contemporary art gallery exhibits Léger, Miró, Max Ernst, and Calder. *Antibes tourist office, 11 pl Gén de Gaulle.* ☎ *04-97-23-11-11. www.antibes juanlespins.com.*

Leave Antibes on the D6107 and follow signposts to Vallauris. Distance: 7km (4 miles).

8 Vallauris. The tacky ceramics capital of the Riviera still attracts lovers of pottery and Picasso with its three-in-one **Musée National de Picasso, Musée Magnelli,** and **Musée de la Céramique,** in the village castle, Place de la Libération

(☎ 04-93-64-71-83; admission 3.25€, 1.70€ reduced; free under 16, mid-June to mid-Sept Wed–Mon 10am–6pm; until 5pm mid-Sept to mid-June).

Picasso lived in Vallauris from 1948 to 1955, and created some 4,000 ceramic pieces. He also decorated a rough stone chapel with two fabulous contrasting paintings: *La Paix* (Peace) and *La Guerre* (War). One floor houses a museum devoted to Abstract Art pioneer Alberto Magnelli; more Picasso ceramics, plus works by regional potters, are on another floor. In the main square, look out for Picasso's sculpture *L'Homme au Mouton* (Man with Sheep), which he created in just one afternoon. *Vallauris tourist office, av Frères Roustan 06220.* ☎ *04-93-63-21 07. www. vallauris-golfe-juan.com.*

From Vallauris, head for the A8 (toward Cannes). Leave the A8 at junction 36 (after 60km/37 miles) and follow signs to St-Tropez. Distance: 95km (59 miles).

The seaside Picasso Museum in Antibes.

9 **St-Tropez.** Well-off or well-connected artists have long flocked to St-Tropez for a break in the sun. Post-Impressionist painter Paul Signac was one of them, and he inspired a host of others bent on capturing the Riviera's light. The **Musée de l'Annonciade** opened in 1955 within a 16th-century chapel on the old port, displaying many of Signac's works, along with other striking Post-Impressionist pieces. *For detailed information, see chapter 6, p 189.*

Leave St-Tropez on the D98a. After 4km (2½ miles), take the N98. Four islands and 10km (6 miles) later, join the D25. After 15km (9 miles), take the D125 toward Le Muy. Join the A8 here and follow signs to Aix. Distance: 135km (83.5 miles).

10 **Aix-en-Provence.** Paul Cézanne and Aix-en-Provence are inseparable. Cézanne was a law student at his father's behest, but his real love was painting the countryside around Aix. Gradually he found recognition and friends among the circle of Impressionist painters in Paris. After outgrowing Impressionism, he begun to juxtapose large patches of color in new ways and to exaggerate lines and relief. His

A sculpture of Paul Cézanne, native son of Aix-en-Provence.

Van Gogh's Café de Nuit.

most prolific works were inspired by Aix's outlying landscape, particularly the **Montagne St-Victoire,** visible from town. Today, visitors can see **Cézanne's atelier** as he left it when he died (see p 118). Contemporary art followers shouldn't miss the stellar collection at the **Fondation Vasarely** (p 119).

From Aix take the A8. After 23km (14 miles), join the A7 and follow the signs for Arles. Distance: 79km (49 miles).

11 **Arles.** In 1888, van Gogh attempted to overcome his gloomy temperament by settling in sunny Arles. Never one for good luck, he arrived to find the sunshine city covered with snow. Nevertheless, he went on to paint 200 canvases in fewer than 15 months here. But it was in Arles that he notoriously lopped off his ear, after a fight with

In Van Gogh's Footsteps

One of the most moving pilgrimages a van Gogh buff can make is to the **Saint-Paul-de-Mausole** asylum, outside St-Rémy (see p 182). After suffering from what was likely undiagnosed bipolar disorder, aggravated by absinthe and lead paint fumes, Vincent checked himself into Saint-Paul-de-Mausole for a year, from 1889 until 1890, the year of his death. In this peaceful sanctuary, he painted 150 canvases, including *Starry Night* and other masterpieces. St-Paul is still a functioning asylum, but visitors can take a self-guided walking tour through the grounds, past hand-wrought signs that picture some of Vincent's most famous paintings on the very sites where he painted them.

fellow artist Paul Gauguin. The **Espace Van Gogh** (see p 125), the **Café Van Gogh** (See p 127), and the **Fondation Van Gogh** all pay tribute to the tortured genius (see p 125 in chapter 6), who would die penniless, without recognition, 2 years later in Provence. *For detailed information, see chapter 6, p 122.*

Café Van Gogh, depicted in the van Gogh painting Café du Nuit.

Best Historic **Architecture**

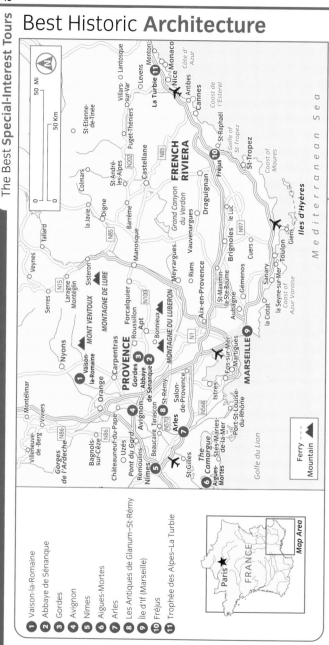

1 Vaison-la-Romaine
2 Abbaye de Sénanque
3 Gordes
4 Avignon
5 Nîmes
6 Aigues-Mortes
7 Arles
8 Les Antiques de Glanum–St-Rémy
9 Île d'If (Marseille)
10 Fréjus
11 Trophée des Alpes–La Turbie

As ancient Rome's first transalpine conquest, Provence has a wealth of ancient architectural wonders and ruins. Later, as Christendom took root and spread, the Middle Ages saw a surge in Romanesque abbeys and churches, followed by France's own home-grown Gothic style. From the 16th to the 18th century, the fortified walls and gates that protected many cities during the religious wars gave way to sumptuous châteaux and classical town houses. The wild 19th century, with its Belle Epoque villas and hotels, left behind some beautiful and extravagant *folies*. And although extensive tourism has spawned plenty of modern eyesores—particularly on the Riviera—a select few 20th-century buildings and art galleries are astonishing. START: **Vaison La Romaine is 56km (35 miles) north of Avignon. Trip length: 7–10 days.**

Roman artifacts in Vaison-la-Romaine.

Travel Tip

For hotels and restaurants, see chapter 6: Avignon p 128; Nîmes p 174; Arles p 122.

1 Vaison-la-Romaine. Built along the banks of the Ouvèze River, Vasio Vocontiorum (Vasion-la-Romaine) flourished under Roman rule for centuries. After the collapse of the Roman Empire and several years of flooding, however, all evidence disappeared under layers of silt and sand. It wasn't until 1907

that the Roman ruins were rediscovered and excavated. Until then, Vaison was a small, amiable medieval village, high on a crag overlooking the river. Its Romanesque **Cathédrale Notre-Dame-de-Nazareth** still has an 11th-century *chevet*, made from one solid block of stone. It is intricately decorated with cornices and friezes. The nave inside has pointed barrel vaulting and an octagonal dome covered with symbols of the evangelists. The adjacent **cloisters** are from the 12th and 13th century, wonderfully

The Abbaye de Sénanque.

decorated with interwoven patterns, figures, and acanthus leaves. The **upper town** *(haute ville)*, with its maze of alleyways, is surrounded by **14th-century fortifications,** the stones of which were taken from the Roman town ruins. There is a good view onto Mont Ventoux from the parvis of the 15th-century church. A dramatic **12th-century château,** built by the Count of Toulouse, stands proud at the highest point of the hill. Back in the lower town, only 15 hectares (37 acres) of kids **Roman Vaison** are accessible; the rest lies forgotten beneath modern buildings. The **Puymin** district is the first you'll see. It was the hub of Roman Vaison, containing the courthouse (praetorium), theater, temples, and shops. In Puymin, the **Maison des Messii** was home to a very important family. Remains of columns, baths, a private temple, dining room, and living rooms are still visible.

One of the most impressive sites is the 34 semicircular rows of stone benches that make up the 1st-century **Antique Theatre.** It would

have seated up to 6,000. The **Portico of Pompey** is a vast 65m (213-foot) array of columns that originally surrounded a garden and pool. You can view artifacts unearthed during excavations in the **Musée Théo Desplans,** where highlights include remarkable white marble statues presented in chronological order, the 3rd-century silver bust of a wealthy patrician, and a six-seater public latrine.

The **bridge** linking the Haute Ville to lower town is 2,000 years old. It's one of the only constructions that survived torrential flooding in 1992, which killed 37 people and destroyed 150 houses. *Most sights are open Nov–Feb 10am–12pm, 2–5pm; Mar, Oct 10–12:30pm, 2–5:30pm; Apr–Sept 9:30am–6pm. Admission to all sites 8€; 3.50€ reduced. Vaison-la-Romaine, av Chanoine Sautel.* ☎ *04-90-36-02-11. www.vaison-la-romaine.com.*

From Vaison, exit on the D938 and head for Carpentras. Leave Carpentras on the D4 and, after 12km (7½ miles), join the D177, the D224, and D15 to Gordes. The Abbey is signposted from the town center. Distance: 54km (33.5 miles).

❷ **Abbaye de Sénanque.** The beauty, fragrance, and peacefulness of this gray-stone, Luberon abbey, set in a valley of lavender fields, is not easily forgotten. It is an almost perfect example of Romanesque Cistercian architecture, with stone walls, plain windows, and barrel-vaulted ceilings. Certain parts of the roof are covered with limestone tiles called *lauzes,* also used on the unusual stone dwellings (*bories*) in nearby Gordes (see below). The dual-columned **cloister** shows superb craftsmanship with delicate, late-12th-century, floral-themed carvings. The barrel-vaulted **nave** leads to the eight-sided dome of the **transept,** in the corner of which lies the tomb of the abbey's 13th-century patron, the Lord of Venasque. At its peak, the **chapterhouse** was a hive of monastic activity. Here on the stone seats lining the walls, monks listened to the abbot's biblical sermons. The **calefactory** was the only heated room in the abbey, enabling the monks to read and write without freezing. It is characterized by a beehive-shaped fireplace. Vast, vaulted, and airy, the dormitory has regular arched windows that bathe the room in light, but you still wouldn't want to sleep there. ☎ *04-90-72-05-72.* *www.senanque.fr. Guided visits only. Times change so call to verify.*

3 **Gordes.** As chic as it is stunning, this dramatic perched village has a fine **Renaissance château,** built on the site of a 12th-century fortress. The 1541 chimney piece in the great hall is a decorative spectacle with ornate pediments,

flowers, and shells. In the village, the labyrinth of paved streets are known as *calades*—recognizable by their steep incline, central gutters, vaulted passageways, and tall, old houses.

Just beyond the village, however, along the D2, lies an architectural conundrum dating back to the Bronze Age—the **Village des Bories** (☎ 04-90-72-02-75; www.gordes-village-des-bories.com; daily 9am–sundown). Bories are peculiar, corbel-vaulted, dry-stone huts, used for 3,000-plus years for human housing, sheepfolds, wine cellars, cereal storage, and bakeries. Gordes has 400 of the 3,000 bories in Provence—many of which were inhabited until the 19th century. The village reconstructs the rural lifestyle of borie dwellers and shows a photo display of borie villages around the world. It's most atmospheric first thing in the morning. *Gordes tourist office, pl Château.* ☎ *04-90-72-02-75. www.gordes-village.com.*

Vaulted stone huts known as bories, outside Gordes.

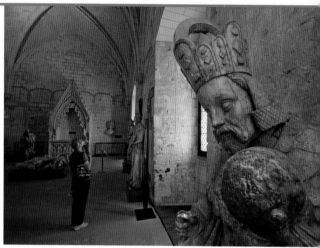

Inside the Palais des Papes in Avignon.

Leave Gordes on the D2. Join the D15, and then the N100, before taking a left onto the D22 and D973. After 4km (2½ miles), join the N7 into Avignon. Distance: 40km (25 miles).

④ Avignon. A jewel in Provence's sparkling crown, the Vaucluse capital can keep architecture enthusiasts busy with enough medieval streets, Renaissance mansions, and Romanesque churches to explore for a lifetime. However, you simply cannot miss the world's biggest Gothic palace—**Le Palais des Papes**—a testimony to the immense power of the papacy in the 14th century. Popes Benedict XII and Clement VI built it in fewer than 20 years (1335–1352). It soars 50m (164 feet) above the town in a massive ensemble of stone towers and sheer walls that hide a maze of passages, chapels, galleries, and halls. Two styles reign: Cistercian (by Benedict XII) and Gothic (by Clement VI). The most visible meeting point of these styles is in the **Cour d'Honneur,** with its machicolated

conclave wing and irregular gothic openings across the façade. Below the **Tour des Anges,** the **treasury** is a beautiful vaulted room with flagstones concealing the pope's secret hiding holes for gold, silver, and precious ornaments. More concealed compartments lie under the **Chamberlain's Bedchamber** on the third floor, which also shows a pretty 14th-century painted beam ceiling and some foliated scrollwork on the walls. The **Grand Tinel** banquet hall is the biggest in the palace, with a keel-vaulted roof that looks like a ship's hull and 18th-century Gobelin tapestries. Frescos by Martini, brought from Notre-Dame-des-Doms cathedral, embellish the bare walls of the **Consistoire,** where the Pope announced the names of his cardinals. It's stripped of most of its decoration, but some original frescos have resisted time. The **Chapels of St-Jean and St-Martial,** the **Pope's Bedroom,** and **Clement VI studium** all contain extraordinary paintwork (see p 129). The **Grande Audience** (Palace of the Great Causes), where 13 ecclesiastical judges formed the Tribunal de la Rota (named after the *rota,* or circular bench, they sat upon), has a vaulted ceiling, set off against a deep-blue starlit sky and the **Fresco of the Prophets,** painted by master Matteo Giovanetti in 1352. *For more information, see chapter 6, p 128.*

Leave Avignon via the Porte de l'Oulle and join the N100. After 20km (12 miles), join the A9 and follow signs to Nîmes. Distance: 51km (32 miles).

5 Nîmes. This ancient city wears its Gallo-Roman vestiges with proud nonchalance. The **Arènes** (arenas, also see p 123, chapter 6) are more complete than Rome's colosseum. The name *arènes* derives from the sand used to soak up blood in the central oval space, *vomitorias* (exits), and corridors. This feat of engineering bears two small carvings of Romulus and Remus, the mythological founders of Rome who were raised by a wolf. You can still sit on the original stone benches and make out holes that would have held poles used to support awnings to shield the crowd from the sun. Medieval residents sought protection within the arena's thick walls, using them as ramparts for a self-contained village. The village

remained until the 19th century, when the buildings and trash (6m/ 6.5 yds deep) were cleared to make way for bullfights. See chapter 6 for fuller coverage of the **Maison Carré,** Nîmes' tremendous Roman temple; the **Temple de Diane** ruins (part of a Roman sanctuary); the **Tour Magne** with its panoramic viewing platform, and the **Castellum** water tower. **Porte Auguste** is the city's best-preserved Roman gate, measuring 6m by 4m (6.5 x 4.5 yds). The **Domitian Way** (the road from Rome to Spain) sliced through Nîmes, so the gates had to be wide enough for horse-drawn chariots to pass. It bears an inscription explaining that the city walls date from 15 B.C. and were 6km (3.75 miles) long. *For more information, see chapter 6, p 174.*

From Nîmes, head for the A9 toward Montpellier. Exit at junction 26 and follow signs for Aigues-Mortes. Distance: 42km (26 miles).

6 Aigues-Mortes. South of Nîmes, this city of the "dead waters" (*aigues mortes* in Provençal) stands alone in the middle of the Camargue's swamps and lagoons. Louis IX and his crusaders once set forth from this former thriving port, but today it is France's most perfectly

Aigues-Mortes, a medieval fortified town in the Camargue.

preserved medieval walled settle-ment, with **ramparts** (1272–1300) that still enclose the entire town. They were built of stone quarried from nearby Beaucaire and Les Baux (see p 109). They are punctuated by 10 gates, 6 towers, a watch path, and overhanging latrines. The 13th-century **Tour de Constance** (☎ 04-66-53-61-55; daily May–Aug 10am–7pm, Sept–Apr until 5pm) is a circular keep with walls 6m (20-ft) thick. Its entrance was protected by a portcullis with embrasures that allowed soldiers to hurl missiles onto enemies. It was mostly used as a prison for Catholic, Calvinist, and finally Huguenot prisoners. From the top, a sweeping panorama over the Midi salt marshes and the Camargue will get your pulse racing. In town, the religious centerpiece is the **Eglise Notre-Dame des Sablons** (rue Jean-Jaurès; no phone). Constructed of wood in 1183, it was rebuilt in stone in 1246 in the ogival style. Its modern stained-glass windows were installed in 1980 as replacements for the badly damaged originals. *Aigues-Mortes tourist board, pl St- Louis 30220.* ☎ *04-66-53-73-00. www.ot-aiguesmortes.fr.*

Leave Aigues on the D979 to the D46. At the second island, take the D58, turning off 3km (2 miles) later onto the D38c. After 5km (3 miles), turn left onto the D570. After 24km (15 miles), Arles is signposted along the N113. Dis-tance: 47km (29 miles).

7 Arles. Known as the "the little Rome of the Gauls," Arles possesses some of France's best-preserved Gallo-Roman legacies. The 136m by 107m (148 x 116 yds) **Arène** is a complex structure of arches, corri-dors, vomitorias, seating for 20,000 spectators, and underground pas-sages for machinery, animals, and gladiators. Mosaics furnished some

The Chateau d'If, overlooking the Côte d'Azur near Marseille.

floors, to facilitate cleaning after bloody battles (also see p 123). Other Roman architectural sites of interest are the **Thermes de Constantin** Roman baths, the **Musée d'Arles Antique, the Théâtre Antique** (the Roman theater), and the **Alycamps** cemetery. *See p 124, chapter 6, for details.*

If you're a fan of the Romanesque, you'll be mesmerized by the intricate detail on the **Eglise St-Trophime's** 12th-century portal, which displays an ancient classical arrangement that suggests a triumphal arch. *For more information, see chapter 6, p 125.*

From Arles, take the D570n. After 10km (6 miles), join the D99 at an island (via Mas-Blanc-des-Alpilles) to St-Rémy. Distance: 26km (16 miles).

8 Les Antiques de Glanum–St-Rémy. St-Rémy's quintessential Provençal streets, graced with 15th- and 16th-century mansions, contrast heavily with its ancient quarters 2km away in Glanum. Here an impressive **triumphal arch** and **mausoleum** mark the site of the oldest Greek-Roman settlement in the region. *For more information, see chapter 6, p 183.*

From St-Rémy, take the D99a toward Cavaillon. Join the A7 toward Aix, then follow signs to Marseille. Distance: 90km (56 miles).

⑨ Île d'If—Marseille. On the sparsely vegetated island of If, François I built a fortress to defend Marseille (1524–28). Later a bastioned curtain wall was added, but the site was never attacked and became a prison for Huguenots and political prisoners. Alexandre Dumas used the château as a setting for the fictional adventures of *The Count of Monte Cristo.* The château's most famous association—with the legendary Man in the Iron Mask—is also apocryphal. See p 53. *Marseille tourist board, 4 La Canebière.* ☎ *04-91-13-89-00. www.marseille-tourisme.com*

From Marseille, take the A7 toward Aix, then join the A51 (toward Nice) and the A8 (toward Nice). Exit at junction 37 and follow signs to Fréjus. Distance: 145km (90 miles).

⑩ Fréjus. The beach resort of Fréjus has a colorful past as a Roman settlement and a flourishing medieval town. As a port town, Fréjus's **ampithéâtre** (rue Henri Vadon; ☎ 04-94-51-34-31) was destined to entertain soldiers rather than wealthy folk, and thus lacked the sophistication of the arenas in Arles and Nîmes. It is currently undergoing extensive renovations to turn it into a 5,000-seater stadium; and as earth is scraped back, archaeologists step in, so you might be lucky enough to see a dig.

Although somewhat dilapidated, Fréjus's **Roman aqueduct** once stretched for 40km (25 miles), bringing water in from Montauroux and Mons. *Fréjus tourist office, 325 r Jean Jaurès.* ☎ *04-94-51-83-83. www.frejus.fr.*

From Fréjus, go back to the A8 (toward Nice). Exit junction 57 for Roquebrune, then follow signs to La Turbie. Distance: 80km (50 miles).

⑪ Trophée des Alpes. La Turbie has a ruined monument erected by Roman emperor Augustus in 6 B.C., to celebrate the subjugation of the French by the Roman armies. The trophy was originally 49m (53 yds) high, topped by a statue of Emperor Octavius Augustus. Only the pedestal remains today, but the miniature replica in the **Musée du Trophée d'Auguste** (rue Albert-1er, La Turbie; ☎ 04-93-41-20-84) will help you imagine the grandeur of the original statue.

*The **Trophée des Alpes** from 6 B.C.*

Provence & the Riviera **for Kids**

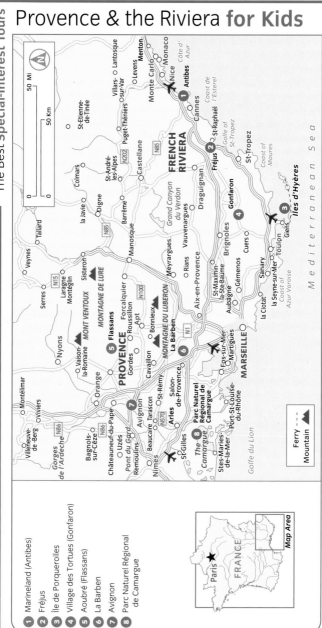

1 Marineland (Antibes)
2 Fréjus
3 Île de Porquerolles
4 Village des Tortues (Gonfaron)
5 Aoubré (Flassans)
6 La Barben
7 Avignon
8 Parc Naturel Régional de Camargue

Ferry - - -
Mountain ▲

Map Area

FRANCE
Paris

Through a child's eyes, the castles and fortified hilltowns of Provence and the Riviera could have come straight from a Disney movie, which makes it easier to lure kids to "cultural attractions" (provided you don't call them that of course!). Then there's the great outdoors, which provides a host of activities, both on land and on sea, for the whole brood. The region is also known for its spectacular wildlife and flora, which gives kids a chance to learn about nature and have fun at the same time. With this tour, we have tried to provide a list of kid-specific attractions that can either be followed in order or mixed in with destinations on other tours. START: **Antibes. Trip length: 436km (270 miles).**

Travel Tip

For hotels and restaurants, see chapter 6: Avignon, p 128.

1 Antibes. Just outside Antibes, near Biot, **Marineland** is an adventure park devoted to the ocean. Excellent live dolphin, killer whale, and sea lion shows reproduce the animal's natural behavior and give them a chance to show off their flips and turns, while splashing delighted audiences. The killer whales and dolphins are particularly endearing, with their wild leaps and languorous rubbing. The 30m (32.5 yd) shark tunnel shows a variety of sharks, with their bristling jaws and streamlined bodies, and a huge stingray over 1.5m (1¾ yds) wide. **The Tropical Aquarium Gallery** has a vibrant display of seahorses, starfish, shrimp, and shoe crabs. The "touch" pool is particularly compelling to curious kids, who can caress skates and rays as they swim through the water.

Don't forget your swimwear. Adjacent to Marineland, **Aquasplash** is the Riviera's biggest water-slide park, with 13 giant toboggans, a "lazy river" where you can relax in a rubber ring, and a wave pool. **La Petite Ferme du Far West** will amuse kids under 13 with cowboy-themed pony rides, an Indian teepee full of distorting mirrors, and a labyrinth of obstacle courses. Finally, the **Adventure Golf** section is a crazy Jurassic-themed golf course with giant dinosaurs—including a mean-looking tyrannosaurus. Combined tickets with Marineland are sold for all attractions. *RN 7, Antibes.* ☎ *08-92-30-06-06. www.marineland.fr. Open May–Sept 10am–6pm. Admission from 28€ adults; from 19€ kids 3–12.*

The Ferris wheel at Marineland near Antibes.

Food on the Farm

Graine & Ficelle is a wee farm, in the flower-strewn hills behind Vence, with an excellent vegetarian Sunday brunch. Small kids can feed the donkeys and fawn over the baby rabbits and hens, while you admire the organic vegetable patch and wait for Isabella Sallusti to prepare the delicious food. Guests eat on communal tables, and, in the spring, baby lambs run around your legs as you dine. Isabella is planning to start cooking classes for kids in 2008. *670 Chemin des Collets, 06640 St-Jeannet.* ☎ *06-85-08-15-64.* Daily, upon advance reservation by telephone or e-mail, graine.ficelle@wanadoo.fr. Sunday brunch & farm visit 31€; 12€ under 18. 2-hour farm visit 11€; 8€ children. No credit cards.

From Antibes, join the D35 (toward Cannes) to the A8. Exit junction 38 and follow signs to Fréjus. Distance: 50km (31 miles).

❷ **Fréjus.** In addition to Fréjus's beaches and Roman Ampithéâtre (see p 94), you and your children might want visit the 20 hectare (50-acre) safari-style **Parc Zoölogique,** zone du Capitou, off A8 (☎ 04-98-11-37-37; www.zoo-frejus.com; daily 10am–6pm June–Aug, until 5pm Mar–May, Sept; and until 4:30pm

Nov–Feb; admission 13€, 9€ kids 3–9). More than 150 different species from five continents roam the park. They range from cute and fluffy mammals to big Asian elephants, wild cats, wolves, birds, and reptiles. The park runs a permanent breeding program to help maintain its many endangered animals, so you may be lucky enough to see newborns, particularly lion or tiger cubs. On a hot day, take a good bottle of sun cream to Fréjus's **Aqualand,** Quartier le

Aquasplash near Antibes.

Capou, RN98 (☎ 08-92-68-66-13; www.aqualand.fr; admission 23€, 18€ 3–12s; open daily June–Sept 10am–6pm). It's a veritable outdoor kingdom of fast-flowing water slides for the whole family. The park's most popular ride is the multicolored *Twister*—a triple whammy slide that twists and turns like a corkscrew. For smaller kids, the *Mini Parc Jungle* provides tame slides and a shallow pool. Your teenagers may want to hang out at *Surf beach,* where they can lounge around a swimming pool and practice looking cool; or, for the more daring, the *Black Hole* slide plunges riders into total darkness. Plenty of fast food and ice cream bars are on hand.

From Fréjus, take the N7 to the A8 (toward Marseille). After 30km (19 miles), join the A57 and follow signs to Hyères. Distance: 94km (58 miles).

③ Île de Porquerolles. Most kids will love the boat trip to this island jam-packed with beaches, forests, and cycle paths. Porquerolles is the largest and westernmost of the Îles d'Hyères (off the shores of Hyères)— a land of rocky capes, pine forests twisted by the mistral, sun-drenched vineyards, and pale ocher houses.

The south coast is rugged, but the north strand, facing the mainland, has sandy beaches bordered by heather, scented myrtles, and pine trees—excellent spots for a family picnic. The 8 by 2km (5 x 1¼ mile) island is best explored on bike. Several companies rent them, but we recommend **Le Cycle Porquerol-lais,** 1 rue de al Ferme (☎ 04-94-58-30-32; www.cycle-porquerollais.com; 13€ day, 9€ children). Outside the village, cycle paths are often bumpy but well marked and great fun for kids with a sense of adventure. The ancient **Fort Ste-Agathe,** built in 1531 by François I, will fire young imaginations. The island has withstood raids, attacks, and occupation

Marineland near Antibes.

by everybody from the Dutch, English, and Turks to the Spaniards, and this fort testifies to its embattled past. Boats to the island, run by **TLV-TVM** (☎ 04-94-58-21-81; from 16€; daily from 7:30am–6pm; times are subject to change), depart south of Hyères at the Tour Fondue on the peninsula of Gien.

From Hyères, take the A570 (toward Toulon). Join the A57 (toward Fréjus). Exit junction 11 and follow signs to Gonfaron. Distance: 46km (29 miles).

④ Village des Tortues-Gon-faron. At the foot of the Massif des Maures mountains, amid fields of lavender and oak, this sanctuary cares for 2,500-plus species of tortoise—particularly the Hermann tortoise, which is almost extinct in France. A series of shaded paths and bridges lead you and your kids through the village into the clinic where staffers nurse sick tortoises back to health before releasing them into the wild. Babies are on view in the hatching room and nursery, and a series of enclosures present the different species, from the most fierce

Turtles from Village des Tortues-Gonfaron.

and exotic, to water tortoises and terrapins. Another exhibition takes visitors back in time to learn about extinct tortoise species and dinosaurs. Staffers are mostly passionate volunteers who offer guided tours about their protection programs. On the way out, you can buy tortoise memorabilia in the gift shop or arrange to sponsor a tortoise for just 30€ a year. *Gonfaron.* ☎ *04-94-78-26-41. www.villagetortues.com. Daily 9am–7pm Mar–Nov. Admission 7€; 4€ children.*

From Gonfaron, take the D39 (Route de Flassans) to Flassans-sur-Issole and follow signs for Parc des Cèdres. 9km (5½ miles).

⑤ Aoubré—Flassans. Within this 30 hectare (74-acre) cedar forest, the whole family can pretend to be primates for the day and move from tree to tree between platforms hoisted high above the forest floor. Routes range in difficulty, but all are highly secure. The **Mowgli Path,** 1m (3 ft) above ground level, has been specially created for 5- to 7-year olds. Older children and brave adults can try the 120m (394-foot) high death slide **(Tyrolienne des Cimes).** Suspended from a harness, you slide down to ground level along a rope. To calm everybody's nerves, the **Petite Ferme** (small farm) provides plenty of cooing opportunities with cute

rabbits, guinea pigs, chickens, and dwarf goats. The **Parc Animalier** (animal park) contains larger deer, wild boar, and donkeys; if your French is good, you can follow an educational tour of local flora and birds. The botanical tour gives an overview of the types of plants that grow in the Massif; the aromatic tour regroups Provence's sweetest-smelling flora; the *tinctoriales* path shows plants formerly used to dye clothing; and the ornithological tour looks at birdlife. *Parc des Cèdres, Flassans.* ☎ *04-94-86-10-92 or 06-12-58-02-26. www.aoubre.fr. Reservations only. Open Sat–Sun, public holidays and school holidays 9am–8pm. Closed Nov–Feb. 19€ adult, 16€ age 8–11; 11€ age 5–7. No credit cards.*

From Flassans, head for Brignoles on the N7, then join the A8 (twd Marseille). You will go by St-Maxime-le-Sainte-Baume and Aix en Provence. After 50km (31 miles), join the N296, following signs for the A51 (toward Marseille). Exit onto the D7n after 3km (2 miles) and follow signs to Celony. Enter St-Cannat and take the D572, then the D22 to La Barben. 99km (61 miles).

⑥ La Barben. On a plateau halfway between Marseille and Avignon, more than 600 animals (120 species) live together harmoniously under the watch of a medieval castle. Visitors will see wolves, giraffes, elephants, llamas, leopards, tigers, and baboons in habitat. A small farm provides petting opportunities for smaller kids, and a minitrain runs to and from the park entrance.

A fascinating reptile house is set within the humid warmth of a restored 12th-century sheepfold. The château's square turrets are visible from most areas in the zoo. Good King René built it just before the 11th century, and it's period furnished. *La Barben.* ☎ *04-90-55-19-12. www.zoo*

labarben.com. Daily 10am–6pm. Admission 13€; 7€ children; free kids under 3. MC, V.

From La Barben, take the D22a to Pélissanne then head for Salon-de-Provence to the A7. Follow signs to Avignon. Distance: 60km (37 miles).

7 Avignon. Avignon makes for a jam-packed family day. The Pont d'Avignon, stretching only halfway across the River, is particularly interesting for kids, who can record their own DVD version of the famous children's song "Sur le Pont d'Avignon." The streets themselves present an atmospheric and eclectic array of 15th- to 18th-century mansions, characterized by big doors with ornate doorknockers. Kids love to seek out the most interesting knockers—from lion heads to hand shapes. The **Petit Train** (a mini tourist train that leaves in front of the Palais des Papes) is a fun way to discover the city (☎ 04-50-60-05-55; www.petittrainavignon.com; daily 10am–7pm; closed Nov–Feb; 7€, 4€ reduced). A boat trip along the Rhône also keeps little minds occupied. Head for the Allées de l'Oulle where Les Grand Bateaux de Provence provide a variety of options—from 1-hour cruises to full-day excursions to cities such as Arles and Châteauneuf du Pape (☎ 04-90-85-62-25; www.mireio.net).

From Avignon, take the D570n to the D35. Turn left onto the D77e, left onto the D34 (left), and right onto the D570 via Arles. From Arles, take the N113 and follow signs for Stes-Maries-de-la-Mer.

8 Parc Naturel Régional de Camargue. The Camargue, where French cowboys ride the range, is an alluvial plain inhabited by wild horses, fighting black bulls, roaming gypsies, pink flamingos, lagoons, salt marshes, and wetlands. It's a paradise for families with children of all ages. The area has the most luxuriant birdlife in Europe and is known for its colonies of pink flamingos *(flamants roses)* and some 400 other bird species, including ibises, egrets, kingfishers, owls, wild ducks, swans, and ferocious birds of prey. Bring a pair of binoculars and head for the area around **Ginès,** a hamlet on N570, 5km (3 miles) north of Camargue's capital, Stes-Maries-de-la-Mer. A memorable way to explore is on the back of a Camarguais horse, which will take you to otherwise inaccessible places. Numerous stables dot the road from Arles to Stes-Maries. They all charge around 80€ to 90€ a day and cater to beginners. Helmets are not traditionally worn in the Camargue; if you're worried, ask for a helmet beforehand. **Note:** Mosquitoes are gluttonous in the reserve. Bring decent repellent or visit in March or April before the swarms descend. The visitors' center *(Maison du Parc)*, with parking and picnic areas, is 4km (2½ miles) south of Stes-Maries de la Mer, at Pont de Gau. *Rd 570, Pont de Gau. ☎ 04-90-97-86-32. www.parc-camargue.fr. Apr–Sept daily (except May 1) 10am–6pm; Oct–Mar open Sat–Thurs (except Dec 25, Jan 1) 9:30am–5pm. Admission free.*

An elephant and giraffe from the zoo in La Barben.

Best **Gardens & Fragrant Sites**

The Best **Special-Interest Tours**

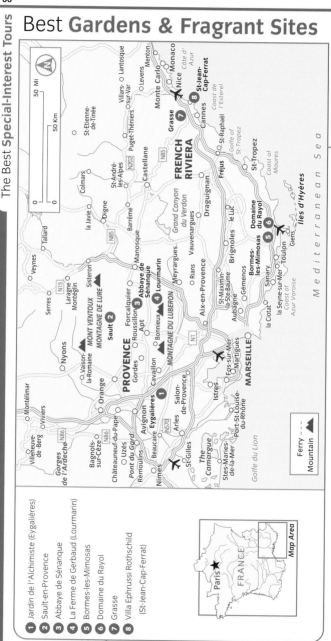

1 Jardin de l'Alchimiste (Eygalières)
2 Sault-en-Provence
3 Abbaye de Sénanque
4 La Ferme de Gerbaud (Lourmarin)
5 Bormes-les-Mimosas
6 Domaine du Rayol
7 Grasse
8 Villa Ephrussi Rothschild (St-Jean-Cap-Ferrat)

Ferry - - -
Mountain ▲

Intense sunshine has penetrated the Provençal landscape for millennia, creating perfect growing conditions for all sorts of aromatic herbs, flowers, fruits, and exotic plants. A 400-year-old perfume industry thrives in Grasse, owing to Queen Catherine de Médici's penchant for perfume-scented leather gloves. As the region's popularity burgeoned among 19th-century aristocrats, so did their desire to create elaborate gardens in which to impress fellow socialites. These floral legacies still stimulate the senses and enrich every visitor's stay today. START: **Eygalières. Trip length: 466 km (289 miles).**

Travel Tip

For hotels and restaurants, see chapter 6.

① Jardin de l'Alchimiste-Eygalières. The majestic 16th-century **Mas de la Brune** château-hotel is luxurious and beautiful (☎ 04-90-90-67-67; www.masdelabrune.com; doubles 200–370€). The draw for most visitors, however, is its unique, atmospheric garden complex. Start your tour along the **Berechit** path—so-called because it spells the name "Berechit" when viewed from above. This leads you to the first garden—**le Jardin Magique** (medicinal plant garden), with plants historically prized for their healing properties. From here, the **Jardin Alchimique** (alchimist's garden) uses stone, water, and specific colored flowers to create ancient alchemist symbols used to divine the meaning of life and even secure immortality. *Mas de la Brune, Eygalières.* ☎ *04-90-90-67-67. www.jardin-alchimiste.com. Oct–May daily 10am–7pm. Admission 6€; 4€ reduced.*

Leave Eygalières on the D74a and take the D99 to Cavaillon. From Cavaillon, take the D2 to Saint-Saturnin-lès-Apt and take the D230, then D943 to Sault. 68km (42 miles).

② Sault-en-Provence. When the lavender blooms in July and August, this hillside town, with its pale buildings and peach roof tiles, looks like an island protruding from a purple sea. The juxtaposition of the flowers with crops of golden corn and white rock is one of the prettiest sights in Provence. Sault's

Provence's hallmark lavender.

A stroll through the blooming streets of Bormes-les-Mimosas.

tourist office (ave de la Promenade; ☎ 04-90-64-01-21; www.saultenprovence.com) has a detailed list of lavender paths you can follow. One of the best ways to learn about lavender cultivation, make your own perfume, and learn how to cook with the plant is to spend time at **La Ferme-aux-Lavandes** (Route du Mont Ventous; ☎ 04-90-64-13-08; by appointment only), a working lavender farm that will take you on an aromatic journey into the heart of lavandiculture. *Sault en Provence tourist office, av Promenade. ☎ 04-90-64-01-21. www.saultenprovence.com.*

Exit Sault on the D943. Take the D140, D60, and D102 to Gordes. The abbey is signposted from here (40km/25 miles).

❸ **Abbaye de Sénanque.** In the zenith of summer, this tranquil Cistercian abbey is engulfed by a carpet of purple, perfumed lavender—rendering it one of the most photographed sites in Provence. Don't let the number of visitors put you off; it is for good reason that the abbey's harmonious yet austere Romanesque architecture, offset by lovely gardens, is so famous. Founded in 1148, it was torched in

1544 during the anti-protestant Vaudois Massacre—Provence's bloodiest event, during which men, women, and children were burned alive. Then in 1580 it was hit by the Plague, before the French Revolution in 1789 and consequent anti-monastic movement almost sealed the abbey's fate for good. Restored by a wealthy industrialist in the 1980s, some monks moved back in to cultivate the lavender and sell other homegrown products to the public. *4km (2½ miles) north of Gordes on D15/D177. ☎ 04-90-72-05-72. www.senanque.fr.*

From Gordes take the D2 and head for the N100 via a series of small roads. Take the D36 via Bonnieux and take the D943 to Lourmarin (30km/18.5 miles).

❹ **La Ferme de Gerbaud (Lourmarin).** The heady scents of Provençal herbs originate from the parched soil of the Lubéron. Join farm owner Paula Marty in Lourmarin for a guided tour through her remote fields. She'll teach you how to recognize the *herbes de Provence* in their natural habitat. She's also a whiz in the kitchen, and, every Thursday from April to September, invites guests to her converted barn to taste dishes flavored with her own herbs. All produce is local, potently flavorful, and organic. Paula also sells her own products (oils, dried herbs, honey, lavender, and herb-flavored cookies) in the farm shop (daily 2–7pm). *Lourmarin.* ☎ *04-90-68-11-83. www.plantes-aromatiques-provence.com. Guided visits Apr–Oct Tue, Thurs, Sat 5pm; Nov–Mar Sun 3pm. Admission 5€; children free.*

From Lourmarin, take the D139 and head for the N7 and N296 toward Aix-Encagnane to the A8 (toward Fréjus). After 12km (7½ miles), join the A52 to Toulon. From Toulon, take A57 to Hyères, then the N98 to Bormes. 156km (97 miles).

⑤ **Bormes-les-Mimosas.** Its name gives it all away: Bormes-les-Mimosas is a center for the fluffy, sweet-scented yellow balls of the mimosa flower (in bloom Jan–Feb). This gorgeous, 12th-century village tumbles delicately down the steep hillside, festooned in flowers year-round. It has been deemed France's most floral village for the past 7 years. Each February, the village bursts alive with the *Corso fleuri*— a parade of innovative and often huge flower sculptures on floats. Also see p 196. *Bormes-les-Mimosas tourist office, 1 pl Gambetta.* ☎ *04-94-01-38-38. www.bormesles mimosas.com.*

From Bormes, take the D559 (via Pramousqiuer) to Rayol. 12km (7½ miles).

⑥ **Domaine du Rayol.** This vast protected domain is one of the most magnificent sites on the coast. Eight gardens re-create plant life from Mediterranean-type climates across the world: agaves from Central America, rare honey palms from Chili, blue gum and eucalyptus trees from Australia, Proteas from South Africa, and bamboo from China. Wild dolphins spend most of the spring in the bay below the gardens. Sometimes they breach the water—a fine reason for you to sign up for Rayol's brand-new marine visit, the *Sentier Marin.* Equipped with flippers, goggles, and a snorkel, you will follow a guide into the sea to observe the aquatic plant life at the bottom of the domain (17€). While you're here, treat yourself to the excellent organic salads and pressed fruit drinks in the **Café des Jardiniers,** back by the main building. *Avenue des Belges. Rayol-Canadel-sur-Mer.* ☎ *04-98-04-44-00. www.domaindurayol.org. Admission 8€; 5€ reduced. Daily 9:30am–sundown or 7:30pm depending on the season.*

From Rayol take the D27 and join the N98 to Ste-Maxime. Take to D125 to Le Muy where you join the A8 (twd Nice). Exit at junction 42 and follow signs to Grasse (110 km/68 miles).

⑦ **Grasse.** The capital of the perfume industry since the Renaissance, Grasse produces three-quarters of the world's essences. The most fragrant town on the Riviera is redolent

Domaine du Rayol on the Côte d'Azur.

with jasmine, roses, violets, daffodils, wild lavender, and other blooms.

As you gape in sticker shock at the price of perfume sold here, remember this: It takes 10,000 flowers to produce 1kg (2⅕ pounds) of jasmine petals and nearly a ton of petals to distill 1 liter (¼ gallons) of essence. To learn about scents and even create your own perfume, don't miss the following two perfumeries. Named after the 18th-century French painter, **Parfumerie Fragonard,** 20 bd Fragonard (☎ 04-93-36-44-65; www.fragonard.com; free admission; open Feb–Oct daily 9am–6:30pm, Nov–Jan daily 9am–12:30pm and 2–6:30pm) has the best villa, the best museum, and the best tour. An English-speaking guide will show you how experts extract "the soul of the flower." After the tour, you can explore the shop and museum, which displays bottles and vases that trace the industry back to ancient times. In the factory of the **Parfumerie Molinard,** 60 bd. Victor-Hugo (☎ 04-93-36-01-62; www.molinard.com; free admission; May–Sept daily 9am–6pm, Oct–Apr Mon–Sat 9am–12:30pm, and 2–6pm), you can watch while *parfumiers* extract the essence of flowers. You'll also learn about the process of converting flowers into essential oils. The museum collection includes antique perfume-bottle labels and a rare assortment of perfume *flacons* by Baccarat and Lalique.

From Grasse, go back to the A8 in the direction of Cannes. Once on the A8 head for Nice, then Promenade des Anglais and Cap. Leave Nice towards Villefranche-sur-Mer, and take D25 to St-Jean-Cap-Ferrat (50km/31 miles).

8 Villa Ephrussi Rothschild—St-Jean-Cap-Ferrat. Known as the Riviera's most perfect villa, this nest of opulence has themed gardens designed to resemble the prow of a ship, suited to the fine sea views over Villefranche and Beaulieu. Fountains, gargoyles, columns, and statues adorn the stone garden; a waterfall splashes over into a rockery next to a replica of Versaille's Temple of Love; the French, Japanese, and tropical gardens compliment each other beautifully. An entire section is planted with cacti, and the rose garden has a surprisingly large number of varieties for the Mediterranean. Inside the house, art treasures litter every room, including an unrivaled collection of drawings by namesake Jean-Honoré Fragonard. *Av. Denis-Séméria.* ☎ *04-93-01-33-09. www.villa-ephrussi.com. Admission 9.50€; 7€ reduced. Mid Feb–mid Oct daily 10am–6pm; Jul–Aug daily 10am–7pm); Nov–Jan Mon–Fri 2–6pm, Sat–Sun 10am–6pm.*

Blooming Calendar

Provence is stunning year-round, but it can take your breath away when flowers are in bloom and fruit is on the tree. Look for **mimosas** and **lemons** in January and February, **roses** in June, **lavender** and **jasmine** in July and August, and **grape vines** heavy with fruit and ripe for harvest in September. ●

The Grasse Perfume Museum.

The Great Outdoors

Best **Beaches**

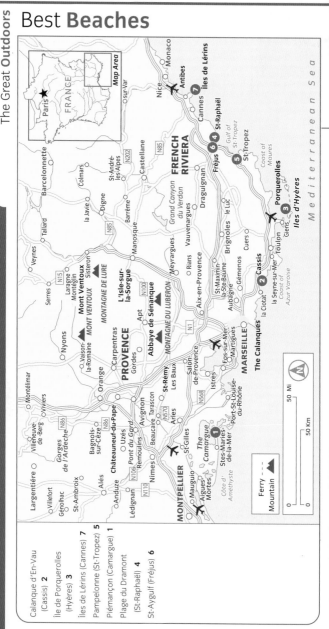

Previous page: A wild horse in the marshy Camargue region.

Contrary to the French Riviera's film and tabloid image, it's not just about bronzing stick figures and celebrities hiding behind Chanel shades. The coastline from the Camargue to Nice is lengthy and varied enough to satisfy a range of beachcombers—whether you seek solace and tranquility in a secluded cove, wild nature, family activities, or a hotspot in which to see and be seen. The region has fabulous shorelines not mentioned here; this list was designed to accommodate a host of needs, tastes, and interests.

Tip

In busy resort areas, restrooms and watering holes usually line the shores. Remote beaches, however, are often without any public facilities, including restrooms and fresh water. Before setting out, be sure to pack food, water, and plenty of sunscreen, and prepare to water the seaweed when nature calls.

Calanque d'En-Vau (Cassis). The Calanques form some of the prettiest and most spectacular beaches in the South of France. Though the name stems from the Provençale word *cala,* meaning steep slope, calanques are actually creeks carved from the chalk cliffs, for 20km (12 miles) between Cassis and Marseille, by now-dry rivers and centuries of

A plunge from the cliffs of the Calanques.

weathering. Flora and fauna flourish here: You'll find a semi-arid environment of viburnum, rosemary, heather, sea lavender, oak, and Allepo pine, plus Europe's largest lizard, the Ocellar (up to 60cm/24 inches long), and Europe's largest snake, the Montpellier Grass Snake (up to 2m/2 yards). **Le Calanque d'En-Vau** is by far the most picturesque, encircled by tall, spiky rocks called *doigts de Dieu* (fingers of God). The small beach is pebbly, but the sea is a beautiful shade of emerald green, and the overall effect is enchanting. You can access the beach on foot or by boat from the port in Cassis. The **Bateliers Cassisains** (☎ 04-42-01-90-83; www.cassis-calanques.com; no credit cards) run a variety of excursions to 3 or 5 *calanques.* Tickets are sold on the boat; reservations aren't required. Walking takes 2 hours from Cassis. You can hire a guide via the Cassis Tourist Office (see p 24), or obtain a map. If you go it alone from Cassis, walk past Port Miou and Port-Pin calanques. Make sure you have decent footwear and water. The route can be steep and uneven, with little shade on sunny days. Be warned, access to the Calanques is limited and often prohibited between July and August, to protect the fragile ecosystem from sun-seekers who come here in droves.

Île de Porquerolles (Hyères).

A short boat crossing from the Hyères Peninsula leads you to an island of pine trees, vineyards, walking and cycling trails, plus several

The Calanque d'En-Vau.

small, sandy beaches—the landscape that reportedly inspired Robert Louis Stevenson to write **Treasure Island.** Hire a bicycle and choose a route to either the silvery sands of the Plage d'Argent; Plage de la Courtade, ideally situated by the Ste-Agathe Fort; or the beautiful Plage Notre Dame—the island's biggest beach, bordered by pines and furnished with a seasonal restaurant. Maps are available at the information center in the village. To hire a bike, try **Le Cycle Porquerollais** *(1 rue de al Ferme;* ☎ *04-94-58-30-32; www. cycle-porquerollais.com; 13€ day, 9€ children).* **TLV-TVM** runs boats to the island *(*☎ *04-94-58-21-81; from 16€; daily from 7:30am–6pm; times are subject to change).* Embark south of Hyères at the Tour Fondue on the peninsula of Gien at the bottom of the D97.

Îles de Lérins (Ste-Marguerite & St-Honorat beaches).
Away from the glitter and the glitterati of Cannes, two offshore islands called the Îles de Lérins offer sanctuary to those wishing to escape the Riviera's glamor queens and kings. **Île St-Honorat** is the smallest of the two, dominated by a fortified Cistercian

monastery, still occupied by monks today. Its remote creeks and beaches are peaceful and inviting, but tourists are expected to dress appropriately while swimming and sunbathing (no nipples or privates). On **Île Ste Marguerite,** you can break up the beach time with nature hikes. Throughout the island, trails run through pine and eucalyptus woods and lead to several small beaches, many of which look out onto Cannes. Certain spots can only be reached by scaling steep cliffs, however, so wear suitable footwear. An old fortress, built by Richelieu and reinforced by Vauban in the early 18th century, contains a marine museum. Ste-Marguerite has several cafes and restaurants near the port, but little elsewhere, and St-Honorat has practically nothing in the line of refreshments. **Trans Côte d'Azur** boats run to both islands from Quai Maubeuf *(*☎ *04-92-98-71-30; www. trans-cote-azur.com; tickets 11€; 5.50€ under 10; MC, V; first departure from Cannes 9am; last return boat to Cannes 6pm, subject to change and weather).*

Pampelonne Beach (St-Tropez).
St-Tropez's public image was forged and burnished on this 9km (5.5 miles) stretch of white sand. A galaxy of stars have bronzed their busts and butts to perfection on this beach, and the mega-wealthy and famous continue reserving places in the exclusive beach clubs. Certain stretches are reserved for nudists. Gays and families also have their own designated areas. The most exclusive beach clubs are **Le Club 55** *(*☎ *04-94-55-55-55; www.leclub55.com);* and **Nikki Beach** *(*☎ *04-94-79-82-04; www.nikki beach.com).* To get there, head eastwards from St-Raphaël along the N98.

Piémançon Beach (Camargue).
This flat, golden stretch of sand, bordered by lonely salt lagoons and

The sands of St-Tropez.

magnificent bird reserves, draws mostly **Camargian** residents and Riviera refugees looking for a peaceful moment away from the crowds. Although the sand can get more populated in warmer months, the beach's relative seclusion keeps the hoards at bay. The Camargue's reputation for virulent mosquitoes is also daunting (see p 59). If you plan to bring children here, be warned that part of this beach has designated areas for nudists perfecting their full-body tans. *To get there, head for Salins de Giraud (D36) and then look out for a sign marked "La Mer." The beach is 1km (⁶⁄₁₀ mile) from the road.*

Plage du Dramont (St-Raphaël). It was on this sand, on

St-Honorat island.

the 15th of August 1944, that the 36th Division of the U.S. Army landed at the end of World War II. Nowadays, the beach is attractive and less commercial than St-Raphaël's other shorelines, and you can watch the French Navy float by on a variety of military boats (from bases nearby). When you've made one sandcastle too many, stretch your legs and follow the signposted, 1-hour walk up to the **Sémaphore du Dramont,** which provides excellent views along the coastline. A second path leads to the **Port of Agay,** a family resort with plenty of watersports and another sandy beach. The nearby **Pointe du Dramont** provides the best view of the tiny, private Ile d'Or (Golden Island), where a 19th-century mock medieval tower stands proudly.

St-Aygulf Beach (Fréjus). Just outside Fréjus, St Aygulf beach is encircled by rocks inside a nature preserve—a world apart from the commercialized, often tacky beaches on this shoreline. A haven for more than 217 species of birds, it protects both fresh and sea water lagoons called Les Etangs de Villepey. The most exciting time to visit is spring, when pink flamingoes and gray herons fly overhead as you soak up the sun. The beach affords a lovely view over the Fréjus Bay.

Best **Hiking & Cycling**

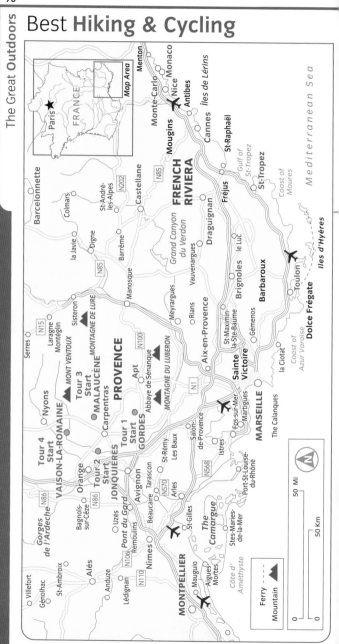

If you're looking to freshen up your town tours with a dose of country air, consider one of these hikes and cycling routes. They are all in one accessible area, the Vaucluse. If you wish to hoof it farther afield, you can contact local tourist offices or the **Fédération Française de la Randonée Pédestre** *(14 rue Riquet, Paris 75019; ☎ 01-44-89-93-90; www.ffrp.asso.fr)*, which covers France's main GR routes (long-distance trails). Provence and the Riviera are littered with places to walk, so you won't be short on routes, wherever you stay. For cycling, you can contact the **Fédération Française de Cyclo-tourisme** *(12 rue Louis-Bernard, Ivry-sur-Seine; ☎ 01-44-16-88-88; www. ffct.org)*. The official tour operator for the Tour de France, **Cyclomundo** *(La Chatelaine; 18 rue Rene Cassin, 74240 Gaillard; ☎ 04-50-87-21-09; www. cyclomundo.com)*, offers guided and self-guided tours for cyclists of all levels, from novices to seasoned riders.

Travel Tip

Don't embark on any of these tours without sufficient water and food, and suitable clothing and footwear. In the summer, weather can get very hot, so don't push yourself too hard. For cycling tours, we recommend a 21-speed mountain bike. Tour 2 can be done either on foot or by bike.

Tour 1: Hiking Gordes to Abbaye de Sénanque.

Postcard-perfect Gordes and the magnificent Abbaye de Sénanque are within ideal hiking distance. We recommend that you pack a picnic, park the car early in Gordes, and

walk down to the monastery. Once you've left Gordes, you won't find refreshment stops en route to the abbey, but the countryside is lovely. Once you're back in Gordes, you can extend your tour down to the **Bories Village.** START: *Gordes. Trip length: 9.5km (6 miles). Time: 3 hours (excluding picnic time).*

① **Gordes.** Gordes is one of France's spectacular *villages percheés*—medieval towns that look as though they're growing from the hilltops where they were built to stave off invaders (for more information see p 88). Start your hike in the **Place du Château,** and take the second road to the right of the

Hikers with a plum view of Gordes.

Tour 1

1 Gordes
2 Abbaye de Sénanque

Tour 2

Tour 3

1 Malaucène
2 Suzette
2b Lafare
2c La Roque Alric

3 Le Barroux
4 Aqueduct sign
5 Third Left
6 Intersection with D90

Tour 4

1 Vaison-la-Romaine
2 Roaix
3 Rasteau
4 Dirt track

5 Cairanne
6 Alley of Plane trees
7 D8
8 Séguret

Le Provençal cafe (not the D15 to Murs), which leads past **La Poste** (post office) on your right.

At the Y-junction, bear right, with the cemetery on your left. Once you pass the cemetery gate, continue straight until the next Y-junction, where you turn left down a road with dry-stone walls on either side. This leads to the D15. Go straight before turning left uphill at the signpost marked **Fontanille.** By this point, you should have walked around **30 minutes.** By a campsite, the road forks again. Go left, look out for some letterboxes, and turn right onto a well-surfaced lane. You will eventually come to another fork in the road. Take the rocky path to the right. It eventually skirts left, but continue straight, with the fields to your right, along a narrow stretch shaded by oak trees. By the time you hit the end of the fields, at a T-junction, you should have been walking for about **an hour.** Turn right at the junction. After 150m (164 yards), turn left down a wide, uneven path. If you are here in summer, get your cameras ready: The path leads you to a valley of lavender, which is splendorous in July and August, when the purple flowers suffuse the air with their delicate scent. Cross the valley, keeping a farm entrance to your right.

At the next fork, stay left along a stony path, from where you can make out the abbey and see the distant Lubéron hills. Near the **Sénanque** hamlet, you'll reach a crossroads. Turn right and head downhill into a wood—an ideal spot for your picnic in the shade. Take your time, because the abbey is closed for lunch from 12pm to 2:30pm. At the next crossroads, head straight along the vehicle-friendly road, which comes out on the D177 (past a big building that belongs to the abbey). Cross the road to climb a path (30m/33 yards downhill on the left), which leads to a crossroads with red and white marks.

This is the GR6/97, which turns left downhill then heads toward the Abbey's long drive, surrounded by rows of lavender.

❷ Abbaye de Sénanque.
Founded by Cistercian monks in the 12th century, the abbey saw much death and destruction before becoming the tranquil retreat it is today. See p 88.

On the D177, look out for traffic and bear right to follow the sign to **Cote de Sénanque.** Just after, turn right and descend a pebbly track with a view onto Gordes. Back on the D177, fork left down a street after 200m. Once you're back in Gordes, turn left back into the center, where a cafe awaits you.

Tour 2: Hiking or Cycling around Jonquières.
The charming village of **Jonquières** doesn't appear elsewhere in this book, making this tour—on foot or two wheels—an ideal opportunity to visit someplace new, while taking in the countryside around

The jagged peaks of Les Dentelles.

A bakery in Malaucène.

Chateauneuf-du-Pape (see p 84), including Mont Ventoux and Les Dentelles de Montmirail in the distance. Once you've left Jonquières, there are no refreshment stops en route—just the vineyards and cornfields of the **Ouvèze plains**. Some of the route is on roads, so look out for traffic.
START: *Jonquières. Trip length: 12km (7.5 miles). Time: 4–5 hours on foot; 1 hour by bike (excluding picnic time).*

1 Jonquières. One of the only villages in France to have **four châteaux,** Jonquières became an important settlement in the 12th century, when it was linked to the House of Orange. Much later, it became famous for its silk

industry. Nowadays it is a quaint village, concentrated around its belfry, with a strong Provençal identity.

Park your car in Jonquières **train station** and take the road heading towards Camaret. At the fire station, turn left and go over the **Via Venaissia** tracks. Take the third road on the right (Chemin des Chèvres) in the direction of the Domaine Duplessis. After 2km (1 mile), you come to a crossroads (with the Chemin des Platrières). Continue straight. About 100m (109 yds) before the D67 (Route d'Orange), turn right toward the **2 Domaine Rigot** vineyards.

Detour from Suzette

At the viewpoint table in Suzette (see p 77), follow signs for "Le Village." Continue on the main road to the D90a, which leads to the market village of **2B Lafare,** laced with steep, charming lanes. Turn left out of the village to **2C La Roque Alric.** Perched on its rocky outcrop, right in the heart of Les Dentelles, it's a world apart from urban noise and haste. Cross the village and head to **Le Barroux** via the D90a, from where you continue your tour back to Malaucène.

A vineyard in Suzette.

Go straight, leaving the Domaine behind on the right. After 500m (545 yds), turn right down a track that follows a small ③ **water channel.** After 1km (⅔ miles), at the end, where you'll see a private property on your left, turn right.

After 300m (327 yds), turn left down the **chemin de Grange Neuve.** At the stop sign head straight, and after 700m (766 yds) turn left onto the chemin du bois de Grange Neuve. At the end of the road, turn left and follow signs to the **centre ville** of Jonquières, crossing back over the Via Venaissia tracks. You will find plenty of moments to marvel at the scenery along the way, so don't forget your camera.

Tour 3: Cycling between Mont Ventoux & Dentelles de Montmirail.

This cycling trip is for those unafraid of a challenge. The terrain is steep, but the unrivaled views make it one of the most rewarding tours around. There are several viewpoints of the **Dentelles de Montmirail**

between **Malaucène** and **Suzette;** look behind you as you ride. Once you get to Suzette, you will have to decide whether to return to Malucène via the pretty perched hamlet of **Le Barroux,** or take a detour through the villages of **Lafare** and **La Roque Alric** in the Dentelles Massif, where the views are breathtaking. START: *Malaucène. Trip length: 22km/14 miles (28km/17*

The rooftops of Le Barroux.

miles by alternative route). Time: 3–4 hours (excluding picnic time).

1 Malaucène. The gateway to Mont Ventoux is a pleasant town with a 14th-century fortified church that was once part of the ramparts. The small streets are filled with fountains and wash houses. The path to the left of the church leads to a viewpoint over the Drôme mountains and Mont Ventoux.

Start in front of the tourist office, on **Place du Mairie.** Head in the direction of Vaison-La-Romaine. At the small island on the edge of Malaucène, turn left toward Suzette. Follow this road until you get to Suzette, where you will have a choice of routes. See the box **"Alternative Route"** if you wish to lengthen your ride (p 75).

2 Suzette. This tiny village charms visitors 410m (448 yds) above sea-level amid rolling hills. Its church is a Romanesque gem, and it has a huge, ceramic viewpoint table, indicating directions for both nearby settlements and faraway cities like Geneva and Milan.

Once you've wandered through the streets take the C2 downhill, to your left toward the perched village of **Le Barroux.**

3 Le Barroux. Come off season and you could easily be in a ghost town. Le Barroux is an exquisite village, with sloping streets, dominated by its 12th-century château. The whole village was burned down in WWII, before being restored to what you see today.

After visiting the village, return to Route de Suzette and turn right towards Monastère (a monastery). Continue along the main road, and follow signs for Aqueduc (aqueduct) **4** Take the third left **5** (1.5km/ 1 mile after the intersection; at the yellow signpost indicating a hiking

trail, choose the right-hand dirt track leading back to Malaucène. You go past the aqueduct and eventually end up on a tarmac surface. Continue on past the monastery and onward to the intersection with the D90.

Here **6**, take the path on the left of the bend. (Cross the mound of earth to avoid crossing the busy ***Départmentale*** road.) Go straight on to the D90. Turn right at the stop sign and cycle back into Malaucène.

Tour 4: Cycling Vaison-la-Romaine & the Pays Voconce. If you're looking for Roman heritage, medieval villages, and vineyards with views onto the Dentelles de Montmirail, this loop will suit you. START: *Vaison-la-Romaine. Trip length: 42km (26 miles). Time: 3–4 hrs (excluding picnic time). Park opposite the Office de Tourisme in Vaison-la-Romaine (ave Chanoine).*

1 Vaison-la-Romaine. The ruins of the old Roman town make for a wonderful visit, before you climb

A fountain in Vaison-la-Romaine.

The Camargue's wild horses.

up the medieval part of town that dominates the hillside. For more information, see p 86.

Begin in front of the **Jardin des 9 Damoiselles.** Take the D975 to St-Quentin's chapel (before the cooperative wine cellar), then join the Route de Villedieu on the left. After 700m (766 yds), turn left down a little road just before Palis (toward Baud). Turn left at the intersection, then right. At the next junction, turn left, then go straight at the cross-roads. *Note:* Use caution; the road is very busy. Turn right at Roaix's Island and enter the village.

2 Roaix is a tiny place, dominated by its château, which is privately owned. It is renowned for its Côte du Rhônes wines.

Cross the village and head straight toward Rasteau. Turn right at the island in front of Rasteau's wine cellar. Turn right at the bend to get to the village square.

3 Rasteau is another small wine village, producing Côte du Rhônes and a dessert wine, aptly named Rasteau. Its wine museum, **Musée du Vigneron** (☎ 04-90-46-11-75),

contains a collection of vintage Châteauneuf-du-Pape.

After visiting the village, return to the D69 (right at the stop sign). Turn right down the path behind the signpost. Turn right at the fork in the road, and right again at the intersection, on an uphill path that leads to a dirt track. **4** Go straight ahead at the junction of three roads (veer to the right, then left); then cycle straight ahead along the hill-side. At the crossroads, go straight ahead.

At the next crossroads, turn left and cycle down towards the centre of **5 Cairanne,** another pretty wine village. Turn left at the stop sign, go straight at the island, then make the first right toward Travaillan.

At the next intersection, turn left under an **6 alley of plane trees.** Continue to the intersection with the D975. Go straight ahead (Mémorial Plan de Dieu). Cross the D24 and head straight to the vine-encircled village of **Violès.** Upon leaving the village, take the small road on the left.

Pony Trails

One of the best places to go horseback riding is in the Alpilles mountains around Les Baux and St-Rémy. Try **Alpilles à Cheval** (Chemin de Constemple, 13990 Fontvieille; ☎ 06-84-51-46-54; http://lesalpillesacheval.free.fr), near les Baux de Provence, or **La Sariette** (Route du mas des Mauniers 13810 Eygalières; ☎ 04-90-95-94-50; www.lasariette.com) near St-Rémy. If you dream of riding a white horse from the Camargue, call **Promenades à Cheval de la Fadaise** (route d'Arles, 13460, Les Saintes-Maries-de-la-Mer; ☎ 04-90-97-86-79). Many schools don't require you to wear a helmet. If you want one, ask when you book. The **Fédération Française d'Equitation** (9 bd MacDonald, 75019 Paris; ☎ 01-53-26-15-50; www.ffe.com) also has useful addresses for riding vacations.

Cross the **7** **D8** and take the Chemin St-André, leading to the wine estate **Domaine St André.** Cross the estate, then go straight. At the intersection near the tennis courts, go straight. At the next intersection, turn right up a road leading to the village of Sablet, before you head downhill to the D7. Turn left, then at the island turn right toward Séguret.

8 **Séguret.** From this picturesque town on a steep hill with a ruined castle, you can marvel at the Dentelles from a scenic overlook.

From Séguret, follow signs for Vaison-la-Romaine. Go straight ahead (toward Roaix), and after 600m (656 yds) turn right onto the Chemin de Bel Air. Cross the bridge

over the Ouvèze river, head past the industrial estate, then at the next island go straight toward the Jardin des 9 Damoiselles.

A clock tower in Séguret.

Best **Golfing**

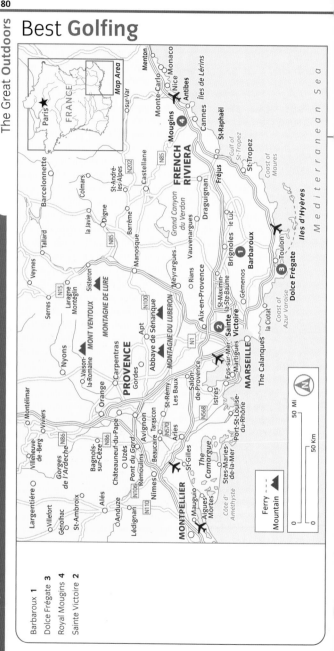

Barbaroux **1**
Dolce Frégate **3**
Royal Mougins **4**
Sainte Victoire **2**

Whether you're looking for a sea view, a backdrop of mountains, or an ultra-chic clubhouse, you'll find a course nonpareil on which to plant a tee and improve your handicap. An excellent destination for golfers, Provence has a multitude of courses for all budgets and all levels of play. Most clubs require membership, but it is possible to rent clubs and play as a visitor. You should expect to pay around 55€ to 75€, excluding club rental, for a day on an 18-hole golf course; exclusive clubs are more costly (see details below).

Barbaroux. This prestigious course near Brignoles is one of Europe's top fifty golf clubs. Eighteen holes unfold over 87 hectares (215 acres) of pine-covered hills, encompassing the biggest green in Europe (69m/75 yds long). In one area, you have to drive your balls over a working vineyard to reach the fairway. Three of six lakes are on the same hole. The course was created by Pete and PB Dye, two of America's most renowned golf architects, in a traditional American design. One of their trademarks is the use of wooden beams to retain the lake. The 4th hole is particularly remarkable, where you have to pass under the green through a tunnel. A special practice area allows you to play off grass. The pro-shop sells all the golf world's latest merchandise. Don't pass by without dining in the club house, with two restaurants that serve excellent French cuisine.

The hotel is unpretentious with 24 rooms and five apartments, an independent terrace, a swimming pool, and tennis courts. *Barbaroux is 10 minutes from the Brignoles highway exit (junction 35), 35 minutes from Aix, and 50 minutes from St-Tropez. Route Cabasse. Brignoles 83170. ☎ 04-94-69-63-63. www. barbaroux.com. 18-holes, 65€; 9-holes, 45€. AE, MC, V.*

Dolce Frégate. Designed by American architect Ronald Fream, this course near Toulon is renowned as one of the prettiest courses in Europe. It affords sea views, salty breeze, vineyards, pines, rock gardens, and aromatic shrubbery. The 18 holes are varied enough to accommodate players of all levels.

The clubhouse adjoins a large, modern hotel, often reserved for weddings and private functions, so be prepared to smile for the bride. Three restaurants fill hungry golfers' bellies, including the gastronomic Le Mas des Vignes, one of the best Provençal restaurants in the region, run by chef Hervé Robert. *From Toulon and Hyères, Dolce Frégate is accessed via the A50. From Marseille via the A7. Route de Bandol; RD 559, St Cyr sur Mer, 83270. ☎ 04-94-29-39-39. http://fregate. dolce.com. 18 holes 55€; 9 holes 40€. AE, MC, V.*

Every hole at St-Victoire affords a view of the mountain peak for which it's named.

Royal Mougins. The village of Mougins is chicer than chic, so it should come as no surprise that the Royal Mougins attracts a moneyed crowd with demanding expectations. Decor here is carefully conceived and wrought—particularly in the clubhouse and restaurant, where posh, steely grays combine with dark wooden furniture and ultra-modern design features. It's nothing if not exclusive. Even the number of non-members allowed to play here is limited to 20 people per day, so phone way in advance if you'd like to hobknob with the high-flyers. The 18-hole championship golf course has a par of 71, and it's renowned for its peaceful, rolling Provençal landscape, dotted with olive trees and stonewalls. The hotel is undergoing an upgrade with 29 new luxury suites in the works, as well as a state-of-the-art spa and health club, set to open during the first half of 2008. *Take the A8 to Cannes (exit junction 42), then the N85 towards Grasse. Take the 3rd exit towards Mougins (N2085). Continue towards Mouans-Sartoux and after the BP gas station, take a left. You'll see a sign for the golf course on your left. 424 ave du Roi, 06250 Mougins. ☎ 04-92-92-49-69.*

www.royalmougins.fr. 18 holes 175€, 9 holes 100€. AE, MC, V.

St-Victoire. Between Marseille and Aix, this 18-hole golf course stands out from the crowd by virtue of its views: Every hole looks onto the majestic Mont St-Victoire—the mountain prized by Cézanne. The beautiful 17th-century ocher Château de l'Arc is the proud centerpiece of the grounds. It used to belong to the painter Bernard Buffet, who painted the chapel. Today it's a four-star hotel with two decent restaurants. The fairways, surrounded by Mediterranean pines, are somewhat of a challenge, with several ponds and three levels of greens, sunken below a multitude of bunkers. The practice areas include putting and pitching zones, plus a driving range on carpet or grass. *To get to Sainte Victoire from Aix, take A8 toward Nice exiting at Le Canet, then head towards Trets on the D6. At the island with the level crossing, turn right. From Marseille, take the A51. Take the Gardanne exit and follow the D6 to the island and level crossing. Domaine Château l'Arc, 13710 Fuveau. ☎ 04-42-29-83-43. www.saintevictoiregolfclub.com. 18 holes 56€; 9 holes 36€. AE, MC, V.* ●

The greens at Royal Mougins.

Vaucluse & the Lubéron

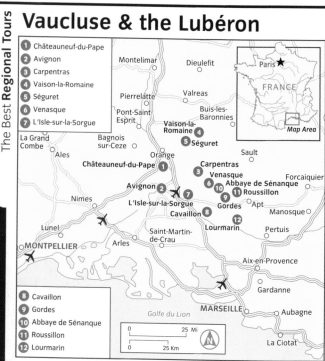

1 Châteauneuf-du-Pape
2 Avignon
3 Carpentras
4 Vaison-la-Romaine
5 Séguret
6 Venasque
7 L'Isle-sur-la-Sorgue

8 Cavaillon
9 Gordes
10 Abbaye de Sénanque
11 Roussillon
12 Lourmarin

Perched villages spring up like mushrooms around many a bend in the hills of Provence's northernmost region. It's an idyllic, kaleidoscopic landscape, adorned by grape vines and fields of lavender and poppy, with bountiful village markets that specialize in truffles, melons, and other seasonal produce. Avignon, capital of the Vaucluse and briefly the seat of Christendom, is a fine cultural center with a world-famous annual theater festival. Provence's best wines come from Châteauneuf-du-Pape, near Avignon. Vaison-la-Romaine is rich with Roman ruins. Isle-sur-la-Sorgue is a motherlode for antiques lovers, and don't miss the pretty village of Fontaine la Vaucluse, with its mysterious water source and castle ruin. **START:** Châteauneuf-du-Pape. Trip Length 7–10 days.

A Note on Hotels & Restaurants

For a full list in Avignon, see p 134 in chapter 6.

1 Châteauneuf-du-Pape. This village gave the most famous Côte du Rhône wine its name. Some 350 domains now constitute the *appellation contrôlée*. The tastefully restored medieval village rolls up a

Previous page: A classic Provençal landscape near Les Baux.

hill toward the old ruin of the **Château des Papes.** Built in 1317 by Pope John XXII, who first planted the surrounding vineyards, it was destroyed during the wars of religion in the 16th century, but it still commands a wonderful view of Avignon and the surrounding countryside. Besides the pretty streets, the main attraction here is the **Musée du Vin,** Le Clos (☎ 04-90-83-70-07; www.brotte.fr; daily). Its displays are relatively interesting, but the highlight is undoubtedly the tasting at the end of the tour. *Châteauneuf-du-Pape tourist office, pl Portail;* ☎ 04-90-83-50-34.

Leave Châteauneuf on the D17, then join the N7. From here follow signs to Avignon. Distance: 17km (11 miles).

② ★★★ **Avignon.** Stunningly beautiful Avignon is dominated by the **Palais des Papes,** formerly inhabited by the 14th-century popes who fled here to escape political infighting in Rome. The town's famous 12th-century half-bridge, the Pont d'Avignon, is deservedly one of France's top tourist magnets.

A wine store in Châteauneuf-du-Pape.

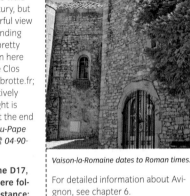

Vaison-la-Romaine dates to Roman times.

For detailed information about Avignon, see chapter 6.

Leave Avignon on the D225 (Route Touristique du Docteur Pons). After 5km (3 miles), take the D942 to Carpentras. Distance: 27km (17 miles).

③ Carpentras. Ruled until 1791 by the Catholic church via Avignon, as part of the **Comtat Venaissin**— a tax-free, military-free papal territory—Carpentras became a haven for Jews expelled by France during the Middle Ages. The town walls crumbled long ago, but the streets still follow their original medieval pattern, which is difficult to drive but a joy to walk. Carpentras is particularly famed as the site of France's oldest synagogue, dating to 1367, opposite the **Hôtel de Ville. Cathédrale St-Siffrein** (place St-Siffrein), has a special entry for converted Jews, the *Porte des Juifs.* The cathedral itself is far more attractive on the outside than on the inside, displaying a mixture of styles. Near the cathedral, look out for a **Roman Arc de Triomphe.**

Despite the historic setting, contemporary Carpentras is down to earth, with a bustling population of 30,000, some of France's most excellent markets (most notably the winter truffle market), and rich Provençal atmosphere. *Carpentras tourist office, pl Aristide Briand;* ☎ *04-90-63-00-78; www.carpentras-ventoux.com.*

From Carpentras, take the D938 via Malaucène to Vaison-la-Romaine. Distance: 30km (19 miles).

④ **Vaison-la-Romaine.** This town is a symbiosis of ancient Rome, the Middle Ages, and modernity. For a full list of attractions, see p 47 in chapter 3. *Vaison-la-Romaine, av Chanoine Sautel;* ☎ *04-90-36-02-11; www.vaison-la-romaine.com.*

Leave Vaison and take the Ave Ulysse Fabre along the D977. After 5km (3 miles) join the island and take the D88 (left) to Séguret. Distance: 9km (5½ miles).

⑤ **Séguret.** After Vaison, spend an hour in this exquisite, quintessential Provençal village. Built into a steep hill, a rabbit's warren of sloping streets lead to a ruined castle. From the village entrance, enter the main street and head toward the 12th-century **St-Denis church,** past a **14th-century belfry** and a **15th-century fountain.** A viewing table provides sweeping vistas over **Les Dentelles** and even the **Massif Central.** *Séguret Mairie (City Hall deals with inquiries), rue Poternes;* ☎ *04-90-46-91-06.*

From Séguret head to the D23 (via the D88) then join the D7. After 17km (11 miles), enter Carpentras, leaving via the D4. After 10km (6 miles), take the D28 to Venasque. Distance: 35km (22 miles).

⑥ ★ **Venasque.** On a warm afternoon, a stroll through Venasque's tranquil streets, past painters and

Fontaine de Vaucluse.

L'Isle-sur-la-Sorgue.

potters, is enchanting. Before Carpentras, Venasque was the seat of the Avignon Comtat bishopric (thus its name, Comtat Venaissin). The village has a **baptistery** (☎ 04-90-66-62-01) dating from the Merovingian period, from the mid-5th to the mid-8th century. Though it was remodeled in the 11th century, it remains one of France's oldest religious edifices. *Venasque tourist office, Grande Rue;* ☎ *04-90-66-11-66;* www.venasque.fr.

Leave Venesque on the D28 and pick up the D4, then the D1 to Pernes-les-Fontaine. Leave Pernes on the D938 (Route de Carpentras) to L'Isle-sur-la-Sorgue. Distance: 22km (14 miles).

❼ L'Isle-sur-la-Sorgue. This wealthy, attractive town owes its name to the Sorgue River, whose crystalline source starts at nearby **Fontaine de Vaucluse** (see p 88). Seventy watermills once pressed the grains and oil that made the town so prosperous. Only nine inoperant wheels remain, but the money rolls in from the antiques industry. More than 300 dealers make it an international center for fine old stuff. Shops are concentrated around ave de la Libération, ave des Quatres Otages, and around the station. On Sundays, *brocanteurs* join in, plying their wares (sometimes junk) at more accessible prices along the water's edge.

The **Collégiale Notre Dame des Anges** is worth visiting just to snap a photo of its cherub-clad, baroque interior. Devoted to the French surrealist poet who was born here, the **Maison Rene Char,** 20 rue du Dr Tallet (☎ 04-90-38-17-41), is a stately 18th-century mansion that hosts temporary modern art exhibitions. *L'Isle-sur-la-Sorgue tourist office, pl Liberté;* ☎ *04-90-38-04-78;* www.oti-delasorgue.fr.

Exit l'Isle-sur-la-Sorgue on the D938 (Route de Cavaillon). After 8km (5 miles) take the D973 to Cavailllon. Distance: 12km (7½ miles).

❽ Cavaillon. Juicy melons are the fruit most associated with this sweet little town. In fact, the area around Cavaillon is used to cultivate a wide range of fruit and vegetables, which adorn stalls here on market days.

Cavaillon began life at the top of the looming St-Jacques hill, but moved down to the current level when the Romans took over the region. A 1st-century **Roman arch** stands proud in place Duclos. Other ancient finds are in the small **Musée Archéologique,** Hôtel Dieu, Porte d'Avignon (☎ 04-90-76-00-34).

Cavaillon's **synagogue** in Hébraïque dates from the 18th century. Like the one in Carpentras, however, it has roots in the 14th century. The **Musée Juif Comtadin,** Rue Hébraïque (☎ 04-90-76-00-34), recounts the history of Judaism in the region. *Cavaillon tourist office, 79 pl François Tourel;*

View from the Top

The Lubéron region of the Vaucluse is particularly hilly and green year-round. The rocky limestone massifs abound with crags, gorges, rolling hills, and perched villages. Much of the area is a national park, protected by dedicated mountain rangers and foresters. It is a fine destination for walking and cycling. **Fontaine de Vaucluse** (D25) is a pretty village with a waterwheel, decent restaurants, and an eerie panoramic castle ruin. It is encircled by a seemingly impenetrable green wall of cliffs, from which springs the Sorgue River in a cascade called the *fontaine* (fountain). Strangely, no one has ever determined the source of the water. To reach the spring, follow the Chemin de la Fontaine uphill. Vast white-capped **Mont Ventoux** rises 1,912m (2,091 yards) above sea level. During the Tour de France, hundreds of professionals huff and puff up the steep slopes to the top. Because it's windy year-round, moisture doesn't have time to condense, which means the views from the summit are often unobstructed by clouds. From a distance, the mount is recognizable by its white limestone tip, covered with snow in winter. **Les Dentelles de Montmirail** are the region's most picturesque mountain ranges, formed by three chalk ridges, topped by ragged crowns, that look more like sharp teeth than the lace *(dentelle)* suggested by their name. Séguret makes for a good stop-off point when you're visiting the Dentelles.

☎ *04-90-71-32-01; www.cavaillon-luberon.fr.*

Leave Cavaillon on the D15 (Route de Gordes). After 12km (7½ miles), join the D2 (via Les Imberts). After 5km (3 miles) turn left onto the Chemin de la Calade and enter Gordes on the D102. Distance: 20km (12 miles).

⑨ Gordes. Quite possibly the most fashionable place in which to have a holiday home if you're a wealthy Parisian, Gordes is a startlingly steep perched village, with prices to match. Its beauty has attracted many a film director—including Ridley Scott, who used Gordes as the setting for his romantic comedy, *A Good Year*, starring Russell Crowe. The village is best

viewed from afar, from where the houses seem to spill higgledy-piggledy down the rock face. The village is crowned by the 16th-century **Château de Gordes** (☎ 04-90-72-02-75), which houses temporary art exhibitions. West of Gordes, you should see the strange **Bories Village,** made up of beehive-shaped, dry-stone huts. For more information, see p 49. *Gordes tourist office, pl Château;* ☎ *04-90-72-02-75; www.gordes-village.com.*

From Gordes, follow signs to the nearby Abbaye de Sénanque.

⑩ Abbaye de Sénanque. One of France's greatest Cistercian monasteries is surrounded by aromatic lavender fields. It is an overwhelming sight in summer when the

The ochre cliffs of Roussillon.

flowers are in bloom. For more details, see chapter 3, p 62. *4km (2½ miles) north of Gordes on D15/D177.* ☎ *04-90-72-05-72. www.senanque.fr.*

Leave Gordes on D102. After 7km (4½ miles) turn left onto Chemin de Joucas and left again onto the D169. Next turn right onto the D105 (rue de la Fontaine) to Roussillon.

⑪ Roussillon. If it weren't for the traditional Provencal houses, all painted a bright peachy hue, Roussillon would look more at home on the red planet Mars than in Provence. The ochre soils and strangely eroded red outcrops surrounding this village lend it an otherworldly romanticism. The town center is enjoyable to wander. Note the belfry-sundial of the Eglise St-Michel.

The real fun is to be had at the **Sentiers des Ocres** (left of the village cemetery, above the car-park; closed Nov–Mar)—an educational path taking you past an old ochre quarry, taking you past weird and wonderful rock formations, and affording some peculiar views. *Roussillon tourist office, pl Poste 84220;*

☎ *04-90-05-60-25; www.roussillon-provence.com.*

Exit Roussillon on the D105, then take the D104, turning right at the island onto the D149. After 1km (⅔ miles) take the D108, then the D149 to Bonnieux. Leave Bonnieux on the D36 and after 5km (3 miles) join the D943 to Lourmarin. Distance: 23km (14 miles).

⑫ Lourmarin. Just when you think you can't take another darling village, Lourmarin eases into view to change your mind. It is easily one of Provence's most charming towns, dominated by its **château,** built high on a crag. Part 15th-century, part Renaissance, it has wonderful chimneys, ornamented with Corinthian columns. The main staircase is a splendid work, ending abruptly with a thin stone pillar and a cupola. Literary buffs might want to visit the town cemetery where lie the remains of former resident Albert Camus, author of *The Stranger* and *The Plague. Lourmarin Marie (City Hall, which fields tourist inquires), Ave Philippe de Girard;* ☎ *04-90-68-10-77.*

The Var & Its Coast

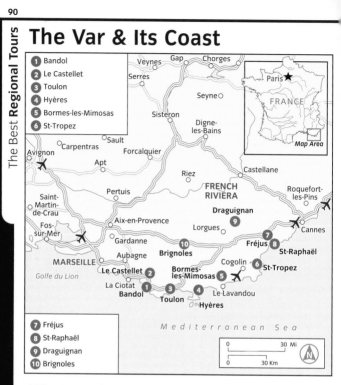

1 Bandol
2 Le Castellet
3 Toulon
4 Hyères
5 Bormes-les-Mimosas
6 St-Tropez

7 Fréjus
8 St-Raphaël
9 Draguignan
10 Brignoles

The Var's rocky outcrops, mountain brooklets, dense forests, luscious vineyards, undulating hills, and beaches speckled with bronzing bodies make for a patchwork of a landscape; no two areas look alike or offer the same attractions. The Var is home to some of the Côte d'Azur's most famous port towns—St-Tropez, St-Raphaël, and Fréjus. If you tire of seaside frivolity and bobbing fishing boats, you can get back down to earth in no-frills coastal Toulon or, farther inland, in Brignoles and Draguignon. This regional tour can be covered in reverse order. START: **Bandol. Trip Length 7–10 days.**

A Note on Hotels & Restaurants

For a full list in St-Tropez, see p 191 and 192 in chapter 6.

1 **Bandol.** If you're looking for a laid-back resort, without the hype of St-Tropez but with a reputation for fine wine, come to Bandol. Unlike most Provençal vintages, Bandol wines are red, full-bodied, and high in tannin, with subtle notes of pepper, cinnamon, and vanilla. The town itself is a popular tourist destination, thanks to four sandy **beaches:** Le Lido, Rènecros, Centrale, and Casino. The streets

around the marina, the Allée Jean-Moulin and Allée Afred-Vivien, are clad in flowers and shaded by pine and palm trees. On Fridays and Sundays, a cheerful market enlivens the center. In warmer months, boat trips run every 30 minutes from the harbor (☎ 04-94-29-44-34) to the tiny offshore island of **Île de Bendor,** noted for its excellent beaches and Provençal craft village. North of Bandol (3km/2miles), the **Jardin Exotique et Zoo de Sanary-Bandol** (☎ 04-94-29-40-38; http://zoosanary.com; daily) is a garden of tropical flora and cacti with an adjacent zoo and a bird sanctuary full of happy, chatty parrots. *Bandol tourist office, all Alfred Vivien; ☎ 04-94-29-41-35; www. bandol.org.*

Leave Bandol on the D559 to the A50 (toward Marseille/Aix-en-Provence). Exit at junction 11 (Circuit du Castellet) and take the D82. Turn right down the Chemin de Château Vieux and enter Le Castellet on the D226. Distance: 11km (7 miles).

❷ **Le Castellet.** In sharp contrast to Toulon, though less than an hour's drive away, this former stronghold owned by the Lords of les Baux sits on a woody hill presiding over vineyards. With its remarkably intact **ramparts, 12th-century church,** and **castle,** it has made

a beautiful backdrop for several movies. Numerous arts and craft shops afford ample incentive to part with your money. Head just beyond the gate by the Place du Mairie (City Hall) to take in the views stretching across the surrounding countryside. You can easily cover the village in 2 hours. *Le Castellet tourist office, Hôtel de Ville; ☎ 04-94-98-57-90; www.tourisme83.com.*

Retrace your steps to the A50, then follow signs to Toulon. You should enter the center on the N8. Distance: 23km (14 miles).

❸ **Toulon.** A far cry from the Var's many quaint fishing villages, France's second largest naval port is stately, distinguished by its nautical heritage. Anti-submarine, anti-missile frigates, and minesweepers line the port, and a nuclear submarine passes through from time to time. The best way to take it in is via **boat tour.** Three companies offer hour-long trips that depart from Quai Cronstadt. Contact the tourist office for more details or call Bateliers de la Côte d'Azur (☎ 04-94-93-07-56), Bateliers de la Rade (☎ 04-94-46-24-65), or Catamaran Côte d'Azur (04-94-46-29-89). You can also retrace Toulon's naval history in the **Musée de la Marine,** Place Monsenergue, Quai de Norfolk (☎ 04-94-02-02-01), next to the stunning old arsenal entrance—one

The landscape around Port Grimaud.

of the only historical sites to have survived WWII.

In the Old Town, you'll find the 900-year-old **Cathédrale Sainte Marie de la Seds** (rue Emile Zola), with its baroque altar and works by Puget; narrow and flaking streets lined with shops, fountains, and cafes; and pretty squares, such as **Place Victor Hugo,** dominated by Toulon's Opera House. The 19th-century part of town, designed by Paris planner Baron Haussmann, is characterized by wide, tree-lined boulevards, cafe terraces, and grand Empire-era fountains such as the **Fontaine de la Fédération** (1889), which spurts proudly on **Place de la Liberté.** If you're looking for a seaside holiday atmosphere, head to the **Mourillon** district, which has several beaches. Look out for **Fort St Louis** on the way, another one of Vauban's 17th-century military constructions. For places to stay and dine in Toulon,

A street in Fréjus.

see p 91. *Toulon tourist office, pl Raimu;* ☎ *04-94-18-53-00; www.toulontourisme.com.*

Leave Toulon on the N8 and follow signs to Hyères along the A57. After 3km (2 miles) it becomes the A570. Enter Hyères on N98 (toward Hyères airport and St-Tropez. Distance: 19km (12 miles).

④ Hyères and its Islands. The oldest winter resort on the coast has 35km (22 miles) of sandy beaches and a charming town center lined with palm trees. The best way to see the sights is to attack the town in three sections: the steep and scenic streets of the **old town,** which leads to the ruined **Château des Aires** and the 1920s artists' haunt, **Villa de Noailles** (be sure to wear comfortable shoes); shopping around **rue Massillon;** and strolling past the sumptuous 19th-century villas of the **modern town** and **Godillot district.** Don't miss the church of St-Louis, on Place de la République, notable for its Provençal Romanesque, and Gothic architecture.

Hyères's unspoiled islands, Les Îles de Hyères, make for an excellent day trip with or without kids. The largest, **Porquerolles,** is famed for its pine forests, beaches, wines, and bumpy cycle paths (for details, see p 57 in chapter 3). **Port-Cros** is a rugged national park with fabulous marine life and walking routes through lush, green forests. If you have a snorkel, goggles, and flippers, you can follow an underwater swimming route and observe the sea creatures in their natural habitat. A plasticized guide helps you to identify the plant and sea life while you swim. For more details, inquire in Hyères's tourist office (see p 25). If you plan to dive, it's useful to visit the park office in the Port-Cros's port. The small, palm-fringed harbor has several watering holes, under the watch of Fort Moulin. Climb up to the top for a sweeping panorama.

Île de Levant was formerly inhabited by Cistercian monks. Nowadays, the French Navy prohibits access to much of the island. In the west, however, the village of Héliopolis is coveted by nudist bathers. During high season, diving activities are open to the public. Inquire at the tourist office in Hyères (see p 25).

For places to stay and dine in Hyères see p 97. *Hyères tourist board, av Ambroise Thomas; ☎ 04-94-01-84-50; www.hyerestourisme.com.*

Leave Hyères on the N98. After 2km (1¼ miles; La Garrigue) take the D559 via La Lond-les-Maures to Bormes. Distance: 20km (12 miles).

❺ Bormes-les-Mimosas. As its name suggests, Bormes-les-Mimosas is famous for mimosa flowers, which it cultivates for export all over the world. Each year in February, a colorful street festival celebrates the harvest (see p 63). As steep as it is pretty, the old town twists and turns through cobbled slopes, covered passages, and a precipitous lane with 83 steps known in Provençal as *rompi-cuo*, or neck-breaker. If you're into churches, visit the 16th-century **Chapelle St François** (next to Wed's market place) built by François de Paule, who delivered the village from the Plague. The **Eglise St-Trophime** is also interesting for its trompe l'oeil frescoes around the choir. History aficionados can learn about Bormes in the **Musée d'Art et d'Histoire,** 103 rue Carnot (☎ 04-94-71-56-60; Tues–Sun).

And if you fancy a tipple in a working winery, stop by the

Bormes-les-Mimosas.

Château de Bregançon (see p 34), which offers samples of its Côte de Provence rosés. Bormes also has a beach suburb called **La Favière** with watersports facilities, beach shops, and a few places to grab food for a picnic on the sandy, family beach. *Bormes Les Mimosas tourist office, 1 pl Gambetta; ☎ 04-94-01-38-38; www.bormesles mimosas.com.*

Exit Bormes on the D559. At La Garrigue, turn right onto the N98. After 30km (19 miles), turn left onto D98a, then immediately right to the D61. At Gassin, rejoin the D98a to St-Tropez. Distance: 40km (25 miles).

❻ St-Tropez. Some consider St-Trop the birthplace of Riviera glamour; others regard it as an epicenter of hedonism. But for the locals, especially out of season, it's still a winning old fishing village with a market and traditional craftsmen. Make up your own mind—preferably from aboard a luxury yacht docked in the marina. For detailed information on St-Tropez, see chapters 6 and 2, p 186 and p 26.

From St-Tropez, take the D98 to Sainte-Maxime, then join the N98 (on the right) to Fréjus. Distance: 36km (22 miles).

❼ Fréjus. Once an important center for Roman merchants, Fréjus still has a **Roman amphitheater** and the remains of an **aqueduct.** The upper town, painted in ochre and peach tones, houses small boutiques, cafes, restaurants, and artists' ateliers. Make sure you set aside an hour to visit the unusual, fortified **Groupe Episcopal** (baptistry, cathedral, cloisters, and archaeological museum) in the old town. Other unique buildings are linked to Fréjus' military role as a center for colonial troops from Africa and Asia at the start of the 20th century. Exotic architectural legacies include a redbrick **Mosquée de Missri** (leave

Docks in St-Raphaël.

The rooftops of Fayence.

Fréjus on Av de Verdun and take the D4 toward Fayence for 3km/2 miles), built by Senegalese soldiers as an exact replica of the Missiri de Djenne mosque in Mali; and the **Hông Hiên Buddhist pagoda,** along the N7 (☎ 04-94-53-25-29), surrounded by an Asian garden with sacred animals and mythological guardians. Less colorful, but equally worthy of your attention, is the **Lanterne d'Auguste,** a landmark in the old port for sailors entering the harbor. The beach area of Fréjus is a long stretch of fine sand known as **Fréjus-Plage,** bordered by tacky bars and amusements. Families are welcome here. If you have kids, you'll appreciate a side trip to Fréjus's **Parc Zoölogique** and **Aqualand** water park. For full detailed information, see chapters 2 and 3. *Fréjus tourist office, 325 rue Jean Jaurès;* ☎ *04-94-51-83-83; www.frejus.fr.*

The Ave du Maréchal de Lattre de Tassigny (D98c) in Fréjus leads to rue Anatole France (D37) in St-Raphaël. Distance: 3km (2 miles).

8 St-Raphaël. A continuation of Fréjus Plage, the resort of St-Raph (as the locals call it) was largely destroyed during WWII and lacks the historic charm of Fréjus's center. What it does have is 36km (22 miles) of coastline—30 beaches and creeks that make it a wonderful spot for bathing, watersports, and beach games. It also lies at the foot of the magnificent **Massif de l'Estérel**— a red volcanic mountain, prized by nature enthusiasts and hikers. For watersports, check out the following companies: **Terrescale** (☎ 04-94-19-19-79; www.terrescale.com; Jun–Sept) runs sea kayaking and diving trips from Dramont beach. **Club Sous l'Eau** (☎ 04-94-95-90-33; www.clubsousleau) offers diving from the pleasure port of Santa Lucia. **Les Bateaux de Saint-Raphael** (☎ 04-94-95-17-46; www.tmr-saintraphael.com) runs boat trips to St Tropez, Les Iles de Lérins near Cannes, and along the Massif de l'Estérel coastline. Also inquire about their nighttime promenades. For water-skiing and parascending, call **Fun Ski School** (☎ 06-07-08-17-17; May–Oct). To discover the Massif de l'Estérel, ask the tourist office for information

about local guides. You could also try **Autres Regards** (☎ 06-08-33-00-68), which provides themed walks on volcanism, local flora and fauna, astrology (at night), and local geology. In summer, access to the Massif can be restricted due to the threat of forest fires. Check before you travel by calling the tourist office (☎ 04-94-19-52-52) or the Forest Commission (☎ 04-98-10-55-41, French only). *St-Raphaël tourist office, Quai Albert 1er; ☎ 04-94-19-52-52; www.saint-raphael.com.*

Go back into Fréjus and take the N98. At the Rond-point de la Miougrano island, take the D98b. At the Rond-point du Harkis island, take the N7 to join the A8. Exit at junction 36 toward St-Tropez, and take the N555 via Le Muy and Trans-en-Provence. Enter Draguignan on the D562. Distance: 34km (21 miles).

9 Draguignan. This former regional capital is a pleasant market town and a gateway to the Var's inland gorges, wild truffle woods, vineyards, and hilltop settlements. Plow through the modern shopping stores, fast food outlets, and 19th-century Haussmann-designed boulevards to reach the old town. The best way to walk is along the **Montée de l'Horloge** towards

Other Villages near Draguignan

It would be a waste to travel as far as Draguignan without visiting the picture-perfect villages that freckle the countryside. Visit **Lorgues,** for its wine and olives; **Barjols,** famed for its numerous stone fountains; **Aups,** for its winter truffle market, old streets, and plane trees; **Villecroze,** noted for its caves, converted into dwellings in the 16th century; and **Fayence,** for weaving and pottery.

The Best Regional Tours

The streets of Fayence.

the clockless 17th-century tower. Continue to **Place du Marché,** where many of the charmingly ramshackle houses sport emblematic blue Provençal shutters, and a market on Saturdays and Wednesdays promises roasted meat, cheeses, charcuterie, honeys, and herbs.

The **Musée des Traditions Provençales,** 15 rue Joseph-Roumanille (☎ 04-94-47-05-72), is a fine little local museum that reconstructs scenes of regional rural life. The **Musée Municipal,** 9 rue de la République (☎ 04-98-10-26-85), is also worth a visit for its Rubens and Renoirs. Don't miss the **Eglise St-Michel** (Place de la Paroisse), which contains a statue of St-Hermentaire, first bishop of Antibes, famed for having slain the dragon that gave Draguignon its name. *Draguignan tourist office, Av Lazare Carnot;* ☎ *04-98-10-51-05; www.dracenie.com.*

From Draguignon, go back to the A8 (toward Hyères/Aix-en-Provence). Exit at junction 35 and follow signs to Brignoles. Distance: 60km (37 miles).

⑩ **Brignoles.** Bustling, medieval Brignoles is a labyrinthian village, with narrow streets that twist and turn within thick 13th-century ramparts. Your first stop should be the tourist office, where you can grab a map and navigate your way past fine houses and old towers. If possible, visit on a market day (Wed on **Place Carami;** Sat at **Place Général de Gaulle** and **Place du 8 Mai**), when locally grown peaches, honey, olives, and oils are sold in abundance to strong-accented locals. **Eglise St-Sauveur** has a wonderfully ornate Romanesque wooden doorway. Admire it on your way up the covered stairway of **rue du Grand Escalier,** which leads to the atmospheric 13th-century Counts Palace, today's **Musée du Pays Brignolais,** Place des Comptes de Provence (☎ 04-94-69-45-18). The highlight here is the Gayole tombstone—a slab demonstrating the transition from pagan to early Christian iconography. *Brignoles tourist office, carrefour Europe;* ☎ *04-94-72-04-21;* www.officedetourisme-brignoles.com.

Where to **Stay & Dine**

L'Hostellerie de l'Abbaye de La Celle LA CELLE   Alain Ducasse manages the restaurant in this 18th-century Benedictine abbey-turned-country inn. Chef Benoit Witz's Provencal cuisine earned a Michelin star in 2006. *10 Pl du General de Gaulle, 83170.* ☎ *33-04-98-05-14-14. www.abbaye-celle.com. Menus 42€–76€; entrees 27€–39€. Doubles 205€–310€; suite 300€–350€. AE, MC, V.*

Hotel du Soleil HYERES   The decor is simple and old-fashioned, but the welcome is warm, the location is central (in the old town), Wi-Fi is free, and rates are reasonable. *Rue du Rampart.* ☎ *04-94-65-16-26. www.hoteldusoleil.com. 22 units. Doubles 40€–90€. MC, V.*

★ **La Corniche Best Western** TOULON   A 15-minute walk from the town center but near Toulon's Mourillon beaches, this well-dressed hotel has tastefully decorated rooms and a restaurant frequented by locals (a reliable indicator of good food). *Littoral Frédéric-Mistral.* ☎ *04-94-41-35-12. www.corniche hotel.com. 25 Units. Doubles 85€–150€. AE, MC, V.*

★★ **L'Aréna** FREJUS   You'll feel like you're sleeping in a large Riviera villa here. Decor is tastefully Provençal, with yellows and blues throughout. The turquoise pool is inviting. The restaurant serves delicacies such as fricassee of lobster and fois-gras. *145 rue Général de Gaulle.* ☎ *04-94-17-09-40. www.arena-hotel.com. 36 units. Doubles 85€–150€. AE, MC, V.*

★★ **Le Haut du Pavé** HYERES   Think perfectly cooked fish, Provençal specialties, fine wine, medieval vaults, and friendly service. Think one of the best restaurants in Hyères. *Place Massillon.* ☎ *04-94-35-20-98. Menu 20€–30€. Lunch and dinner Wed–Sun.*

Hostellerie de l'Abbaye de La Celle.

The Riviera & Monaco

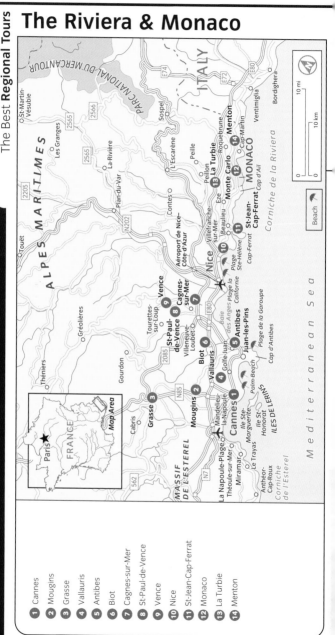

1 Cannes
2 Mougins
3 Grasse
4 Vallauris
5 Antibes
6 Biot
7 Cagnes-sur-Mer
8 St-Paul-de-Vence
9 Vence
10 Nice
11 St-Jean-Cap-Ferrat
12 Monaco
13 La Turbie
14 Menton

The Riviera and Monaco encompass the best and the worst of the south of France. On the one hand, there are all those tall, concrete, post-War constructions monopolizing sea views along some of France's most spectacular coastline. On the other, there's the definitive glamour of towns such as Cannes and Monte Carlo; there's the legacy of artists such as Henri Matisse, Auguste Renoir, Jean Cocteau, and Pablo Picasso; and there's a subtropical climate that supports extraordinary gardens and citrus groves. When the coast gets to be too glitzy and expensive, relief is a brief trip inland, in villages such as Haut de Cagnes, Mougins, St-Paul-de-Vence, or the perfume capital, Grasse. START: **Cannes. Trip length 7–10 days.**

A Note on Hotels & Restaurants

For a full list, see chapter 6: in Cannes see p 142 and 143; in Nice see p 171 and 172; in Monaco see p 163.

❶ Cannes. The legendary film festival has fixed Cannes on the map as an epicenter of wealth, fame, and adulating stargazers and paparazzi. You could spend a day looking around town, shopping, and salivating over designer merchandise, before winding down over a cocktail in a trendy bar or hotel. Once you've explored the city center, you could embark on a day trip to Cannes's offshore islands, the **Îles de Lérins,** with their nature trails, pebbly beaches, and breathtaking views

across the sea onto Cannes. Cannes is also an ideal base from which to explore nearby villages such as **Mougins** (see below) and the town of **Grasse** (see below). *For more on Cannes, see p 136 in chapter 6. For more on the islands, see p 68 in chapter 4.*

Leave Cannes via Le Cannet district on the D6285. At the Rondpoint Winston Churchill, join the D3 and follow signposts to Mougins. Distance: 7km (4 miles).

❷ ★ Mougins. As with most of the Riviera's hilltop villages, Mougins was adopted by artists (Surrealists Francis Picabia and Cocteau, in the case of Mougins). Picasso also came here with Man-Ray, and the Spaniard was so short of money, he resorted to painting the walls of his

A view of Cannes.

room just to pay his rent. He came back a wealthier man in 1961, and he and his last love, Jacqueline Roque, bought a house they named **L'Antre du Minotaur** (the Minotaur's Lair). You can still see it today, opposite the pretty **Notre-Dame-de-Vie** chapel just southeast of the village. Mougins collects a lot of elite runoff from Cannes—a mon-eyed population responsible for restoring the village's wonderful medieval houses, all built upon the lines of ancient ramparts. Art lives on here inside the numerous art galleries. The **Musée de la Photographie**, 67 rue de l'Eglise/Porte Sarrazine (☎ 04-93-75-85-67), exhibits lesser-known works by celebrated photographers such as Robert Doisneau. For refreshments in Mougins, head for the elm-shaded **Place du Commandant Lamy,** lined with restaurants and cafes. The nearby golf course, **Royal Mougins,** is a chic choice for anyone looking to hit off a tee or two. *See p 82 in chapter 4. Mougins tourist office, 96 av Moulin de la Croix;* ☎ *04-93-75-87-67; www. mougins-coteazur.org.*

Leave Mougins on the Ave du Moulin de la Croix, then turn left onto the D35. At the Rond-point de Tournamy, turn right onto ave St-Martin. After 100m (109 yards), take the D6185 and follow the signs to Grasse (D9 and D4). Distance: 13km (8 miles).

❸ **Grasse.** The fragrance capital of the world has been making scents since the Renaissance. You could easily spend a languorous half-day in the famous perfume factories of **Fragonard** and **Molinard** (see p 64 in chapter 3) and in the revamped **Musée Interna-tional de la Parfumérie,** 8 Place du Cours (☎ 04-97-05-58-00; www.museesdegrasse.com; Wed–Mon; closed Nov–early Dec

Pottery from Vallauris.

and lunch), which recounts the history of perfume and cosmetics over the last 1,000 years. Grasse's colorful, often flaking *centre-ville* may charm you away from the scent of Fragonard for a spell. Wander the narrow streets, linked by old arches, steep ramps, and staircases, before entering the **Cathédrale Notre-Dame-du-Puy**—a magnificent example of Lombard-influenced Romanesque architecture. The **Musée d'Art et d'Histoire de Provence,** 2 rue Mirabeau (☎ 04-93-36-80-20; www.museesdegrasse. com; Wed–Mon; closed Nov–early Dec and lunch times), is set inside the magnificent 18th-century Clapier-Cabris mansion—former home to Revolutionary politician Honoré Mirabeau's sister. Its collections portray 19th-century life in Provence. The **Villa Musée Jean-Honoré Fragonard,** 23 bd Fragonard (☎ 04-97-05-58-00; www. museesdegrasse.com; Wed–Mon; closed Nov–early Dec and lunch), is the mansion where the 18th-century artist sought cover when he fell out of favor with powerful Revolutionaries. Today it is a cultural center devoted to art, with a stairwell that displays Masonic allegories painted by Fragonard's 13-year-old son. For a panoramic stroll, head to the **Jardin de la Princesse Pauline** (access from ave Thiers, bd Alice de Rothschild, bd de la Reine-Jeanne)—an ornamental garden affording excellent views over Grasse, the Esterel, and the Massif du Tanneron. For more on Grasse, see p 63 in chapter 3. *Grasse tourist board, 22 cours Honoré Cresp;* ☎ *04-93-36-66-66; www.grasse.fr.*

Retrace your steps to the D6185 and enter St-Basile, bypassing Cannes. At St-Basile, take the D35 toward Vallauris and follow the signs. Enter Vaullauris on the D135. Distance: 20km (12 miles).

❹ **Vallauris.** Despite standing out for its rare grid plan, conceived in the 16th century after the town was razed in 1390, tacky Vallauris would have little to offer were it not for Picasso, who took up pottery here. Indeed, don't put aside more than an hour, unless you visit the **Musée National de Picasso** and adjacent **Musée Magnelli** and **Musée de la Céramique** (see p 43), or live and die for ceramics—a tradition that continues here, although most workshops qualify as tourist traps. *Vallauris tourist board, av Frères Roustan 06220;* ☎ *04-93-63-21 07; www.vallauris-golfe-juan.com.*

Leave Vallauris on the D135. After 2km (1 mile) turn left onto D6007. Turn left at the first island, then right. At the next island, take the D6107 to Antibes. Distance: 9km (5½ miles).

❺ ★★ **Antibes.** The largest pleasure port on the Riviera is an ideal base for visiting the smaller villages of Biot, Haut-de-Cagnes, St-Paul-de-Vence, and Vence. As a result, you could spend 2 nights here—more if you plan to sunbathe (the main beach is La Gravette). Antipolis (Antibes) began life around 500 B.C.

as a Greek trading post. After Ligurian assaults, a tremulous spell under the Romans, and further barbaric invasions, it eventually fell to the Lords of Grasse, then the bishops of Antibes, and, in the 14th century, the Grimaldis of Monaco. Henry IV of France bought it back in 1608 as a defense post against the kingdom of Savoy. Today the **Château Grimaldi** houses the **Musée Picasso** (also see p 43), which displays a collection of works donated by the artist. The picturesque streets of old Antibes are lively year-round. One of the region's best produce markets, **Le Marché Provençal** (Tue–Sun), is on Cours Masséna. While you're there, don't miss **Balades en Provence** at N 25 (☎ 04-93-34-93-00)—a wonderful boutique selling olive oils, pesto, honeys, and the favored drink of all hedonists, absinthe. Try it in the bar downstairs, but don't count on a meeting with the Green Fairy: Absinthe lost its hallucinogenic properties years ago. To best rub shoulders with the yachterati, head to **Port Vauban,** where you'll see some of the grandest vessels on the coast. Over the port, the **Fort Carré,** ave du 11 Novembre (☎ 06-14-89-17-45; www.antibes-juanlespins.com; Tues–Sun 10am–4:30pm winter, until 6pm Jul 15–Sept 15), is a fine example of the

The market in Antibes.

A glassblower in Biot.

star-shaped defenses designed in the 17th century by Marquis de Vauban, Louis XIV's military genius. Guided tours are available in English.

Inside the ramparts, the **Eglise Notre-Dame de l'Immaculée Conception** was built over a Roman temple devoted to Diana. It's decorated in ochres, reds, and penetrating blues. The belfry is a converted 12th-century watchtower. South of the marina, the small **Musée Archéologique,** Bastion St André (☎ 04-92-90-54-35), covers 4,000 years of Provençal history. Within an old 19th-century school building, the **Musée Peynet,** Place Nationale (☎ 04-92-90-54-30) contains hundreds of works by Raymond Peynet (1908–1999), one of France's most successful cartoonists. For shopping, **rue Sade,** between Cours Masséna and Place Nationale, is lined with quaint shops. If you're in Antibes with kids, don't miss the sea life at **Marineland** just outside the center (see p 55). *Antibes tourist board, 11 pl Gén de Gaulle; ☎ 04-97-23-11-11; www.antibesjuanlespins.com.*

From Antibes, take the D6007 (Bd du Général Vautrin) and turn right onto the D704 (Route d'Antibes) to Biot. Distance: 6.5km (4 miles).

6 **Biot.** Biot is a tiny perched village famous for its flowers (roses,

carnations, and mimosa) and blown glass, strewn with pretty bubbles. It's easy to circumnavigate, and the tourist office publishes a very good self-guided map. Once you've taken in the sights, head out of the village along the D4 (Chemin de Combes) to watch live glassblowing at the **Verrerie de Biot** (☎ 04-93-65-03-00; www.verreriebiot.com; daily), which has a shop and adjacent art gallery that showcases contemporary glass-themed pieces. Farther along the D4, the **Musée National Fernand Léger** is a treat for fans of cubism. *Biot tourist office, rue St-Sébastien; ☎ 04-93-65-78-00; www.biot.fr.*

Leave Biot via the D4. After 3km (2 miles), turn left onto the D6007. After another 3km (2 miles), turn right onto the D241, then continue on the D6098. After 2km (1 mile), turn left onto the D341. Distance: 10km (6 miles).

7 **Cagnes-sur-Mer.** This town is in fact three separate divisions: **Cros-de-Cagnes,** which covers the seafront, is of little interest aside from a crowded pebbly beach, tacky restaurants, and watersports rentals. **Cagnes-sur-Mer,** farther inland, contains the former home of artist Renoir, whose estate, **Les Collettes,** is now a moving museum. **Haut-de-Cagnes**—a gem of a village perched high above the coast in medieval, chocolate-box glory— is a magnet for contemporary art, thanks to the UNESCO-sponsored International Painting Festival that takes place here each summer. The village's fortified **Château-Musée-Grimaldi** (☎ 04-92-02-47-30; www.cagnes-tourisme.com; Wed–Mon) is home to an olive tree museum, a modern art museum, and the fabulous **Donation Suzy Solidor,** a collection of more than 40 portraits by Raoul Dufy, Cocteau, and Tamara de Lempicka. *Cagnes*

tourist office, pl du Dr Maurel;
☎ *04-92-02-85-05; www.cagnes-tourisme.com.*

Leave Cagnes via D136. At the first island, take D336. At the second, turn left onto the D436. Continue on D2 for 3km (2 miles), and after a short stint on D7, rejoin D2 on the right into Saint-Paul de Vence. Distance: 7km (4 miles).

⑧ St-Paul-de-Vence. Picture-perfect St-Paul is another delightful village full of pretty, medieval streets lined with art galleries, and crafts and antiques shops. Visit on market day to soak up Provençal life: **Marché d'Yvette** sells fruit and vegetables at the village entrance in the old washhouse (Tue, Thurs, Sat); every Saturday morning, the **Marché aux Fleurs** peddles flowers here too. Every Wednesday a country market sells regional produce on Place de Gaulle. Art lovers come especially to see the spectacular **Fondation Maeght** (see p 41). *Saint-Paul-de-Vence tourist office, 2 r Grande;* ☎ *04-93-32-86-95; www.saint-pauldevence.com.*

Take the D2 out of St Paul and follow signs to Vence. Distance: 6km (4 miles).

The streets of St-Paul-de-Vence.

⑨ Vence. This former Episcopal town, loved dearly by writer D. H. Lawrence, who died here in 1930, has retained much of its medieval charm. Part-ruined rampart walls still encircle the old town. You can take in sweeping views over the Alps from **Boulevard Paul André,** which follows the old ramparts. **Porte Peyra,** one of five original gates, leads to **Place Peyra,** the site of the former Roman forum, today a lovely square with an urn-shaped fountain. The old 17th-century **Château de Villeneuve,** 2 place du Frène (☎ 04-93-24-24-23), with its 13th-century watchtower, contains the **Fondation Emilie Hughes,** which shows works by 20th-century masters and holds regular temporary art exhibitions. The town's centerpiece is the **Cathédrale Notre-Dame de la Nativité,** built on top of a Roman temple to Mars. Don't miss the Matisse-decorated **Chapelle du Rosaire,** just north of the center. See p 41. *Vence tourist office, 8 pl Grand Jardin;* ☎ *04-93-58-06-38; www.vence.fr.*

From Vence, take the D36 to Cagnes-sur-Mer, where you can join the A8 autoroute to Nice. Exit junction 50. Distance: 23km (14 miles).

⑩ Nice. Thanks to its stunning setting in the Baie des Anges, a climate to die for, and wonderful culinary and cultural traditions, Nice is one of the most charming cities on the Riviera. Allocate at least 2 days for the town—more if you plan to use it as a base for exploring the region. For complete coverage of Nice, see chapters 3 and 6.

From Nice, follow the D6098 for 8km (5 miles) via Villefranche-sur-Mer. Join the D125, then the D25 to Cap-Ferrat. Distance: 11km (7 miles).

La Turbie's Roman Trophée des Alpes.

⓫ St-Jean-Cap-Ferrat. Snuggled between the resorts of Beaulieu and Villefranche, the Cap-Ferrat peninsula affords some of the best views over the sea from its coastal roads and footpaths. The main town, **St-Jean-Cap-Ferrat,** is a former fishing village with old houses that smile down over the pleasure boats in harbor. For the best views walk up to the 19th-century chapel at **Pointe St-Hospice,** or drive round to the **Phare** (lighthouse). Once you've climbed the 164 steps to the top, you can see as far as Italy, the Alps, and the Esterel. The peninsula is lined with some of the grandest villa's on the coast—the highlight of which is the astoundingly beautiful **Villa Ephrussi-de-Rothschild** and gardens (see p 64).

Leave St-Jean-Cap-Ferrat on the D25, and at ave Jean Monnet, join the D125 to Beaulieu. Leave Beaulieu on the D6098 to Monaco. Distance: 15km (9 miles).

⓬ Monaco. Governed by the Grimaldi family since the 13th century, the principality of Monaco is the tax-free playground of the mega-rich and famous. You needn't worry about crime here: Big Brother is watching from practically every street corner, and there is 1 cop for every 55 inhabitants. Monte Carlo, with its fancy casino and shops, is where much of

the action goes down, but you'll find excellent museums, an aquarium, and the Grimaldi family château to visit just across the port on La Rocher. *For complete coverage of Monaco, see chapter 6.*

Leave Monaco via D6098. Join the D51 and enter Beausoleil. Leave Beausoleil on the D53 and after 4km (2½ miles) turn left onto D2564 to La Turbie. Distance: 7km (4 miles).

⓭ La Turbie. Built upon the Grande Corniche road, at the base of the Tête de Chien (dog's head) headland over Monaco, this hilltop village is mainly famous for the **Trophée des Alpes** (Alpine Trophy), one of the tallest and most spectacular Roman ruins in the region (see p 53). If possible come late afternoon to climb the trophy, and then stay for sunset when the lights of Monaco begin to twinkle over the jagged coastline. *La Turbie tourist office, Place Detras;* ☎ *04-93-41-21-15; www.ville-la-turbie.fr.*

Perched Village Hopping

If Provence's hilltop settlements compel you to see more, whip out your map and drive from La Turbie to the stunningly attractive villages of **Contes, Coaraze, Eze, Peillon, Peille,** or **Roquebrune.**

Leave La Turbie on the D2564 to the A8 and follow signs to Menton. Distance: 17km (11 miles).

⓮ Menton. The warmest spot on the Riviera is the lemon capital of France, with an annual lemon festival in February, which draws in crowds of festive onlookers. The streets of the old town are colorful and inviting. Shops, cafes, and houses with Belle Epoque façades along the main pedestrian thoroughfare, **rue St-Michel,** are intermingled with citrus trees. A stroll through the bustling **covered market** will stimulate your senses with luscious local produce. The **Basilique St-Michel-Archange,** with its fine medley of Baroque ornamentations, is the largest church of its kind in the region. Jean Cocteau is associated with Menton, thanks to the **Salle des Mariages** he decorated in the City Hall, and to the **Musée Jean Cocteau,** devoted to his art (for both). The **Musée des Beaux-Arts** (see p 169), inside the **Palais Carnolès,** showcases works from the 12th to the 15th century, and has a sumptuous citrus garden. Another fine garden is the **Jardin du Val Rameh** (from Promenade de la Mer, take the Chemin de St-Jacques), which has a startling array of sub-tropical flora that thrive on panoramic terraces with views over the town and the sea. *Menton tourist office, 8 av Boyer;* ☎ *04-92-41-76-76;* www.menton.fr.

Where to Stay & Dine

In addition to Cannes, Nice, and Monaco, Antibes makes for a fine base. Stay at the wonderful **La Jabotte:** a gem of a hotel with exquisite, personalized decor. It's a 10-minute walk from the old town, opposite the beach, and Tommy the dog is the star of the house (13 ave Max Maurey, Cap d'Antibes; ☎ 04-93-61-45-89; www.jabotte.com; doubles from 57€–176€). For lunch or dinner, dine at **Le Comptoir de la Tourraque,** where you will find textbook gourmet French cuisine for around 35€ (1 rue Tourraque; ☎ 04-93-95-24-86).

Relaxing outside La Jabotte.

Bouches du Rhône & Rhône Delta

1. Nîmes
2. Camargue
3. Aigues-Mortes
4. Arles
5. St-Rémy
6. Les Baux
7. Salon de Provence
8. Aix-en-Provence
9. Marseille
10. Les Calanques
11. Cassis

Most of the Bouche du Rhône's attractions lie inland, on the Rhône River, which fans into the sea through the Camargue, French cowboy country. In ancient times, the Romans inhabited much of the Rhône Valley. Their legacy endures in Arles, Aix-en-Provence, and Nîmes. Farther inland toward the Alpilles mountains, St-Remy is quintessentially Provençal, and nearby Les Baux teeters atop a rocky outcrop. Back along the coast, Marseille and the fishing town of Cassis are popular destinations, linked together by dozens of stony creeks called Calanques. This tour can also be covered in reverse order. START: **Nîmes. Trip length: 7–10 days.**

① **Nîmes.** An incredibly sturdy set of Roman ruins will be the highlight of this tour for many historical architecture lovers. Geographically in Languedoc-Roussillon, Nîme's traditions and proximity to the Rhône make it thoroughly Provençal in spirit. While you're there, don't miss the **Pont du Gard** (25km/16 miles northeast along the N86, then D6086), the tallest of all Roman aqueducts (48m/52 yds). *For more details on Nîmes, see p 174 in chapter 6, and p 51 in chapter 3.*

A Note on Hotels & Restaurants

For a full list in these towns, see Nîmes, p 178 and 179; in Arles, p 127; in St-Rémy, see p 184 and 185; in Aix-en-Provence, p 121; and in Marseille, p 155 and 156.

From Nîmes join the A54 autoroute (toward Arles) and leave at junction 4 to follow signs to Stes-Maries-de-la-Mer, capital of the Camargue. Distance: 65km (40 miles).

2 Camargue. Unique to the region in every way, the Camargue has its own traditions, and it's home to *gardians*, France's cowboys. They herd and care for white horses and black bulls, and live in distinctive, low, whitewashed *mas*, or farmhouses. A haunting, flat region of rice paddies and salt marshes, it attracts rare birds, including pink flamingos. One of the best places to observe our feathered friends is in the **Parc Ornithologique du Pont-de-Gau,** off the D570 (☎ 04-90-97-82-62; www.parcornithologique.com; daily), where more than 400 species of migrating birds visit annually. While you're there, check out the **Centre d'Information du PNRC** (☎ 04-90-97-86-32; Apr–Sept daily; Oct–Mar Sat–Thurs), also in Pont-de-Gau. It commands excellent views over the lagoon and chronicles the history of the Camargue. Just 4km (2½ miles) south of here is the region's capital, **Saintes-Maries-de-la-Mer.** It is named after three Marys: Mary Magdalene, her sister Mary Jacobea, and Mary Salome, mother of the apostles James and John. According to legend they set sail after the crucifixion, landing with their servant Sarah in Saintes-Maries, where they built a shrine. Their arrival is celebrated in May and October, when residents carry a statue to the sea for a blessing. Despite the crowds in summer, cheery Saintes-Maries feels like a traditional fisherman's town year-round. The local Gypsy population's presence is most evident in the town center, where you will find shops strewn with colorful Romany souvenirs. The Romanesque **Eglise de Notre-Dame-de-la-Mer** is a gem of a fortified church. Climb up to the rooftop walkway encircling the church for a view over the sea, the town, and the Camargue plains. Back inside the church, on the north side of the nave above the altar, you can see the three Marys' boat, which locals parade around town in May and October during the celebrations. In the crypt lie the relics of St. Sarah.

Along the D570, 10km (6 miles) southwest of Arles, the **Musée de la Camargue,** Parc Naturel Regional de Camargue, Mas du Pont de Rousty (☎ 04-90-97-10-82; Apr–Sept daily, Oct–Mar Wed–Mon), a fabulous museum, is set inside an old 19th-century *mas.* It is devoted to traditional Camargue life and the

A Camargue cowboy.

108

The Best Regional Tours

The Camargue police station.

flora and fauna. The museum is also affiliated with a 3.5km (2 miles) educational trail that allows you to observe local husbandry and agricultural activities.

The main roads through the Camargue are the D36, D36C, D570, and D37. The **Salin de Giraud,** just off the D36, provides a viewing point over the salt pans in the east. To fully appreciate the strange beauty of this region, go off the beaten track on foot, bike, or horseback. Ask for detailed maps at the tourist office in Nîmes, Arles, Aigues-Mortes, or Sainte-Maries. The wonderful **Le Mas de Peint** hotel and working farm in Le Sambuc (see Where to Stay, below), offers excellent horseback riding excursions across their land, where they raise horses and bulls used in local bullfights. *For more information, see chapter 3 and chapter 4.*

Leave Saintes-Maries and join the D570 via La Brouztière. Turn left onto D85, then right onto the D38, and left again onto the D38a. Join the D58 and after 12km (7½ miles), at the island, join the D46. At the next island, take the D979 to Aigues-Mortes. Distance: 31km (19 miles).

3 Aigues-Mortes. The turreted silhouette of Aigues-Mortes is

impressive any time of day, but it's especially beguiling at sunset. The medieval town's defensive curtain wall rises gallantly from the flat plains of the Camargue. Built to stave off outsiders, it now welcomes them into the town's grid-patterned streets via a series of ancient *portes* (gates). You could easily spend an entire lazy day here. Start by touring the **ramparts,** then take a break in one of the many cafes around **Place St-Louis.** The tourist office runs excellent 2-hour guided tours. Once you've taken in the towers and chapels, try a boat trip along the **Grau-du-Roi canal.** The Pescalune Barge leaves at the foot of Tour de Constance (☎ 04-66-53-81-21). *For more information, see p 19.*

Leave Aigues-Mortes on the D979 and join the D46. At the second island, join the D58 and then the D38c. After 5km (3 miles), turn left onto the D570 toward the N113. From here, follow signs to Arles. Distance: 46km (29 miles).

4 Arles. The Romans and Vincent van Gogh put this little town on the map. The Romans left behind an **arena,** a **theatre,** relics, and ruined baths. Van Gogh left behind more than 200 paintings and drawings of Arles and its surrounding countryside. *For a full list of attractions, see chapter 6, p 15 in chapter 2, and p 44 in chapter 3.*

Leave Arles on the D570n and after 15km (9 miles) turn right onto the D99 to St-Rémy. Distance: 25km (16 miles).

5 St-Rémy. This quintessentially Provençal market town was the birthplace of Nostradamus, who later lived in Salon-de-Provence (below, p 110). Its streets are lined with 15th- and 16th-century mansions, including the Marquis de Sade's family home, now a museum displaying local Roman finds. The nearby settlement of **Glanum** is another trove of Roman and Greek artifacts, a short drive or 30-minute walk from the town center along the D5. Van Gogh's presence is felt nearby here too, in the **Monastère St-Paul-de-Mausolée** (5km/3 miles along D5), where he convalesced after cutting off his ear in Arles. *For full listings, see chapter 6, and p 13 in chapter 2.*

Leave St-Rémy on the D5. After 7km (4 miles), join the D27 to Les Baux. Distance: 10km (6 miles).

6 Les Baux. Possibly the most dramatic fortified village in France, Les Baux commands spectacular views across the **Val d'Enfer, Les Alpilles** mountains, and, on a good day, the **Camargue.** This vantage, coupled with the town's beautiful, winding streets, attracts hoards of visitors each summer. Visit off season or develop nerves of steel, but, whatever you do, don't miss it. Set amid vineyards and olive groves, it is famous for its wines and oils, all

sold in typical Provençal boutiques. You can enter the 10th-century **ruined citadel** at the **Tour-du-Brau,** which also houses the **Musée d'Histoire des Baux de Provence,** rue du Trena (☎ 04-90-54-55-56), a museum devoted to Les Baux's history. Back in the main village, two contrasting churches are the 12th-century **Eglise St-Vincent** and next door **Chapelle des Pénitents Blancs.** Just opposite the village, an old quarry is the site where the mineralogist Pierre Berthier discovered bauxite (the principle component of aluminum) in 1822, naming it after the town. Today, part of the quarry has become the spectacular **Cathédrale d'Images**—an eerie light and sound show inside an old tunnel, route de Maillane D27 (☎ 04-90-54-38-65; www.cathedrale-images.com). Cars cannot drive up to the village, so leave your vehicle near the Porte Mage gate. *For more information, see chapter 2 p 14 and chapter 3 p 35.*

The rooftops of Stes-Maries-de-la-Mer.

Leave Les Baux on the D27. After 2km (1 mile), turn right onto the D5 and enter Maussane-les-Alpilles. Leave the town on the D17, regaining the D5 after Mouriès. At the island, join the D113 toward Salon-de-Provence. Distance: 32km (20 miles).

7 Salon-de-Provence. Salon's most famous inhabitant was the physician and astrologer Nostradamus, who wrote his celebrated book of predictions, *Les Centuries,* here. Published in 1555, it attracted much attention. The Vatican banned it for foretelling the downfall of the papacy and King Charles IX appointed Nostradamus as his personal physician. A CD-guided tour leads you through a series of kitschy waxwork tableaux at the **Maison de Nostadamus,** rue Nostradamus (☎ 04-90-56-64-31), the house in which the seer spent the last 19 years of his life. You can also visit his tomb, just outside the city wall, in the Gothic **Collégiale de St-Laurent.** Another pretty church is the 13th-century **Eglise de St-Michel,** with its five-bay arcaded tower. Shadowing over Salon is the **Château de l'Emperi,** Montée du Puech (☎ 04-90-56-22-36; Wed–Mon). Built between the 10th and 13th centuries by the Bishops of Arles, it houses a military museum, covering the history of the French Army from the reign of the Sun King to 1918. **City Hall** (Hôtel de Ville), the shops on **Cours Gimon,** and the cafes on **Place Croustillat** are the hub of modern life.

The town is particularly famous for its olives and soap. Most of the *savon de Marseille* actually comes from Salon. Around the station, look out for Belle Epoque follies, built by Salon's prosperous soap barons in the 1900s. *Salon de Provence tourist*

A sidewalk café in St-Remy.

office, 56 cours Gimon 13300; ☎ *04-90-56-27-60; www.visitsalonde provence.com.*

From Salon, leave along the D538, heading towards the A54 (toward Aix). Join the A7 for 10km (6 miles), then the A8. Exit at junction 31 and follow signs to the center. Distance: 40km (25 miles).

8 Aix-en-Provence. This former Roman spa town, nestled beneath the Mont St-Victoire, was once the capital of Provence. Now it's best-known as the home of Emile Zola and Paul Cézanne. Today, the town is a chic jamboree of fountains, Renaissance mansions, medieval streets, cafes, restaurants, and boulevards shaded by plane trees. *For full listings see chapters 6, 2, and 3.*

From Aix join the A8, then follow signs to Marseille (via A51 and A7). Distance: 35km (21 miles).

9 Marseille. France's oldest city has been a trading hub and center of immigration for millennia. It's split into quarters you could liken to urban villages, and you need at least 2 days to get a feel for the place, longer to get your bearings, and a lifetime to see and understand the ancient town and its chalky coastline. Grab a boat from the **Vieux Port** on Quai des Belges to visit the **Îles de Frioul** offshore. The main island is the **Île d'If,** dominated by the 16th-century fortress that inspired Alexandre Dumas to write *The Count of Montecristo. For more information see p 144 chapter 6, p 20 chapter 2, and p 33 chapter 3.*

The direct route from Marseille to Cassis is along the D559. Along the coastline, you will notice the Calanques, access to which are signposted. Marseille and Cassis are 30km (19 miles) apart.

⑩ **Les Calanques.** These spectacular slashes in the limestone cliffs between Marseille and Cassis are the craggy sea edges of a 5,000-hectare (12,355 acre) national park—home to rare flora and fauna (including Europe's largest snake and lizard) and birdlife. In the coves, some locals are lucky enough to have family *cabanons*—tiny, old fisherman's huts passed down from generation to generation. The only way to access most of the Calanques is on foot, but pack plenty of water and wear decent shoes before you set out. The only Calanque fully accessible by car on the Cassis side is **Port Miou.** It has the longest beach, and it's nearly always invaded by pleasure boats. The Calanques close to Marseille are flatter and wider, with some limited parking facilities. From Marseille toward Cassis, the best Calanques are **Les Goudes,** a tiny fishing village set amid impressive cliffs, with a few local restaurants; **Callelongue,** with its many cabins and *cabanons*; **Sormiou,** widely considered the best Calanque, with a tiny port, a

beach, and seafood restaurants; **Morgiou,** separated from Sormiou by the Cap Morgiou, which has a wonderful viewing point; **Sugiton,** with its turquoise water (coveted by nudists); **En-Vau,** the prettiest of them all (see p 67); **Port-Pin,** surrounded by pines; and Port Miou. At sunset, don't miss the heart-stopping views over the Calanques along the **Route des Crêtes.** (See p 25; take D559 east from Cassis and watch for a signposted road on your right, then turn left at Pas de la Colle.) If you fancy diving around the Calanques, contact the **Centre Cassidain de Plongée** (3 rue Michel Arnaud; ☎ 04-42-01-89-16; www.cassis-services-plongee.fr); and for walking and rock climbing, call **Massilia Sport Aventure** (☎ 06-12-39-59-59; www.massilia-sport-aventure.com). *To see the Calanques by boat, see En Vau on p 67 in chapter 4.*

⑪ **Cassis.** This pretty fishing port, sheltered by the Cap Canaille outcrop, is famous for its pretty streets and excellent seafood. *For more information, see chapters 2 and 4.*

Marseille's city hall and port.

Where to **Stay & Dine**

★★ **Château de Cassis** CASSIS
Every nook and cranny is charmed
in this beautifully restored château,
where old armor stands alongside
contemporary art. The views over
Cassis and the coast will stay etched
in your memory. Rooms are sublime.
Lunch is 45€, dinner is 75€.
Traverse du Château. ☎ *04-42-01-
63-20. www.chateaudecassis.com.
Doubles 190€–470€. MC, V.*

Hôtel Angleterre SALON DE
PROVENCE   The decor here can be
kitschy (check out the frescoes in
the lobby); but the price is right, the
service friendly, the rooms comfortable, and the location central. *98
cours Carnot.* ☎ *04-90-56-01-10.
www.hotel-dangleterre.biz. 26 units.
Doubles 47€–60€. Parking 7€.
MC, V.*

★★ **Le Mas de Peint** CAMARGUE
White horses, bulls, and genuine
gardians wander around this beautiful 500-hectare (1,235 acre) property, which organizes excellent

horseback excursions into the
Camargue. The great, country
kitchen–diner combo churns out lip-
smacking gourmet food, and the
chef gives cooking lessons. *Le Sambuc via D570 and D36.* ☎ *04-90-
97-20-62. www.masdepeint.com.
11 units. Doubles 205€–381€. Half-
board available. MC, V.*

★ **L'Eau à la Bouche** SALON DE
PROVENCE   The fruits of the sea
served here come straight from the
fishmongers next door. The veranda
is an agreeable spot in summer.
Place Morgan. ☎ *04-90-56-41-93.
Menus 25€. MC, V. Tues–Sun lunch.*

★ **Nino** CASSIS   Smack bang on
the pretty port, Nino serves some of
the best seafood and Provençal cuisine in town. The three brand-new
bedrooms feel like the inside of a
luxury yacht. *1 quai Jean Jacques
Barthélemy.* ☎ *04-42-01-74-32.
www.nino-cassis.com. 3 units. Doubles 210€–350€. AE, MC, V.* ●

A room at the farmstead Le Mas de Peint.

6 The Best Cities & Towns

Aix-en-Provence

1 Cours Mirabeau
2 Café des Deux Garçons
3 Fontaine des Neuf Canons
4 Quartier Mazarin
5 Musée Granet
6 City Hall
7 Rue Gaston-de-Saporta
8 André Genis
9 Musée du Vieil Aix
10 Cathédrale St-Sauveur
11 Atelier Paul Cézanne
12 Pavillon de Vendôme
13 Fondation Vasarely
14 Musée d'Histoire Naturelle
15 Thermes Sextius
16 Cité du Livre
17 Musée des Tapisseries
18 Montagne St-Victoire

Where to Stay
Grand Hôtel Nègre Coste 27
Hôtel Artéa 22
Hôtel des Augustins 24
La Villa Gallici 19

Where to Dine
Le Formal 23
Le Papagayo 20
Le Passage 25

Nightlife
La Belle Epoque 26
Le Mistral 28
Le Scatt Club 21

P Parking
i Tourist Information

Previous page: The streets of St-Rémy.

Provence's former capital, demi-Parisian Aix is chic and contemporary, save for its elegant 17th- and 18th-century setting. Its tree-lined avenues, stately ***hôtels particuliers,*** graceful fountains, and exquisitely detailed façades have long inspired artists and writers. Both Paul Cézanne and author Emile Zola lived here, and visitors can follow in their footsteps via themed walks organized by the tourist office. For more than 600 years, the University of Aix-en-Provence has infused the town with intellectual energy; today, the large student population congregates on busy cafe terraces, soaking up the sun between classes. Aix is also a renowned spa town, built over a natural spring, and the largest center in France for processed almonds, used to make the delicious local specialty, Calissons d'Aix.
START: **Aix is 80km (50 miles) southeast of Arles and 32km (20 miles) north of Marseille.**

❶ ★★ **Cours Mirabeau.** Built in the 1650s as a promenade for the wealthy, this boulevard is the social hub of Aix. The once privately owned aristocratic mansions *(hôtels particuliers),* with finely carved doorways and wrought-iron balconies, are now official buildings or banks, but their splendor endures. Each *hôtel* has a story; the most bloodthirsty goes to the **Hôtel d'Iosard de Vauvenargues** (N°10), where in 1784, Bruno d'Entrecasteaux murdered his wife. The largest mansion is **L'Hôtel de**

The main plaza in Aix.

Forbin (N°20). Built in 1656, it is remarkable for its simplicity and symmetry.

In complete contrast, the opulence of the **Hôtel d'Espagnet** (N°38), reflects the social success of its owner, Pierre Maurel, whose booming textile business allowed him to climb the social ladder and join France's noble classes. The balcony, supported by giant Atlases, is typical of Aix's baroque architectural style. The right-hand side has fewer mansions but more cafes, and it catches the sun. Next to passage Agard, you'll find **Cézanne's childhood home** (today a shop called La Plume d'Or).

Take a Break

❷ **Café des Deux Garçons.** Once a hangout for Cézanne, Zola, and their chums, this cafe is an essential stop in Aix. *53 Cours Mirabeau.* ☎ *04-42-26-00-51.* **$.**

❸ **Fontaine des Neuf Canons.** Built over a natural hot spring, Aix has always been associated with water; the word *aix,* in fact, means "water source." Over time, the whole town was ornamented with

The Atlas figures that support the Hôtel d'Espagnet.

graceful fountains, three of which adorn the Cours Mirabeau. The **Fontaine des Neuf Canons** (rue Clémenceau) marks the center of the Cours and dates from 1691. Water from the moss-coated **Fontaine Moussue** (rue de Nazareth and rue Laroque) issues forth at a steaming 34°C (93°F). **Fontaine du Roi René** (just before Place Forbin) is a 19th-century ode to Good King René,

who introduced the Muscat grape to the region in the 15th century.

4 ★★ **Quartier Mazarin.** Archbishop Mazarin designed this grid-patterned district in the 17th century as a "luxury housing estate" for Aix's haute bourgeoisie and Parliament members. As you saunter through the restful squares and exquisite façades, you'll come across hidden art galleries, atmospheric antiques shops, and Aix's first Gothic building, the late 13th-century ★ **St-Jean-de-Malte Priory.** Built in honour of the Knights of Malta, it was the burial site of the counts of Provence and is now part of the Musée Granet (see below). *Rue Cardinale and rue du 4 Septembre.*

5 ★ **Musée Granet.** The former commander's palace, the *Palais de Malte* (1676) houses major painting collections from the great European schools of the 16th to 20th centuries. The Masters' A-list includes Rubens, Van Loo, Ingres, Rembrandt, and Cézanne. 🕐 *1 hr. Place St Jean-de-Malte.* ☎ *04-42-52-87-80. Free. Wed–Sat, Mon noon–6pm; closed Tues, Sun.*

The calissons d'Aix, *made from a medieval recipe.*

The streets of Aix.

6 City Hall. The Hôtel-de-Ville is a 17th-century masterpiece by Pierre Pavillon. Step through the wrought-iron gate into a pretty paved courtyard with classical pilasters separating the buildings. The square is dominated by a stunning 16th century belfry with an astronomic clock, built in 1661 embellished by four wooden statues that represent the seasons. *Place de l'Hôtel-de-Ville.*

7 ★★ Rue Gaston-de-Saporta. In ancient times, this bustling semi-pedestrian street was a road. Today it heaves with commerce. Between shops are several sumptuous mansions: N°23, the Hôtel Maynier-D'Oppède, was rebuilt in 1730 and holds summer concerts in its courtyard; Louis XIV stayed at N°19, the Hôtel du Chateaurenard, in 1660; and N°17 houses the Museum of old Aix (see below).

Take a Break

8 André Genis. For four generations, the Genis family has satisfied sweet-toothed locals with their crunchy *biscotins* (grilled hazelnuts in a biscuit coating, flavored with orange-flower) and their divine *Calissons d'Aix*. Legend says Good King René of Aix concocted this almond dessert to win the trust of his young second wife, Jeanne, on their wedding night in 1473. Until she was ready, he sublimated his own advances with a symbolic, petal-shaped *calisson*—which literally means "sweet caress." Like the dessert, the name endured. *1 rue Gaston de Saporta.* ☎ *04-42-23-30-64.* *$.*

9 Musée du Vieil Aix (Museum of old Aix). This magnificent 17th-century town house, clad in sumptuous friezes and majestic staircases, competes with its exhibitions, which include paintings, screens, ceramics, wooden puppets, and *santons*. Since the 18th century, Provençal families have traditionally hand-crafted Christmas nativity scenes. The figurines, called *santons*, represent the holy family, the magi, oxen, asses, and ordinary tradesfolk. Aix is a center for this craft, and the **Santons**

Aix cathedral.

Fouque workshop, 65 Cours Gambetta (☎ 04-42-26-33-38), is the best. ⏱ *45 min. 17 rue Gaston-de-Saporta.* ☎ *04-42-21-43-55. Admission 4€; free under 14. Tues–Sun 10am–12pm, 2–5pm (2:30–6pm Apr–Oct); closed public holidays.*

⑩ ★★★ Cathédrale St-Sauveur. This architectural hodge-podge was built on the site of a temple to Apollo from the 5th to the 18th century. To the south, a 12th-century Romanesque gate joins a Roman wall; to the north a colossal 14th-century bell tower flanks a richly carved gothic gate (15th–16th c.). Inside, cross the chancel to the stirring 12th-century cloisters, with pillared galleries casting dramatic shadows on the floor. ⏱ *30 min. Place de l'Université.* ☎ *04-42-23-45-65. Free admission. Daily 7:30am–12pm, 2–6pm.*

⑪ ★ Atelier Paul Cézanne. The major forerunner of Cubism, Cézanne lived and worked in this unassuming house uphill from the cathedral. It remains much as he left it in 1906; even his coat still hangs on the wall. Here he painted his celebrated *The Bathers*. ⏱ *50 min. 9 av. Paul-Cézanne (head north along rue Pasteur).* ☎ *04-42-21-06-53. www.atelier-cezanne.com. Admission 5.50€ adults, 2€ 13–25 yr, free under 12. Open Apr–June, Sept daily 10am–noon, 2:30–6pm; July–Aug daily 10am–6pm; Oct–Mar daily 10am–noon, 2–5pm. Closed public holidays.*

⑫ Pavillon de Vendôme. When the duke of Vendôme was forced to enter the clergy in 1665, he built this sumptuous palace and gardens as a secret love nest for his mistresses. The entrance is supported by two well-muscled Atlases, and the rooms contain interesting Provençal furniture and paintings. ⏱ *40 min. 32 rue Célony.* ☎ *04-42-21-05-78. Admission 2.50€; under 25 free. Wed–Mon 10am–6pm.*

★★★ Aix Markets

An orgy for the senses, from 8am until noon, Aix's vast street markets take over **Place des Prêcheurs** and **Place de la Madeleine** every Tuesday, Thursday, and Saturday. On the same days, a wonderful flower market showers color onto the square in front of the **Hôtel de Ville** (city hall), and an antiques fair fills **Place Verdun**. A daily farmers market, selling fresh local produce, also sets up beneath the plane trees on **Place Richelme**.

Aix After Dark

La Belle Epoque, bar 29 cours Mirabeau (☎ 04-42-27-65-66), is popular for its large terrace and attractive happy hour. Pretty people (Aix has plenty) flock to **Le Mistral** nightclub, 3 rue Frédéric-Mistral (☎ 04-42-38-16-49), for a late-night bop. For a variety of live music, **Le Scatt Club,** 11 rue de la Verrerie (☎ 04-42-23-00-23), is a crowded den that maintains notoriously late hours.

⓭ ★ Fondation Vasarely. Much of Aix's charm derives from its old buildings, but this modern structure is refreshing, made from black and white metal, shaped like honeycomb. Designed by Hungarian artist Victor Vasarely in the 1970s, it houses his avant-garde collections (often wild geometric tableaux), explores the boundaries between art and architecture, and promotes Aix's art on a national and international scale. ⏱ *1 hr. 1 av Marcel Pagnol.* ☎ *04-42-20-01-09. www. fondationvasarely.fr. Admission 7€; reduced 4€. Mon–Sat 10am–6pm.*

⓮ Musée d'Histoire Naturelle. In the Jurassic era, Aix-en-Provence was a breeding ground for Megaloolithid dinosaurs. Fossil lovers should visit just to admire 553 of the 1,000 Titanosaurus eggs found in Aix—the greatest number in the world. ⏱ *45 min. 6 rue Espariat.* ☎ *04-42-27-91-27. www.museum-aix-en-provence.org. Admission 2.50€. Free under 25. Open Wed–Mon (daily school holidays) 10am–12pm, 1pm–5pm.*

⓯ ★★★ Thermes Sextius. Aix lies on the site of a 10,000-year-old hot spring, enriched in calcium and magnesium, which served as the baths of Aix's founder, Roman Emperor Augustus Sextius, in 122 B.C. If you're feeling flush, pamper

The modern spa built on the grounds of the Roman Thermes Sextius.

The grounds of La Villa Gallici.

yourself at the modern spa, where remains of the original thermal pool are visible at the entrance. *55 ave des Thermes.* ☎ *04-42-23-81-82. www.thermes-sextius.com. Basic treatments: 82€–120€. Mon–Fri 8:30am–8:30pm, Sat 9:30am–7:30pm, Sun 9:30am–2:30pm.*

🔟 **Cité du Livre.** In an old match factory, the Méjanes library holds some 80,000 tomes left by the marquis de Méjannes in 1786. It also seconds as the official headquarters of the contemporary Preljocaj Ballet (www.preljocaj.org). *8–10 rue des Allumettes.* ☎ *04-42-91-98-88. www.citedulivre-aix.com. Opening hours vary.*

🔟 **Musée des Tapisseries.** This former archbishop's palace houses three series of important tapestries from the 17th and 18th centuries, including the world's only example of *The History of Don Quixote,* by Natoire (1735). ⏱ *40 min. 28 place des Martyrs de la Résistance.* ☎ *04-42-23-09-91. Admission 2.50€. Wed–Mon 10am–12:30pm, 1:30–5pm. Closed public holidays.*

🔟 ★★★ **Montagne St-Victoire.** It's easy to understand why this limestone range, 1,011m (3,297 ft) tall and 7km (4 miles) wide, obsessed Cézanne. He painted it more than 60 times. Picasso, however, got the final word: The Spaniard is buried on its north slopes at the Château de Vauvenargues, where he lived until his death in 1973. *From Aix, Vauvenargues is 15km (9 miles) northeast along the D10.*

Where to **Stay & Dine**

★ **Grand Hôtel Nègre Coste**
COURS MIRABEAU This 17th-century town house is popular with musicians who flock to Aix for the summer festivals (see p 196). Rooms are excellent value and parking is available. *33 cours Mirabeau.* ☎ *04-42-27-74-22. www.hotelnegrecoste.com. 37 units. Doubles 85€–145€. MC, V.*

Hôtel Artéa HISTORIC CENTER
The best budget hotel in town is in a stately 19th-century house with bright, clean rooms. *4 bd de la République.* ☎ *04-42-27-36-00. www.hotel-artea-aix-en-provence. com. 42 units. Doubles 72€–87€. AE, MC, V.*

★ **Hôtel des Augustins** COURS
MIRABEAU History lovers enjoy this quirky hotel—first a 12th-century chapel, then an auberge where Martin Luther stayed after his excommunication from Rome. *3 rue de la Masse.* ☎ *04-42-27-28-59. www.hotel-augustins.com. 29 units. Doubles 97€–240€. AE, MC, V.*

★★★ **La Villa Gallici** NORTH OF
HISTORIC CENTER This relentlessly chic inn has charming rooms richly infused with the decorative traditions of Aix, a pool, and Aix's finest restaurant (Le Clos de la Violette). *Av. de la Violette (impasse des Grands Pins).* ☎ *04-42-23-29-23. www.villagallici.com. 22 units. Doubles 220€–900€. AE, DC, MC, V.*

★★★ **Le Formal** COURS
MIRABEAU *FRENCH* Join the local gastronomes for chef Jean-Luc's succulent foie-gras, locally produced cheeses, fresh lobster, and solid wine list. *32 rue Espariat.* ☎ *04-42-27-08-31. Menus: lunch*

17€–21€; dinner 29€–44€. AE, MC, V. Open Tues–Fri noon–2pm, 7–10:30pm; Sat 7–10:30pm.

Le Papagayo HISTORIC CENTER
SALADS Cheap food and copious salads are served with a smile on this bustling, sun-filled square. *22 place Forum des Cardeurs.* ☎ *04-42-23-98-35. Menus 14€–18€, salads 10€. Lunch daily (May–Aug noon–3pm lunch & dinner daily). No credit cards.*

★ **Le Passage** QUARTIER
MAZARIN *FRENCH FUSION* This converted warehouse is Aix's most fashionable address, combining fun design with great food, art exhibitions, live music, and even cooking classes. *10 rue Villar.* ☎ *04-42-37-09; www.le-passage.fr. Menus 22€–35€; a la carte 40€. AE, MC, V. Open daily 10am–midnight; closed some public holidays.*

Le Passage.

Arles

Where to Stay

Hôtel Calendal **18**
Hôtel d'Arlatan **14**
Grand Hôtel Nord-Pinus **13**
Hôtel Le Cloître **20**

Where to Dine

La Charcuterie **15**
La Gueule du Loup **17**
Le Café Van Gogh **16**
Le Cilantro **19**

1 Musée d'Arles Antique
2 Les Arènes
3 Thermes de Constantin
4 Théâtre Antique
5 Musée Réattu
6 Place du Forum
7 Espace Van Gogh
8 Fondation Van Gogh
9 Église St-Trophime
10 Musée Arlaten
11 Hôtel de Ville
12 Les Alyscamps

P Parking
i Tourist Information

0 — 1/8 mile
0 — 125 meters

FRANCE
Paris ★
Arles ●

Arles is the gateway to the Camargue delta, French cowboy country. Once a Greek trading post and then a Roman colony, Arles is one of Europe's best-preserved Gallo-Roman cities, with ancient monuments casually woven into the town fabric of narrow medieval alleys, several superb Romanesque structures, modest homes with blue-shuttered windows, and cafes you may recognize from the paintings of Vincent van Gogh. Residents are generally friendly, with a strong identity influenced by the nearby Catalan regions of France and Spain. Bullfights and paella are common, and locals often wear traditional Arlésian costume during Arles' frequent festivals and the *course camargue*. START: **Arles is 32km (20 miles) southeast of Nimes, 36km (22 miles) south of Avignon, and 80km (50 miles) west of Aix-en-Provence.**

Money-Saving Travel Tip

Buy a **Pass Monument** (14€; 12€ reduced) from the tourist office and enter Arles' sites and museums for free.

1 ★ **Musée d'Arles Antique.** Although it's away from the old center, visit this museum before the rest of Roman Arles: A series of model replicas show how the ancient city would have looked, which will help you to visualize the ruins later. Collections include Roman Christian sarcophagi, sculptures, mosaics, and inscriptions from the Augustinian period to the 6th century A.D. ⏱ *45 min. Presqu'ile du Cirque Romain.* ☎ *04-90-18-88-88. www.arles-antique.cg13.fr. Admission 5.50€, 4€ reduced. Apr–Oct 9am–7pm; Nov–Mar 10am–5pm. Closed some public holidays.*

2 ★★★ **Les Arènes.** Built at the end of the 1st century, this oval arena measures 136 by 107m (149 × 117 yards). With space for 20,000 spectator seats, it was the largest Roman monument in Gaul. Today,

An aerial view of Arles.

Say Olé!

Arles' ties to Spain are strong, and polemical bullfights (*corridas*, or *course camarguaise*) take place between Easter and late September. The bull is only killed during the Easter *corridas*; otherwise, fighters (*raseteurs*) use long forks to grab trinkets hanging from a cord between the bull's lyre-shaped horns. Seats range from 15€ to 85€ (see contacts below).

Provençal and Spanish bullfights have replaced the Romans' bloody affrays. Amazingly, it was transformed into a fortress during the early Middle Ages and contained 200 houses and two chapels. You can still see three of the four watchtowers that surveyed the city. ⏱ *45 min. Rond Point des Arènes.* ☎ 08-91-70-03-70. www.arenes-arles.fr. *Admission 5.50€; 4€ concession. Nov–Feb 10am–4:40pm, Mar–Apr, Oct 9am–5:30pm, May–Sept 9am–6pm.*

Travel Tip

Tickets for Les Arènes and the Thermes de Constantin may be combined.

❸ Thermes de Constantin.
These ruins of 4th-century baths were the Romans' preferred meeting place. *Rue Dominique Maïsto.* ☎ 04-90-49-38-20.

❹ Théâtre Antique. In the
1st century B.C., pantomimes and mimes would have played to audiences of 12,000 here. It was almost lost forever when medieval folk used its stones as a quarry. The remaining seating—twin marble columns, stage, and orchestra—are still impressive, however, and you could be lucky enough to see an archaeological dig. ⏱ *25 min. rue de la*

Calade. ☎ 04-90-49-36-25. *Admission 3€, 2.20€ reduced. Nov–Feb 10am–4:30pm, Mar–Apr, Oct 9am–5:30pm (closed 11:30am–2pm), May–Sept 9am–6pm).*

❺ ★ Musée Réattu. The former
collection of local painter Jacques Réattu includes dozens of works by Picasso, pieces signed by Dufy and Zadkine, and some particularly special 16th-century Arras tapestries. ⏱ *45 min. rue Grand Prieuré. Admission 4€; 3€ concession. Nov–Feb 1–5pm; Mar–Jun, mid-Sept–Oct 10am–noon, 1:45–6pm; Jul–mid-Sept 10am–6:30pm.*

A bullfight in Arles' Roman arena.

An outdoor café near Arles' arena.

6 Place du Forum. On the site of the original Roman forum, this coveted square buzzes with cafes and restaurants that fill up beneath the erudite gaze of a statue of Frédéric Mistral.

7 ★★ Espace van Gogh. Vincent van Gogh spent only 15 months in Arles (from 1888), yet through the filter of his neuroses and what he called the town's "different light," he painted more than 300 writhingly vivid scenes now prized by museums and collectors. The town ironically owns none, but this library, bookshop, and exhibition space—set in the former hospital where the misunderstood genius stayed—looks just as it did on his canvases. *Place du Dr Félix Rey.* ☎ *04-90-49-37-53. Free. Daily 7:30am–7pm.*

8 ★ Fondation van Gogh. This exhibition space pays homage to Vincent with tribute works by artists such as Francis Bacon and Roy Lichtenstein. *24 bis Rond Point des Arènes.* ☎ *04-90-49-94-04. Admission 7€; 5€ concession. Apr–mid-Oct 10am–7pm daily, mid-Oct–Mar 9:30am–12pm, 2–5:30pm.*

9 ★★★ Eglise St-Trophime. Opposite an Egyptian obelisk taken from the Roman circus across the Rhône, this church's 12th-century portal is one of the finest achievements of the southern Romanesque style. Frederick Barbarossa was crowned king of Arles here in 1178. Don't miss the spectacular Gothic and Romanesque cloister, noted for its carvings. ⏱ *35 min. Place de la République.* ☎ *04-90-49-33-53. Free admission to church; cloister 3.50€, 2.60€ reduced. Daily 8:30am–6:30pm. Church daily 8:30am–6:30pm. Cloister Nov–Feb daily 10am–4:30pm; Mar–Apr, Oct daily 9–11:30am, 2–5:30pm; May–Sept daily 9am–6pm.*

The gardens of the Espace van Gogh.

The bar at the Grand Hôtel Nord-Pinus.

⑩ ★★ **Musée Arlaten.** The poet Frédéric Mistral led a movement to establish modern Provençal as a literary language. He founded this local folklore museum, filled with fascinating costumes and artifacts, using the money from his Nobel Prize for literature in 1904. 🕐 *45 min. 29 rue de la République.* ☎ *04-90-93-58-11. Admission 4€, 3€ reduced. Oct–Mar 9:30am–12:30pm, 2–4pm; Apr–May, Sept until 5pm; Jun–Aug 9:30am–1pm, 2–5pm.*

⑪ ★ **Hôtel de Ville.** While you're on place de la République, enter the city hall and look up at the unusual flat vaulting—a pure 17th-century marvel by Jules Hardouin Mansard, architect of Versailles, south of Paris.

⑫ ★★ **Les Alycamps.** Many tombs were looted, but the main alley of this ancient sacred burial ground is still as atmospheric as when van Gogh painted it. *Ave des Alycamps. Admission 3.50€, 2.60€ concession. Nov–Feb 10am–4:30pm, Mar–Apr, Oct 9am–5:30pm (closed 11:30am–2pm), May–Sept 9am–6pm).*

A room at the Grand Hôtel Nord-Pinus.

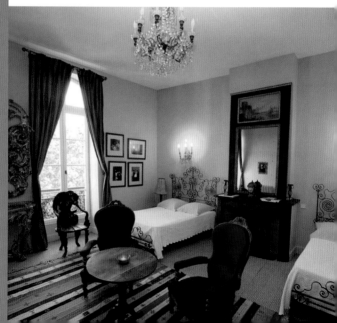

Where to **Stay**

Where to **Dine**

★★ **Grand Hôtel Nord-Pinus**
FORUM CENTER   Expect glamor,
even theater: Rooms are richly
upholstered, and representations
of bullfights decorate most public
areas. *14 place du Forum.* ☎ *04-
90-93-44-44. www.nord-pinus.com.
26 units. Doubles 137€–275€. MC,
V, AE.*

★ kids **Hôtel Calendal** ARENES
This place has an unbeatable position overlooking the arena. Rooms
are basic, but there are kid's games
in the shaded garden, and the
restaurant serves simple buffet
food. *5 rue Porte de Laure.* ☎ *04-
90-96-11-89. www.lecalendal.com.
34 units. 84€–99€ double; parking
10€. MC, V.*

★★★ **Hôtel d'Arlatan** MEDIEVAL
CENTER   Roman vestiges lie
underfoot in the lobby of this 15th-
century residence with a walled
courtyard pool. Rooms are furnished with authentic Provençal
antiques. *26 rue du Sauvage.* ☎ *04-
90-93-56-66. www.hotel-arlatan.fr.
47 units. Doubles 85€–155€; parking 14€. AE, MC, V. Closed Jan.*

Hôtel Le Cloître THEATRE
ANTIQUE   This atmospheric
budget option, with 12th-century
Romanesque vaults, used to be a
cloister. Rooms are lean on amenities but still a good value. *16 rue du
Cloître.* ☎ *04-90-96-29-50. www.
hotelcloitre.com. 30 units. Doubles
47€–65€; parking 5€. MC, V. Closed
mid-Nov–mid-Mar.*

★ **La Charcuterie** MEDIEVAL
CENTER *LYONNAIS*   The cheery
owner is proud of his Lyonnais
origins and the top-class sausages
and hams his Lyonnais restaurant
cooks so well. Wash everything
down with a local Côte du Rhone.
51 rue des Arènes. ☎ *04-90-96-56-
96. www.lacharcuterie.camargue.fr.
Menu 15€; a la carte 25€–30€.
MC, V. noon–1:30pm, 7:30–9:30pm
Tues–Sat (plus Sun & Mon in May,
July & Aug). Closed Aug 1–15, Dec
23–Jan 6.*

La Gueule du Loup ARENES
PROVENÇAL   In a stone-fronted
house near the ancient arena, this
cozy restaurant serves scrumptious
dishes such as bull filet braised in red
wine or monkfish in saffron sauce.
Reservations recommended. *39 rue
des Arènes.* ☎ *04-90-96-96-69. Fixed-
price menu 25€. MC, V. noon–1:30pm,
7:30–9:30pm Tues–Sat; 7:30pm–
9:30pm Mon. Closed 1 week in Nov &
mid-Jan to mid-Feb.*

Le Café van Gogh ARENES
CAFE   The famous yellow cafe
van Gogh chose for his work
Café la Nuit. 11 place du Forum.
☎ *04-90-96-44-56.*

★★★ **Le Cilantro** ARENES
FRENCH FUSION   Enjoy ultra-modern surroundings, inventive cocktails, excellent wine, and chef
Jérôme Laurent's successful culinary inventions (think tuna with
foie-gras—surprising but delicious).
31 rue Porte-de-Laure. ☎ *04-90-
18-25-05. Lunch Menus 20€–25€;
Dinner Menus 40€–50€. MC, V.
Noon–3pm, 7pm–midnight Tues–Fri.
7pm–midnight Mon & Sat.*

Avignon

Where to Stay
Hôtel Colbert 22
Hôtel de Garlande 19
Hôtel de l'Atelier 13
Hôtel Europe 17
La Mirande 14

Where to Dine
Christian Etienne 16
Hiély-Lucullus 18
La Compagnie des
. Comptoirs 21
L'Ami Voyage en
Compagnie 20

Nightlife
Théâtre-Opéra 15

1 Palais des Papes
2 Pont St-Bénézet
(Pont d'Avignon)
3 Musée du Petit Palais
4 Café de la Comédie
5 Musée Angladon
6 Rue des Teinturiers
7 Musée Lapidaire
8 Musée Calvet
9 Chapelle des
Pénitents Gris
10 Collection Lambert
11 Place de l'Horloge
12 Villeneuve-lez-Avignon

✝ Church
Ⓟ Parking
ⓘ Tourist Information

Once the center of Christendom, Avignon is still one of Europe's most elegant and captivating medieval cities, bordered by the Rhône River, and encircled by medieval ramparts. The papacy was headquartered here in the 14th century (during what the Romans called the Babylonian Captivity), and the church's legacy prevails, centered on the Palais du Papes (pope's palace). Avignon's city walls encompass architectural treasures, petite bustling squares, and animated cafe culture. Its festivals, museums, and progressive, contemporary attitude toward film and theater have earned it the distinction of being one of the European Capitals of Culture for the millennium. Accommodations are nearly impossible to find during the summer months and festivals, between July and September, unless you book well ahead. START: **Avignon is 37km (23 miles) northeast of Arles and 45km (28 miles) east of Nîmes.**

The fortified city of Avignon.

① ★★★ Palais des Papes.
Dominating Avignon from a hilltop, this 14th-century monument—headquarters of a schismatic group of cardinals who came close to destroying the authority of the popes in Rome—is one of the most notorious palaces in the Christian world. Although stripped of most of its finery, some treasures are still visible. The Chapels of St-Jean and St-Martial contain 14th-century frescoes attributed to the school of Matteo Giovanetti. The pope's bedroom in the Tour des Anges is decorated in tempera foliage on which birds and squirrels perch. In a secular vein, the studium (stag room)—the study of Clement VI—was frescoed in 1343 with hunting scenes. For wine buffs, the monument's very own *bouteillerie* (wine house) offers *dégustations* (tastings) during visiting hours.
🕐 *1 hr. Place du Palais des Papes.* ☎ *04-90-27-50-00. www.palais-des-papes.com. Admission (including audio-guide) 9.50€; 7.50€ reduced (7.50€ and 6€ Nov to mid-Mar). Daily July 9am–8pm; Apr–June & Aug–Oct 9am–7pm; Nov–Mar 9:30am–5:45pm.*

A mime performing at the Festival d'Avignon.

Money-Saving Tip

Buy a combined ticket for the Pont d'Avignon and Palais des Papes; or get an Avignon Pass (at any attraction) and pay full rate for your first visit then a reduced rate at all other museums in Avignon and Villeneuve-lez-Avignon.

2 ★★★ kids **Pont St-Bénézet (Pont d'Avignon).** Spanning the Rhône, much of this 12th-century monument was washed away during floods several hundred years ago. Today it has only 4 of its original 22 arches. On one pier is the two-story

Chapelle St-Nicolas—one story in Romanesque style, the other in Gothic. As a fun extra, record your version of the famous song about the bridge, *Sur le pont d'Avignon,* on DVD (5€). Or watch the bridge live 24/7 on www.earthtv.com. ⏱ *50 min. Pont St Bénézet.* ☎ *04-32-74-32-74. www. palais-des-papes.com. Admission: 3.50€; 3€ concession (4€ and 3.30€ reduced mid-Mar–Oct). Mid-Mar–July, Oct 9am–7pm; July–Sept 9am–8pm (until 9pm during festival); Nov—mid-March 9:30am to 5:45pm.*

3 **Musée du Petit Palais.** Overshadowed by its giant neighbor, Le Palais des Papes, this wonderful museum contains an important collection of paintings from the Italian and Avignon schools of the 13th to 16th century. Several galleries also display Roman and Gothic sculptures. ⏱ *45 min. Place du Palais des Papes.* ☎ *04-90-86-44-58. www.petit-palais.org. Admission 6€; 2€ reduced. June–Sept Wed–Mon 10am–1pm, 2–6pm; Oct–May Wed–Mon 9:30am–1pm, 2–5:30pm. Closed public holidays.*

Take a Break

Café de la Comédie. Grab a table, a coffee, and a salad in the shade of a plane tree, while looking out at the Renaissance façade of Avignon's first theater. *15 pl Crillon.* ☎ *04-90-85-74-85. $.*

Festival d'Avignon

Created by actor Jean Vilar in 1947 and known throughout the land as merely "the festival," this world-acclaimed jamboree of top-notch theater now encompasses the official Festival d'Avignon as well as a simultaneous fringe festival. This is *the* time to visit (or steer clear), when for 3 weeks in July, every inch of available floorspace (including sidewalks and parking lots) becomes a stage. www.festival-avignon.com.

The Musée Anglodon.

⑤ ★★ Musée Anglodon.

Jacques Doucet (1853–1929) was a Belle Epoque dandy, dilettante, and designer of Parisian haute couture. He also collected works of art. He died a pauper, but his former home contains 6th-century Buddhas, Louis XVI chairs, and canvases by Cézanne, Sisley, Degas, Modigliani, Picasso, Max Jacob, and van Gogh. ⏱ *45 min. 5 rue Laboureur.* ☎ *04-90-82-29-03. www.anglodon.com. Admission 6€; 4€ concession. Tue–Sun 1–6pm (closed Mon in winter).*

Love Boat

Avignon is enchanting by night when the monuments are lit. However, a summer dinner cruise along the Rhône is even more enthralling when love is in the air. **GBP Boats** (☎ 04-90-85-62-25; www.avignon-et-provence.com/mireio) leave from Allées de l'Oulle.

⑥ ★ Rue des Teinturiers.

Named after the textile-working Indians who lived here in the 13th century, this picturesque, cobbled street, shaded by plane trees, is one of the city's most atmospheric spots. Waterwheels still wind along-side the River Sorgue, while locals relax in cafes, secondhand book-stores, and art galleries.

⑦ Musée Lapidaire.

A 17th-century Jesuit church houses this archaeological museum, filled with

A waterwheel on the Rue des Teinturiers.

The Place d'Horloge.

fascinating Gallo-Roman statues, gargoyles, Etruscan artifacts, mosaics, and glass. ⏱ *45 min. 27 rue de la République.* ☎ *04-90-85-75-38. www.musee-lapidaire.org. Admission 2€; 1€ reduced. Wed–Mon 10am–1pm & 2–6pm.*

8 ★ **Musée Calvet.** This wonderfully restored fine arts museum has lovely colonnaded rooms that surround a courtyard. Inside Gobelin tapestries adorn the ground floor. French paintings from the 18th and 19th century, silverware, clocks, and old locks make up other parts of a surprisingly wide-ranging collection of artifacts, including a good section of Impressionist and modern works. ⏱ *45 min. 65 rue Joseph Vernet.* ☎ *04-90-86-33-84. www.musee-calvet.org. Admission 6€; 3€ concession. Wed–Mon 10am–1pm & 2–6pm.*

9 **Chapelle des Pénitents Gris.** Tucked away on rue des Teinturiers by a little bridge, the pretty 13th-century **Chapelle des Penitents Gris** was the scene of a miracle,

when in 1433 flood water reputedly parted like the Red Sea to save it from destruction. *8 rue des Teinturiers. Open Tues, Sat 2–5pm.*

10 ★★★ **Collection Lambert.** Created in 2000 by Parisian art dealer Yvon Lambert, this remarkable gallery presents more than 350

Yvon Lambert at the Lambert Collection.

Buying Avignon's Wares

Les Halles, on Place Pie, is a bustling covered market (7am–1pm) that doubles as a cooking school every Saturday morning (11am–12pm), when chefs display their culinary talents before enthusiastic gastronomes. **Place Carmes** holds a morning flower and flea market on weekends. For high-street brands, head to **rue République.** The pedestrian streets around **rue des Marchands** are a maze of boutiques, and several famous designers flock to **rue St Agricol.** Avignon's oldest shop, **Mouret,** is a time-warp hatter, 20 rue des Marchands (☎ 04-90-85-39-38; www.chapelier.com), and **La Tropézienne** sells a rainbow of artisan-crafted sugary delights, 22 rue St Agricol (☎ 04-90-86-24-72; www.latropezienne.net).

The Mouret hat shop.

works from his personal collection—a testimony to his passionate engagement in several art movements—from Minimal, Conceptual, and Land Art from the '60s and '70s, to painting from the '80s, and photography and video from the '90s. ⏱ *50 min. 5 rue Violette.* ☎ *04-90-16-56-20. www.collectionlambert. com. Admission 5.50€; 4€ concession. July–Aug daily 11am–7pm, Sept–Jun Tues–Sun 11am–6pm.*

⓫ ★★ **Place de l'Horloge.**
With its cafes, national theater, 19th-century city hall, and adjoining 15th-century clock tower, this vast, shaded square is the hub of Avignon life. During the Festival d'Avignon it becomes the home of a swirling carousel of *artistes.*

⓬ ★★ **Villeneuve-lez-Avignon.**
This sleepy village opposite Avignon, just across the Rhône, contains some architectural gems built by the pope's cardinals. These include France's largest Carthusian monastery, the **Chartreuse du Val-de-Bénédiction,** rue de la République (☎ 04-90-15-24-24); the hauntingly beautiful **Eglise Notre-Dame,** Place Meissonier (☎ 04-90-25-46-24), built in 1333; the **Fort & Abbaye St-André,** Mont Andaon (☎ 04-90-25-45-35), founded in 1360 by Jean-le-Bon to serve as a symbol of might to the pontifical powers across the river; and the region's richest repository of medieval painting and sculpture in the **Musée Pierre de Luxembourg,** rue de la République (☎ 04-90-27-49-66).

Where to **Stay**

Hôtel Colbert CENTER This budget hotel is a winner, balancing charm with cheap prices in the heart of town. Rooms are small but clean (with air-conditioning), and breakfast is served in a pretty walled patio. *7 rue Agricol Perdiguier.* ☎ *04-90-86-20-20. www.lecolbert-hotel.com. 15 units. Doubles 45€–104€. MC, V.*

★ Hotel de Garlande CENTER Down a discreet side street near the Palais des Papes and Place de l'Horloge, you can't ask for anything more central, nor for anything more charming for your money. This old mansion has just 12 rooms, all dressed in warm and cozy tones, and the friendly staff members treat you like a family friend. *20 rue Galante.* ☎ *04-90-80-08-85. www.hoteldegarlande.com. 12 units. Doubles 72€–115€. MC, V.*

★★ Hôtel de l'Atelier VILLENEUVE-LEZ-AVIGNON Hidden in the heart of Villeneuve-lez-Avignon, 2 minutes from the Pierre de Luxembourg museum, this 16th-century house has great nostalgic style: Soft, pale colored rooms have high beamed ceilings and neatly tiled bathrooms. A rear garden with potted orange and fig trees provides fruit and shade for breakfast. *5 rue de la Foire, Villeneuve-lez-Avignon.*

☎ *04-90-25-01-84. www.hotel delatelier.com. 23 units. Doubles 53€–104€. MC, V.*

★★★ Hotel Europe CRILLON Sleep in this splendid 1580 town house, and you'll follow in the footsteps of Napoléon, Victor Hugo, Tennessee Williams, and Dalí. Rooms are spacious and tastefully clad in antiques, while the shaded courtyard is a fine spot for breakfast or dinner. *12 place Crillon.* ☎ *04-90-14-76-76. www.hotel-d-europe.fr. 44 units. Doubles 165€–792€. AE, DC, MC, V.*

★★★ La Mirande PALAIS DES PAPES This nest of opulence displays 2 centuries of decorative art, from the 1700s Salon Chinois to the Salon Rouge, with striped walls in Rothschild red. Rooms are huge, the garden is a tranquil haven, and the restaurant is Avignon's finest. Once a month, cooking lessons are organized in the vaulted basement kitchens. Parking 25€. *4 place de la Mirande.* ☎ *04-90-85-93-93. www. la-mirande.fr. 21 units. Doubles 295€–820€. AE, MC, V.*

The entrance to La Mirande.

A room at La Mirande.

Where to **Dine**

★★ **Christian Etienne** PALAIS DES PAPES *PROVENÇAL* This 12th-century dining room, still clad in early-16th-century frescoes honoring the marriage of Anne de Bretagne to the French king in 1491, reaches new culinary heights. If you're on a budget, opt for the half-price lunch menu. Or splurge on a dinner specialty such as filet of perch with Châteauneuf-du-Pape. Reservations required. *10 rue Mons.* ☎ *04-90-86-16-50. www.christian-etienne.fr. Fixed-price lunch 35€; fixed-price dinner 62€–117€. AE, MC, V. Noon–2pm, 7pm–10pm Tues–Sat. Closed early Aug & late Dec–Jan.*

★★★ **Hiély-Lucullus** HORLOGE *CONTEMPORARY FRENCH* Stunning Belle Epoque decor enhances grand, innovative cuisine such as St-Jacques scallops in a coconut crust, and Litchi mousse served with raspberries and sauterne jelly. Wine and service is faultless every time. Reservations required. *5 rue de la République.* ☎ *04-90-86-17-07. Fixed-price menu 29€–48€. Menu gastronomique including wine 83€. AE, MC, V. Noon–3pm, 7pm–9pm daily.*

★★ **La Compagnie des Comptoirs** CENTER *MEDITERRANEAN* Beneath the high ceilings of what was originally a 1363 Benedictine convent, dissolved during the French

The dining room at Hiély-Lucullus.

Revolution, prepare your taste buds for the Pourcel brothers' colonial sensations such as caramelized onion tart with smoked swordfish and orange vinaigrette. After dinner the restaurant becomes a popular lounge-bar. Reservations recommended. *83 rue Joseph-Vernet.* ☎ *04-90-85-99-04. www.la compagniedescomptoirs.com. Mains 14€. Menus 26€–45€. AE, MC, V. Restaurant open Tues–Sat noon–2pm, 7pm–10pm; lounge-bar Tues–Sat 6pm–1am.*

★★★ **L'Ami Voyage en Compagnie** This is a secret the locals would prefer to keep: a family-run cafe-cum-antique-bookstore that serves hearty, local cuisine, and decent wine. *5 rue Prévot Place St Didier.* ☎ *04-90-87-41-51. Mains 8€–14€. No credit cards. Mon–Sat 10am–7pm; closed 2 weeks late Aug & 1 week Feb.*

A Night at the Opera

Inside this festoon of 19th-century architecture, Avignon's **Théâtre-Opéra** makes for a perfect evening's entertainment with ongoing opera, ballet, chamber music, comedy, and symphony music concerts year-round. After the show, end your evening with a drink in one of the bars on Place de l'Horloge. *Place de l'Horloge.* ☎ *04-90-82-42-42. Box office Mon–Sat 11am–6pm. Tickets 5€–80€.*

Cannes

La Croisette 1
Allée des Stars 2
Pointe de la Croisette 3
La Malmaison 4
The Majestic Palace Hôtel 5
The Harbor 6
Le Suquet 7

Plage de La Bocca 8
La Table de Lucullus 9
Musée de la Castre 10
Eglise Notre-Dame de l'Espérance 11
Les Îles de Lérins 12
Château de La Napoule 13

Where to Stay
3.14 28
Cézanne 27
Grand Hôtel 25

Hôtel Molière 26
Martinez 31
Villa Tosca 20

Where to Dine
La Plage 30
Le Méchant Loup 16
Le Mesclun 15
Punto e Pasta 17

Shopping
Agnès B 21
Rue Meynadier 19
Rue d'Antibes 23

Nightlife
Au Bureau 18
Bar des Célébrités 29
Morisson's Irish Pub 22
Palme d'Or 31
The Quays 14
Tantra/Le Loft 24

Thanks to its world-acclaimed film festival, this tinsel town on the Riviera is a gloriously excessive place to visit, even when the red carpet is starless. Bronzed beauties, megastars, groupies, and curious first-timers arrive in droves to experience the decadence. Sandwiched between the red rocks of the Esterel and two peaceful offshore islands (Îles des Lérins), Cannes has attracted high-fashion crowds since 1834, when British Chancellor Lord Brougham stopped here to avoid an outbreak of cholera in Nice. He built a grand home, invited all his friends, and turned Cannes into a winter playground for the English aristocracy. More than a mere resort today, it has become a working port and a busy conference center 365 days a year. START: **Cannes is 37km (23 miles) east of Fréjus and 34km (21 miles) west of Nice.**

❶ ★★ La Croisette. Lined with palm trees, luxury hotels, private beaches, designer shops, and expensive restaurants, this elegant, 3km (2 miles) promenade is where every film star and tourist visiting Cannes ultimately ends up lingering. Just east of the old port, at the top of La Croisette, lies the "bunker"—Cannes' Palais des Festivals—home to miles' worth of that iconic red carpet, a 2,400-seat auditorium, the Debussy Theatre, broadcasting studios, and the tourist office. Guided tours are available 2 days a week. Ask at the tourist office in the Palais des Festivals on La Croisette. ☎ 04-92-99-84-23 or 04-93-39-01-01. www.palaisdesfestivals.com.

La Croisette, Cannes' seaside promenade.

Tip

Unless you're bent on star-spotting or fond of crushing crowds and exorbitant prices, avoid Cannes during the film festival in May and from July through September.

❷ kids Allée des Stars. Between the Palais des Festivals and the gardens, kids (and adults) love the trail of more than 200 hand prints of celebrities who have walked Cannes' red carpet during the film festival.

❸ ★ Pointe de la Croisette. Stroll eastward along the Croisette to this excellent vantage point, with views over La Napoule bay, Cannes, the Esterel, and Îles de Lérins. In the Middle Ages, a cross (croissette) lay here, facing the islands in defiance of the Saracen invaders. Today, artificial beaches and the **Palm Beach Casino** complex, with traditional games and slot machines, draw in

Cannes Film Festival

In 1939, French minister Jean Zay chose Cannes' sunny shores as the venue for an international film festival. WWII broke out, however, and so the first Cannes Film Festival (www.festival-cannes.fr) didn't take place until 1946, in a specially built Palais des Festival on the site of today's Hilton hotel. According to legend, architects forgot to include a projection window and had to chisel out a hole in front of crowds of impatient VIPs. The festival's popularity and renown grew to include star-studded juries presided over by the likes of Jean Cocteau, Marcel Pagnol, and, more recently, David Lynch. For 3 weeks in May each year, in the new Palais des Festi-

Whoopi Goldberg's hand-print on the Allée des Stars.

vals, celebrities confront frenzied hordes to promote their films and their image, meet directors, and party until sundown.

the crowds. *Place Franklin Roosevelt.* ☎ *04-97-06-36-90. www.lepalm beach.com. Daily 11am–4am (5am summer).*

❹ ★ **La Malmaison.** This 19th-century pavilion, a former games and tearoom, is all that remains of

The Hotel Martinez.

the Grand Hotel, demolished and replaced in 1963. Today Cannes' Cultural Authority manages the space for temporary art exhibitions. *47 La Croisette.* ☎ *04-97-06-44-90. Admission 4€, 2€ reduced. Wed–Mon 10:30am–1pm, 3–6pm. Closed during festivals and between exhibitions.*

❺ ★★★ **The Majestic Palace Hotel.** Cannes' four iconic palace hotels, dotted along the Croisette, are veritable legends—purpose-built palaces, with private beaches and spas for Cannes' rich and famous clientele. The **Majestic,** built in 1926, N°10 (☎ 04-92-98-77-00; www.lucienbarriere.com), is part of the Lucien Barrière casino group and has three Venetian-style saloons from the 18th-century, 330 rooms, and 2 swish bars and restaurants. The oldest is the sumptuous **Carlton Intercontinental,** N°58 (☎ 04-93-06-40-06; www.ichotels group.com), built in 1912 by Charles

The Hotel Martinez dock.

6 The Harbor. Lines of fishing boats and luxury yachts bob lazily on the port at the foot of **Le Suquet** (see below), Cannes' old town. The west side is lined with shops and restaurants. Boats for the Lérins islands also embark from here. Near the port, the **Allée de la Liberté** is a shaded square where a daily flower market (food and antiques on weekends, 10am–6pm) gives way to *pétanque* matches in the afternoon.

7 ★ Le Suquet. Perched on the slopes of Mont Chevalier, a hill over-looking modern Cannes, the old town has one of the best covered markets on the Riviera, rue Forville (produce daily 8am–1pm; Mon antiques). Its streets are mainly pedestrian-only, jam-packed with restaurants. Rue Perrissol leads to Place du Castre with its 12th-century fortified château, church, bell tower, and **Musée de la Castre** (see p 140).

Dalmas. Its two, white *coupoles* were reputedly modelled on the breasts of a Gypsy courtesan called La Belle Otéro. The **Martinez,** N°73 (see p 142), is a 1927 Art Deco land-mark with the largest suite in the world. Measuring a phenomenal 1,000 sq m (1,196 sq yds), it costs 35,000€ a night. New kid on the block, the **Noga Hilton,** N°50 (☎ 04-92-99-70-00; www.hilton cannes.com), with its panoramic terrace, was built on the site of the original Palais de Festivals in 1992.

8 Plage de la Bocca. Most of Cannes' sand is privately owned. Much of the 3km (2 mile)-long Plage de la Bocca, however, west of Le Suquet (see above), is open to the public. The trouble is finding room to pitch your towel.

The Hotel Carlton.

The Best Cities & Towns

🍴 ★★ **La Table de Lucullus.**
Away from the glitz and glamor of
La Croisette, join loud shoppers
from Forville Market for some cheap
and delicious tapas (think fresh sardines, vegetable tarts, and shellfish)
in a friendly, unpretentious bistro
(a rarity in this town). *4 place du
Marché-Forville.* ☎ *04-93-39-32-74.
Mains 9.50€. No credit cards.
Noon–2pm Tue–Sun.*

🔟 ★ **Musée de la Castre.** This
11th- to 12th-century castle was
built by the Lérins monks to watch
over Cannes' port. It offers breathtaking views, from the 12th-century
watchtower, and houses a small but
fascinating collection of archaeological and ethnological items from five
continents, as well as 19th-century
paintings by local artists. ⏱ *45 min.
Place de la Castre.* ☎ *04-93-38-55-
26. Admission 3€; 2€ reduced.
Tues–Sun 10am–1pm, 2–5pm (until
6pm Apr–Jun, Sept). Daily 10am–7pm
Jul–Aug. Late night Wed until 9pm
Jun–Sept. Closed public holidays.*

⓫ **Eglise Notre-Dame de l'E-
spérence.** Just behind the Musée
du Castre, this 17th-century Gothic
church has sheltered the sacred

The Hotel Carlton's stretch of sand.

Le Suquet tower.

bones of St-Honorat since 1788.
1 place du Castre. Open daily.

⓬ 🧒 ★★★ **Les Îles de Lérins.**
In contrast to downtown Cannes'
effervescence, the offshore islands
of St-Honorat and Ste-Marguerite are
hauntingly peaceful and teeming
with wildlife, just a 15-minute boat
ride offshore. **Île St-Honorat** is a
striking, pine-studded religious back-
water, founded in the 4th century, and
now home to Cistercian monks
who make and sell their own wines.
Laypersons can visit the monastery,
but discretion is imperative. **Île Ste
Marguerite** is more touristy and
ideal for a hike, swim, and a picnic.
The star attraction is the **Musée de
la Mer,** set inside the **Fort Royal**
prison that Alexandre Dumas made
famous in his novel *The Man in the
Iron Mask*. Nature trails *(sentiers)*
are well indicated all around the
island, and the **Plongée Club de
Cannes** (☎ 04-93-38-67-57; www.
plongee-sylpha.com) takes tourists
diving around the island to see the
wealth of aquatic flora and fauna.
*Musée de la Mer (Marine Museum),
Fort Royal.* ☎ *04-93-43-18-17.
Admission 3€; 2€ reduced. Oct–Mar*

Shopping in Cannes

In Cannes, your budget will dictate the street you shop on. **Rue Meynadier** has the cheapest stores, tempting food and craft displays, and tourist trappings. Try **La Ferme Savoyarde,** N°22 (☎ 04-93-39-63-68), for the best cheese in Cannes. **Rue d'Antibes, La Croisette,** and the streets that link the two are a paradise for luxury shoppers. Grab inspiration at **Christian Lacroix,** 14 bd de la Croisette, then spend in **Agnès B,** 3 rue des Frères Casonova, before finding the perfect shoes at **Jacques Loup,** 21 rue d'Antibes. For regional goodies (crockery, oils, and liquors) try **Cannolive,** 16 rue Venizelos (☎ 04-93-39-08-19), and for a novel to read on the beach, browse the wide selection at **Cannes English Bookshop,** 11 rue Bivouac-Napoléon (☎ 04-93-99-40-08).

Tues–Sun 10:30am–4:45pm; Apr–Sept 10:30am–5:45pm; closed public holidays & lunch Jan–June. Catch Trans Côte d'Azur. Boats to both islands from Quai Maubeuf (☎ 04-92-98-71-30; www.trans-cote-azur.com; tickets 11€, 5.50€ under 10; MC, V; 1st departure from Cannes 9am; last return boat to Cannes 6pm).

The chic boutiques of Cannes.

⓭ Château de la Napoule. In 1918, after a scandalous love affair, rich Americans Marie and Henry Clews moved to France to shun society and invent their own world. The result is this fairy-tale castle, rebuilt from medieval ruins, entirely decorated in their own artistic creations—a grotesque, sculpted menagerie of gargoyles, monkeys, gnomes, and mythological creatures. *7km (4 miles) west of Cannes in Mandlieu La-Napoule. ☎ 04-93-49-95-05. www.chateau-lanapoule. com. Daily 10am–6pm (from 2–6pm Mon–Fri Nov–Feb). Admission 3.50€ gardens; 6€ guided visit (11:30am, 2:30pm, 3:30pm and 4:30pm); 7–17yrs 4€.*

Where to **Stay**

★★★ **3.14** CROISETTE This fun, psychedelic hideaway is decorated in bright colors according to feng shui principles. Decor on each floor is inspired by a different continent. Spoil yourself in the rooftop spa, pool, and trendy beach restaurant. *5 rue François Einesy.* ☎ *04-92-99-72-00. www.3-14hotel.com. 96 units. Doubles 150€–650€. AE, MC, V.*

★★ **Cézanne** CENTER NORTH Cannes' newest boutique hotel (with its private beach) mixes bold colors and sleek contemporary design at a pleasant distance from the hurly-burly of the Croisette. *40 bd d'Alsace.* ☎ *04-92-59-41-00. www.hotel-cezanne.com. 29 units. Doubles 120€–200€. AE, MC, V.*

★★ **Grand Hôtel** CROISETTE This neo-1960s luxury hotel is flash but surprisingly peaceful, thanks to its setting away from the Croisette. Its retro-chic restaurant, le Pré-Carré, serves excellent food. *45 La Croisette.* ☎ *04-93-38-15-45. www.grand-hotel-cannes.com. 76 units. Doubles 200€–410€. AE, MC, V.*

★★ **Hôtel Molière** CENTER This is the preferred haunt for journalist and film critics during the festival. Rooms are old-fashioned, but several have a balcony overlooking a pretty garden. *5–7 rue Molière.* ☎ *04-93-38-16-16. www.hotel-moliere.com. 24 units. Doubles 74€–135€ w/breakfast. MC, V.*

★ **Martinez** CROISETTE Art Deco–style razzle-dazzle wows guests in this palatial hotel with wonderful sea views, a private beach, three gourmet restaurants, a cocktail bar, a heated pool, and a sumptuous spa by Givenchy. *73 La Croisette.* ☎ *04-92-98-73-00. www. hotel-martinez.com. 412 units. Doubles 270€–520€. AE, MC, V.*

★★★ **Villa Tosca** CENTER Right in the center of Cannes' shopping district, this small, elegant hotel is refreshingly unpretentious, with comfortable rooms. *11 rue Hoche.* ☎ *04-93-38-34-40. www.villa-tosca. com. 22 units. Doubles 61€–119€. AE, MC, V.*

The café at the Hotel Carlton.

Where to **Dine**

★★ **La Plage** CROISETTE
MEDITERRANEAN The 3.14 hotel's turquoise restaurant, with a surreal plastic ball theme, is very popular with trendy locals looking for good Mediterranean food and a prime location on the Croisette beach. *3.14 Plage Bd de la Croisette. ☎ 04-93-94-25-43. www.3-14hotel.com. Menus 29€–31€. AE, MC, V. Noon–2:30pm, 7–11pm daily.*

★★★ **Le Méchant Loup** LE SOU-QUET *PROVENCAL BRASSERIE* A charming, rustic spot that serves large portions of top-notch brasserie food, including wonder-fully fresh seafood platters. *23 rue St Antoine. ☎ 04-93-99-06-22. Menus 15€–30€. MC, V. Daily 7pm–midnight.*

★ **Le Mesclun** LE SOUQUET
FRENCH GOURMET Warm tones and wooden paneling give this place an intimate feel, while dishes like fricassee of lobster in wild mushroom sauce, and a heavenly crème-brûlée tantalize taste buds. *16 rue Saint-Antoine. ☎ 04-93-99-45-19. www.lemesclun-restaurant. com. Menus 35€. AE, MC, V. Thur–Tues 7:30–11pm.*

★★ **Punto e Pasta** CENTER *ITAL-IAN* Delicious, well-priced pasta dishes, served in a cozy dining room with a pasta-themed decor. *68 rue Meynadier. ☎ 04-93-39-78-36. Mains 12€–18€. MC, V. Open Mon–Fri noon–2pm, 7pm–11pm. Sat 7pm–11pm (subject to change; call to verify).*

Cannes After Dark

Nightlife takes three basic forms in this glitzy town:

- **Star-Studded Tables d'hautes:** Sup or dine while celebrity-spotting at the Carlton's legendary **Bar des Célébrités** and 7th floor hideaway, the **Casino Club** (passport and smart dress required). With its three Michelin stars, the **Palme d'Or** restaurant or ground floor cocktail bar at the Martinez (see p 142) also get constant VIP business.
- **Lounge-Bar Restaurants:** Several chic eateries stay open all night as a bar and disco. Join the mixed clientele at **Au Bureau,** 49 rue Félix Faure (☎ 04-93-68-56-36; www.aubureau-cannes. com; daily from 5pm); and at the trendy **Tantra** and upstairs bar **Le Loft,** 13 rue Docteur Gérard Monod (☎ 04-93-39-40-46; www. dalton-group.com; daily evening).
- **Humble Pubs:** Morisson's Irish Pub stages live music 3 nights a week, 10 rue Teisseriere (☎ 04-92-98-16-17; www.morissons pub.com; daily evening); and **The Quays** serves beer to locals and others near the old Port, 17 quai St Pierre (☎ 04-93-39-27-84; www.quayspub.com; daily evening).

Marseille

Where to Stay
Hôtel Bellevue **28**
Hôtel Hermès **29**
Hôtel Lutetia **33**
La Maison du Petit Canard **26**
Tonic Hotel **35**

Where to Dine
Chez Madie les Galipettes **27**
La Part des Anges **36**
Le Café des Épices **30**
Le Miramar **31**
Une Table au Sud **32**

Nightlife
Cabaret Aléatoire de
la Friche **34**
La Caravelle **28**
Trolleybus **37**

1. Basilique de Notre-Dame-de-la-Garde
2. Vieux Port
3. City Hall
4. Maison Diamantée
5. The Forts
6. Canebière
7. Cours Julien
8. Grand Théâtre
9. Musée Cantini
10. Musée d'Histoire de Marseille
11. Palais Longchamp
12. Musée Grobet-Labadie
13. Le Panier
14. Musée des Docks Romains
15. Vieille Charité
16. La Joliette Docks
17. Cathédrale de la Major
18. Abbaye St-Victor
23. L'Estaque

Information ⓘ
Church ✝

0   1/8 mile
0   125 meters

PARC DU
PHARO

→ To
Château d'If

Bassin
de la Grande
Joliette

Vieux Port

Tunnel St-Laurent

Fort St-Jean
Fort St-Nicolas
Fort d'Entrecasteaux

av.
Pasteur

bd. Charles-Livon

place
St-Victor

Théâtre de
la Criée

JARDIN PUGET

ESTRANGIN-
PRÉFECTURE

Palais de Justice

place de
la Préfecture

rue Paradise
rue Grignan
rue Montgrand
rue Francis-Davso
rue St-Saëns
rue Breteuil
rue Pierre-Puget
Cours Pierre-Puget

Opéra

rue St-Ferréol
rue de Rome
rue Dieudé
rue d'Aubagne
Cours Julien
rue des 3 Mages
La Canebière
Allées · Gambetta
rue St-Bazile

CINQ AVENUE
LONGCHAMP

Cours Julien

bd. Garibaldi
bd. Dugommier

Cours Belsance
Cours St-Louis

Musée de
la Marine

JARDIN DES
VESTIGES

rue H.-Barbusse
rue des Dominicains
rue de la République

Hôtel-Dieu

Hôtel de Ville

quai des Belges
VIEUX-PORT
quai du Port
rue Caisserie
rue de la Loge

Cathédrale
de la Major

rue de l'Évêché

JOLIETTE

bd. des Dames

rue du Petit-Mossu/Trinquet

Esplanade de la Tourette
av. Vaudoyer
quai de la Tourette

rue Neuve Ste-Catherine
rue Sainte
bd. de la Corse
av. de la Corse

FRANCE
Paris ★
Marseille ★

Southern Marseille

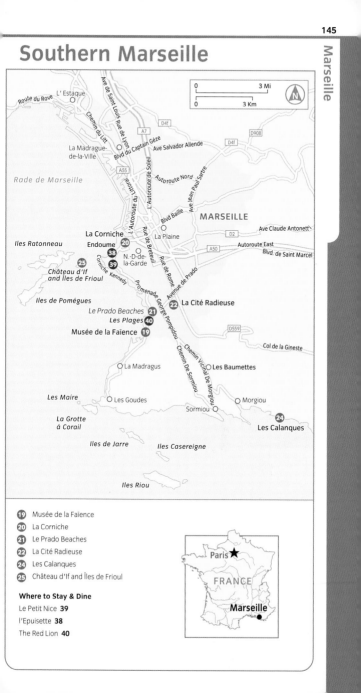

19 Musée de la Faïence
20 La Corniche
21 Le Prado Beaches
22 La Cité Radieuse
24 Les Calanques
25 Château d'If and Îles de Frioul

Where to Stay & Dine
Le Petit Nice **39**
l'Epuisette **38**
The Red Lion **40**

The Best Cities & Towns

France's first city has been a crossroads of culture, trade, and immigration for more than 2 millennia, since the Phoenicians founded it in 600 B.C. Today Marseille remains a fast-paced, forward-thinking port where Provençal traditions meet exotic influences from North Africa and the Middle East. Flanked by white cliffs, and facing the sea, its stepped streets and tranquil squares contrast with bustling 19th-century thoroughfares, souk-like markets, chic shops, and the colorful Vieux Port where fishmongers animate the boat-lined quayside. As Marseille grew, it gobbled up much of the coastline, so stay an extra day or two to visit the outlying urban villages, beaches, and offshore islands that make this city one of the most captivating places on the Mediterranean. START: **Marseille is 32km (20 miles) south of Aix-en-Provence and 30km (19 miles) west of Cassis.**

The golden Madonna atop the Basilique de Notre-Dame-de-la-Garde.

Transportation Tips

Public transport in Marseille is excellent—a cheap and user-friendly subway (Metro) and modern tramway cover most sites. To get your bearings, hop on the tourist bus. It covers more than 18km (11 miles) of the city's key sites. The tour begins at the Vieux Port and lasts for 1½ hours. One-day pass 17€; 2-days 20€. First tour 10am; last tour 4:15pm. Closed Jan.

① ★★★ **Basilique de Notre-Dame-de-la-Garde.** This Romanesque-Byzantine-style church, crowning a limestone mount, is the symbol of Marseille. Built by Henri Espérandieu in the mid–19th century, and topped by a 9m (30-ft.) gilded statue of the Virgin, it's visible from miles around. From its terrace, admire the sweeping panoramas over the entire city, Marseille's offshore islands, and the sea. Its interior is sumptuously decorated with colored marble and mosaic facings, and an exquisite marble Mater Dolorosa by Carpeaux is in the vaulted crypt. *Rue Fort-du-Sanctuaire.* ⏱ *1 hr.* ☎ *04-91-13-40-80. Free admission. Daily 7am–7pm summer, 7:30am–5:30pm winter. Metro: Vieux Port.*

② ★★★ **Vieux Port.** The history of Marseille and the Vieux Port are inseparable. Greek-Phoenicians landed here in 600 B.C., taking over a small Celto-Ligurian settlement. Legend has it that modern "Massalia" (or Marseille) was born of a love affair between Phoenician soldier Protis, and Gyptis, daughter of the Ligurian chieftain, who fell for his good looks. In the 12th century, ships from Marseille took crusaders to the Holy Land, and in 1666, Louis XIV built two emblematic forts at the harbor entrance. In 1943,

Marseille's ancient port.

Quai du Port. Built upon the site of a 13th-century trading center, it symbolized the city's great political status under Louis XIV. To sail across the port, take the ferry boat in front of City Hall (on Quai du Port, near the cross street rue de la Mairie) to Place aux Huiles. *Quai du Port. Mairie closed to visitors. Ferry boat daily 7am–7:30pm (☎ 04-91-91-45-62; .50€ one way, .80€ round-trip). Metro: Vieux Port.*

Fresh Fish Market

Every morning from 8am to 1pm, head to **Quai des Belges** and listen to the velvety drawl of Provençal fishmongers hawking their catches. Metro: Vieux Port.

most of the Quai du Port was dynamited by the Nazis. All but the 17th-century City Hall remains. The surrounding restaurants and apartments are tasteful post-war constructions, built to plans by Fernand Pouillon. On the north side of the port, take a break in the Cours d'Estienne d'Orves, a giant courtyard lined with restaurants, art galleries, and theaters. *Metro: Vieux Port.*

❸ City Hall. The 17th-century City Hall (or Mairie) was the only building to survive WWII Nazi bombing on the

❹ Maison Diamantée. Built in 1570, this atmospheric house is one of the oldest in Marseille. Its name results from the diamond-shaped stones that decorate its façade. Regular temporary exhibitions related to the traditions and popular history of Marseille are held here. ⏱ *30 min. 2 rue de la Prison.* ☎ *04-91-55-28-68. Dec–May Tues–Sun 10am–5pm; June–Nov 11am–6pm. Closed public holidays. Admission*

A fisherman with the day's catch.

2€ adult; 1€ concession. Metro: Vieux Port.

5 ★ **The Forts.** The prosperity of Marseille's traders encouraged rebellion against Louis XIV. The Sun King built Fort St-Nicolas (closed to visitors), near today's Pharo gardens, to control both the city's defenses and contain the rebels. He later gained complete military control by reinforcing the 12th-century Fort St-Jean, on the north entrance. Today, Fort St-Jean affords fine views over the harbor and contains the MUCEM, a museum on Mediterranean Civilizations. 🕐 *45 min. Esplanade St Jean.* ☎ *04-96-13-80-90. www.mucem.eu. Open Wed–Mon 1–7pm; closed public holidays. Admission 3.50€ adult; 2.50€ concession. Metro: Vieux Port.*

6 **Canebière.** Marseille's illustrious thoroughfare was another of Louis XIV's urban designs. In the 19th century, splendid Haussman-style buildings were added, creating most of what you see today. American soldiers from WWII nicknamed it "Can a'

Fort St-Jean and the cathedral.

Beer," but the name really stems from *canbe,* the hemp used to make rigging for boats. The best façade belongs to the oldest stock-exchange in France (founded by Henri IV in 1599), with intricate stone carvings that represent trade and navigation. It also doubles as a Maritime museum. 🕐 *1 hr. Musée de la Marine et de l'Economie de Marseille. 9 La Canebière.* ☎ *04-91-39-33-33. www.ccimp.com. Admission 2€ adult; 1€ child. Open daily 10am–6:30pm; closed public holidays. Metro: Vieux Port.*

7 **Cours Julien.** We love this bohemian spot for a coffee break, lunch, or dinner. Try **Le Sud du Haut** for traditional dishes, 80 Cours Julien (☎ 04-91-92-66-64), then wander around trendy boutiques where artists design their own clothes and objects.

8 **Grand Théâtre.** The originality of the opera house stems from its two styles: 18th-century neoclassical and Art Deco. Inaugurated as a temple to music and dance in 1787, it burned down in 1919, save for the walls and columns. As you gaze upward, contemplate the text inscribed on the top cornice: "Art receives beauty from Aphrodite, rhythm from Apollo, balance from Pallas, and movement and life from Dionysus." *2 rue Molière.* ☎ *04-91-55-11-10. Tickets 8€–75€. Metro: Vieux Port.*

9 ★ **Musée Cantini.** If you love Fauvism, surrealism, and post-war art, this 17th-century private mansion won't disappoint, with leading works by Francis Bacon, Raoul Dufy, Max Ernst, Fernand Léger, Henri Matisse, Joan Miro, Dennis Hopper, and Pablo Picasso. 🕐 *1 hr. 19 rue Grignan.* ☎ *04-91-54-77-75. Dec–May Tues–Sun 10am–5pm;*

Jun–Nov 11am–6pm; closed public holidays. Admission 3€ adult; 1.50€ concession. Metro: Estrangin/ Préfecture.

⑩ Musée d'Histoire de Marseille. Hidden away in the Bourse shopping mall, this museum tells the story of Marseille from prehistory to Gallo-Roman times through archaeological finds, models, and documents. Visitors wander through an archaeological garden where excavations on 1st-century Greek fortifications are sometimes underway, and you can see the remains of a 3rd-century Roman merchant shipwreck. *1 hr. Centre Bourse, square Belsunce.* ☎ *04-91-90-42-22. Open Mon–Sat 12–7pm; closed public holidays. Admission 2€ adults; 1€ concession. Metro: Vieux Port.*

⑪ ★★ Palais Longchamp. Striking and elaborate, this Second Empire palace is a hymn to the glory of water—something the city lacked until an 85km (53 mile) canal was constructed in 1848 to channel water from the Durance River. A

A cafe on Cours Julien.

magnificent half-circle colonnade frames a giant fountain symbolizing the Durance, surrounded by allegories of vine and wheat, on a chariot drawn by bulls from the Camargue. The fountain is flanked by the Fine Arts Museum (closed until 2012), the Natural History Museum, and a pretty park behind. *1 hr. Musée d'Histoire Naturelle, Palais Longchamp.* ☎ *04-91-14-59-50. www.museum-marseille.org. Admission 4€ adult; 2€ concession. Open Tues–Sun 10am–5pm; closed public holidays. Metro: Cinq Avenues/ Longchamp.*

⑫ ★★★ Musée Grobet-Labadie. Opposite the Palais Longchamp, this sumptuous bourgeois home was bequeathed to the city in 1919, and contains one of the most eclectic art collections in the region. Its original decor has been scrupulously maintained, displaying 10 salons, bedrooms, boudoirs, and libraries laden with treasures: paintings by Fragonard, Constable, and Monticelli; 18th-century furniture; medieval trinkets; Renaissance etchings; and a rare abundance of Aubusson and Gobelin tapestries.

Marseille's infamous thoroughfare, the Canebière.

🕐 1½. 140 bd Longchamp. ☎ 04-91-62-21-82. Oct–May open Tues–Sun 10am–5pm; June–Sept 11am–6pm; closed public holidays. Admission 2€ adult; 1€ concession. Metro: Cinq-Avenues.

⓭ ★★ **Le Panier.** The hill on the north side of the Vieux Port is Marseille's oldest district, known as Le Panier. It was here that the Phoenicians first settled, and it has subsequently remained a magnet for immigration. Even today, as you wander along its narrow medieval stairwells and passageways, you'll hear a variety of languages, smell exotic cooking, and see wash drying in windows. Metro: Vieux Port/Colbert.

⓮ **Musée des Docks Romains.** This maritime museum covers Roman port activity in Marseille from 600 B.C. to A.D. 400 and woos visitors with fascinating objects recovered from local Roman shipwrecks. 🕐 40 min. Place Vivaux. ☎ 04-91-91-24-62. Oct–May open Tues–Sun 10am–5pm; Jun–Sept 11am–6pm; closed public holidays. Admission 1€. Metro: Vieux Port.

⓯ ★★★ **Vieille Charité.** This former 17th-century workhouse is one of Marseille's most gorgeous settings. It almost disappeared entirely until Le Corbusier campaigned to have it classified as a historic monument. Its centerpiece is a baroque chapel, by Pierre Puget, with a fabulous ovoid dome. The surrounding arcaded galleries contain the **Musée d'archéologie méditerranéenne** (Mediterranean Archaeological Museum) and the **Musée des Arts Africains, Océaniens & Amerindiens** (MAAOA or Museum of African, Oceanic, and Native American Art), which includes a fascinating display of shrunken heads. 🕐 2 ½ hr. 2 rue de la Charité. ☎ 04-91-14-58-59. www.marseille.fr. Open Oct–May Tues–Sun 10am–5pm; June–Sept Tues–Sun 11am–6pm; closed public holidays. Admission 2€ per museum; 1€ 10–17 yrs; free under 10. Metro: Joliette.

⓰ **La Joliette Docks.** After the glorious 19th century, Marseille's wealth and power eroded, leaving widespread poverty and a reputation for crime. Nowhere was this more evident than at La Joliette Docks: Once the pride of Marseille and the largest port in Europe, it became a playground for druggies and petty criminals. This has now changed, thanks to the Euroméditerranée—a

The Palais Longchamp.

European-led rehabilitation program that has transformed the docks into a business district, soon to be adorned with emblematic skyscrapers, restaurants, and a promenade. To see how this area of Marseille will look in the future, head for the **Compagnie des Docks et Entrepôts**—a revamped brick warehouse of offices, shops, restaurants, and the Euroméditeranée showroom. ⏱ *30 min. Les Docks, Atrium 10.3, 10 place de la Joliette.* ☎ *04-91-14-45-00. www.euro mediterranee.fr. Open Mon–Fri 10am–1pm, 2–6pm (5pm Fri). Metro: Joliette.*

🔟⑦ ★★ **Cathédrale de la Major.** In between the Panier and the Joliette Docks, this neo-Byzantine beauty, built between 1852 and 1893, was modelled on Saint Sophia of Constantinople. It houses the tombs of the bishops of Marseille. Its white stone and green stone cladding recall Notre-Dame-de-la-Garde (in the distance on the opposite side of the port), also designed by Espérandieu. Part of the building is a former 12th-century cathedral, sacrificed during the new construction. Regular organ concerts take place here. ⏱ *30 min. Place de la Major.* ☎ *04-91-90-53-57. Open Daily. Metro: Joliette.*

🔟⑧ ★★ **Abbaye St-Victor.** Founded in A.D. 416, this intriguing example of religious architecture looks more like a medieval fortress than an actual abbey. This is because Abbot Guillaume Grimoard (future Pope Urban V of Avignon) had it fortified in the 14th century, following the barbarian invasions. The crypts form a full-scale underground church and contain the Black Virgin—a painted, walnut statue of Our Lady of Confession. Each year on February 2nd, she leads a procession around Marseille commemorating the legendary arrival by boat of the three Saintes Maries.

The Marseille cathedral.

To celebrate this event, boat-shaped cookies called *navettes*, flavored with orange zest and orange-flower, are sold throughout the city. ⏱ *30 min. Place St-Victor.* ☎ *04-96-11-22-60. Open daily. Admission for Crypt.*

Treat Yourself

The best *navettes* come from **Le Four des Navettes**, 136 rue Sainte (☎ 04-91-33-32-12; www.fourdes navettes.com), the oldest bakery in Marseille dating from 1731.

🔟⑨ ★★ **Musée de la Faïence.** Sublimely situated between the sea and the hills in Parc Montredon, this ceramics museum is set in the wonderful 19th-century Château Pastré. During WWII it was a sanctuary for the intelligentsia and for threatened Jews. Since 1995, it has showcased more than 1,500 ceramic items representing 7,000 years of history, including some spectacular faïence

The city's old Pannier neighborhood.

pottery—an art that reached its peak in Marseille in the 18th century. ⏱ 1½ hours. 157 ave de Montredon. ☎ 04-91-72-43-47. www.marseille.fr. Admission: 2€; 10–17yrs 1€; under 10 free. 10am–5pm Oct–May, 11am–6pm Jun–Sept Tue–Sun; closed some public holidays. Bus 19. Get off at

Abbaye St-Victor.

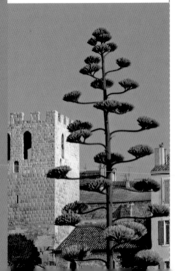

Madrague de Montredon. A mini-train transports visitors to the château via the gardens every 30 min.

㉐ **La Corniche.** Beginning at the pretty **Parc du Pharo** peninsula (with its Napoleon III palace and sea views over the islands, the Corniche runs 5km (3 miles) along the south coast. The President J. F. Kennedy stretch is dominated by late-19th-century villas and a sturdy viaduct that crosses the Auffe Valley. Don't miss the camera candy snugged behind the aqueduct in the **Vallon des Auffes Port**—a jumble of candy-colored traditional Marseille boats called *pointus*, fisherman's houses, and top-class seaside restaurants (see where to dine, p 156) with stunning views of shallow jade-green Mediterranean waters leading to the deeper blue waters off the Côte d'Azur. **Strange fact:** When the Mistral wind is blowing across the Corniche, the Frioul Islands and the Château d'If offshore appear closer to the mainland.

㉑ ★ kids Le Prado Beaches.
Composed of landfill from metro
excavations, the Prado Beaches
are where the locals work up a tan.
Roucas Blanc beach has a bike
track, children's play area, volleyball
court, and solarium. By day, **Escalé
Borely** beach is a fine spot for wind-
surfing, before it reels in the party
crowds at night. The pebbled **Bonn-
eveine** beaches are for water-skiers
and sea-scooters, and **Plage de la
Vieille Chapelle** has yet more kids'
facilities. *Metro: Castellane/Rond
Point du Prado, then bus 19.*

㉒ ★ La Cité Radieuse. In the
1950s, Le Corbusier changed the
face of modern architecture with
his Cité Radieuse—a revolutionary
18-story village of 337 apartments,
schools, shops, sports facilities, a
theater, and a hotel. Although it's a
private residence, visitors are welcome. Opt for an organized tour or
go it alone, but don't miss the roof:
Its Dali-esque features have earned
it the nickname Maison du Fada
(crackpot's house), and the sea
views are tremendous. ⏱ *1 hr. 280
bd Michelet.* ☎ *04-91-16-78-00.
www.marseille-citeradieuse.org.
Metro: Rond Point du Prado. Rond
Point du Pardo then bus 21(S) or 22(S)
to Le Corbusier. For a guided visit,
make a request via email to contact@
marseille-citeradieuse.org.*

㉓ ★★ L'Estaque. In the northern-
most part of Marseille, you'll find a
fishing port forever associated with
Impressionism, Fauvism, and Cubism.
Paul Cézanne, Georges Braque,
Raoul Dufy, August Macke, André
Derain, August Renoir, and Adolphe
Monticelli flocked here between
1860 and 1920 to paint the eclectic
scenery. A signposted walking tour
begins at the harbor's jetty and pres-
ents the district's colorful history.
Don't forget to try the *chichis*—the
Estaque's delicious donut specialties.
Take bus 35 from the Vieux Port or
*drive from Place de la Joliette to bd
Dunkerque, then onto the Littoral
highway and follow the Estaque exit.*

㉔ ★★★ Les Calanques. Within
15 minutes from the city, you're into
the Calanques massif—a 20km (12
mile) stretch of rocky creeks along
the coastline between Marseille and
Cassis. Their paradisiacal beaches
and dramatic white cliffs attract walk-
ers and sunbathers alike. They are
home to exceptional protected
wildlife, including Peregrine falcons
and Bonelli's Eagles. Wear good
shoes, take plenty of water, and
watch your step—paths are often
steep and uneven. For a relaxed
approach by boat, excursions begin
at the Vieux Port. For detailed maps,
guided walks, and information on getting there by public transport, ask at
the tourist office. Access is prohibited
from July to mid-Sept. *G.A.C.M boat
trips, Quai des Belges.* ☎ *04-91-55-
50-09. Open all year. Times vary.
Metro: Vieux Port.*

**㉕ ★★★ Chateau d'If and Îles
de Frioul.** From Marseille's mainland you can see the mysterious

The Vallon des Auffes Port.

The Iles de Frioul, off the coast of Marseille.

silhouettes of four limestone islands: Pomègues, Ratonneau, If, and Tiboulen. The Île d'If is world famous for its 16th-century fortress, built under François I as a military stronghold, and the setting of Alexandre Dumas's epic

Inside the Château d'If.

tale, *The Count of Monte Cristo.* Although Monte Cristo was a fictional character, many real rebels, villains, and slaves were imprisoned here. In the 17th century, hundreds of Protestants also perished in the château's dank dungeons. The untamed Mediterranean environment of the Frioul islands is captivating. They constitute a refuge for flora and fauna such as sea lavender, the sand lily, and the yellow-legged gull. Summer concerts are held in the Hôpital Caroline on Ratonneau Island—a former hospice for yellow fever patients. Pomègues houses the world's first official organic fish farm, and Port Frioul accommodates pleasure boats and yachts. G.A.C.M Boat crossings. ⏱ *25 min. Quai des Belges.* ☎ *04-91-55-50-09. Open all year; times vary (call for details). Metro: Vieux Port.*

Where to **Stay**

★★ Hôtel Bellevue VIEUX PORT
An Old Port location with views onto
Notre-Dame-de-la-Garde, plus Marseille's trendiest tapas bar downstairs (La Caravelle, see p 157).
Rooms are small but comfortable.
34 Quai du Port. ☎ *04-96-17-05-40.*
*www.hotel-bellevue-marseille.fr. 18
units. Doubles 92€–122€ w/break-
fast. AE, MC, V. Metro: Vieux Port.*

★ Hôtel Hermes VIEUX PORT
Recently renovated, with several
rooms overlooking the port and
Notre-Dame-de-la-Garde, this
modern hotel is surprisingly calm
despite its central location. *2 rue
Bonneterie.* ☎ *04-96-11-63-63.*
*www.hotelmarseille.com. 28 units.
Doubles 65€–95€ w/breakfast. AE,
MC, V. Metro: Vieux Port.*

Hôtel Lutetia GARE ST-CHARLES
Clean rooms, good atmosphere,
and friendly staff—all just 200m
(656 ft) from Marseille's train station.
38 Allée Leon Gambetta. ☎ *04-91-
50-81-78. www.hotelmarseille.com.
29 units. Doubles 63€–79€ w/break-
fast. AE, MC, V. Metro: Gare St
Charles.*

La Maison du Petit Canard
PANIER   The "house of the little
duck" bursts with character. Choose

between self-contained apartments
or a B&B plan. The generous hosts
cook hearty meals for just 15€ upon
request. *2 Impasse Sainte Françoise.*
☎ *04-91-91-40-31. http://maison.
petit.canard.free.fr. 4 independent
studios, 1 room. Doubles 46€–75€.
No credit cards. Metro: Joliette.*

★★★ Le Petit Nice CORNICHE
The most chic hotel and restaurant in
Marseille opened in 1917. Set in two
mansions, rooms are spacious and
brilliantly clad in plush fabrics. For a
real treat, request one of four rooms
inspired by the Cubist movement.
Corniche Président-J.-F.-Kennedy.
☎ *04-91-59-25-92. www.petitnice-
passedat.com. 16 units. Doubles
210€–870€ double w/breakfast.
AE, MC, V.*

★★ Tonic Hotel VIEUX PORT
Bright, trendy, and utterly central,
this new hotel offers spacious
rooms, 16 of which have views onto
the bustling Vieux Port. The all-
white breakfast room doubles as a
hip restaurant, La Maison Blanche.
43 quai des Belges. ☎ *04-91-55-67-
46. www.tonichotel.com. 56 units.
Doubles 161€–295€ w/breakfast.
AE, DC, MC, V. Metro: Vieux Port.*

Tonic Hotel, with views of the port.

The Best Cities & Towns

Where to **Dine**

Dining Tip

If you plan to try *bouillabaise*, be sure your restaurant prepares it according to traditional methods; otherwise it's not the real deal. Prepared properly, it's going to cost you both time and money. It's also going to require at least 24 hours notice, so the chef can order fish fresh for you that morning.

★★★ kids **Chez Madie les Galipettes** VIEUX PORT PROVENÇALE Dreamy cuisine, including *alibofis* (sweet breads), and fish grilled to perfection. *138 quai du Port.* ☎ *04-91-90-40-87. Lunch menu 15€, dinner menu 22€–28€. MC, V. Mon–Fri noon–2pm, 8–10:30pm; Sat 8–10:30pm. Metro: Vieux Port.*

★ **La Part des Anges** ESTIENNE D'ORVRES WINE BAR Over 250 types of wine are on the list, plus hearty cheese and meat platters. *33 rue Sainte.* ☎ *04-91-33-48-18. www.lapartdesanges.com. Mains 6€–14€; a la Carte 17€–31€. AE, MC, V. Open Mon–Sat 9am–2am; Sun 9am–1pm, 6pm–2am. Metro: Vieux Port.*

★ **Le Café des Epices** PANIER MODERN PROVENCAL A relaxed bistro with high end, inventive cuisine. Try the chocolate cake with tomato sorbet. *4 rue Lacydon.*

Traditional bouillabaise at Miramar.

☎ *04-91-91-22-69. Menus 19€–35€. MC, V. 12:30–2:30pm, 7pm–10pm Tues–Fri; 12:30pm–2:30pm. Sat. Metro: Vieux Port.*

★★★ **Le Miramar** VIEUX PORT BOUILLABAISSE Bouillabaisse aficionados flock to sample chef Christian Buffa's version, which may be the culinary highlight of your trip. Reservations required. *12 quai du Port.* ☎ *04-91-91-10-40. www.miramar.com. Main courses 30€–50€; bouillabaisse from 50€ per person*

Marseille Shopping

Marseille has many ways of making you spend, but shopping has to be the most pleasurable. Check out the souk market area on Place du Marché des Capucins, then the high street and designer offerings on rue St Ferréol, rue Sainte, and rue de la Tour, before heading to the quirky boutiques and galleries around Cours Julien.

Marseille After Dark

For a late-night boogie, try the Trolley Bus, 24 quai de Rive-Neuve (☎ 04-91-54-30-45; www.letrolley.com), which plays an eclectic selection of music. Fight for a spot on the balcony at **La Caravelle ★★**, 34 Quai du Port (☎ 04-91-90-36-64), and enjoy the vintage surroundings, a breathtaking port view, and free tapas. **The Red Lion,** 231 Ave Mendès-France (☎ 04-91-25-17-17), is a fine English-style pub at the Prado beaches, and the **Cabaret Aléatoire de la Friche ★**, 41 rue Jobin (☎ 04-95-04-95-04), is a cutting-edge disco with occasional live concerts.

(minimum 2). AE, MC, V. Noon–2:30pm, 7–11pm Tues–Sat. Metro: Vieux Port.

★★ Le Petit Nice CORNICHE CONTEMPORARY FRENCH Two Michelin stars and views to die for over the Île d'If and the sea. Anse de Maldormé, Corniche, J. F. Kennedy. ☎ 04-91-59-25-92. www.petitnice-passedat.com. Menus 50€–170€. AE, MC, V. 12:30–2pm, 7:30–10pm Tues–Sat. Open Mon 7:30pm–10pm May–Sept. Bus 83 (get off at the terminus Endoume Eglise).

L'Epuisette CORNICHE SEAFOOD The bouillabaisse (among the city's finest) is on par with the setting—jutting over the water, visible through glass on the floor, on a pretty port. Vallon des Auffes. ☎ 04-91-52-17-82. www.l-epuisette.com. Menu 45€–95€. AE, MC, V. Tues–Sat noon–2pm, 7:30–9:30pm. Bus 83 (get off Vallon des Auffes).

★★ Une Table au Sud VIEUX PORT MODERN PROVENCAL See and be seen tucking into creative cuisine such as chestnut and sea urchin soup. Reservations required. 1 Quai du Port. ☎ 04-91-90-63-53. www.unetableausud.com. Lunch 30€–55€, dinner 43€–55€. AE, MC, V. Tues–Sat noon–2pm, 7–10:30pm. Closed Aug & Dec 23–27. Metro: Vieux Port.

The port lit up at night.

Monaco

1. Les Grands Appartements du Palais
2. Musée Océanographique
3. The Casino
4. Café de Paris
5. Avenue Princesse Grace & Beaches
6. Collection des Voitures Anciennes
7. Jardin Exotique

Where to Stay
Hôtel Colombus **8**
Hôtel de France **12**
Métropole **15**

Where to Dine
Bar et Boeuf **16**
Crêperie du Rocher **9**
Quai des Artistes **10**

Shopping
Galeries du
Métropole **14**
Rue Grimaldi **13**
Rue Princesse
Caroline **11**

Glamorous Monaco is a feudal anomaly. Controlled by the Grimaldi family since 1297, it's the only European state (outside of the Vatican) to have an autocratic leader. Taking up some of the most choice coastline on the Côte d'Azur, between Nice and the Italian border, it is exempt of all taxes and gains most of its revenues from gambling and tourism. Its world-famous casino, exclusive boutiques, luxury hotels, and annual Formula 1 Grand Prix make the principality a veritable playground for international jet-setters and the wintering wealthy. Monaco is split into five districts: Monaco-Ville (the old town on the rock *La Rocher*), Fontevieille (west), Moneghetti (northwest), Monte-Carlo (the central hub of luxury around the casino and opera house), and the busy La Condamine port area. To call Monaco from outside the borders add 00-377 at the beginning of the number. START: **Monaco is 21km (13 miles) east of Nice.**

Travel Tips

Monaco is small but steep. The best way to get around is on the **City Bus** (☎ 97-70-22-22; www.cam.mc; tickets 1€). Only cars registered in Monaco or with an 06 license plate (Alpes-Maritimes) are allowed access to La Rocher. Other vehicles should park at Chemin des Pêcheurs carpark, which is linked to Monaco-Ville by a lift. Other parking, found throughout town, is free for the first hour. Swimwear is prohibited in the street, and suitable attire is required in all public places and religious buildings.

The Musée Océanographique.

1 ★★★ **Les Grands Apparte-ments du Palais.** Monaco's royal family resides here at the Palais du Prince, which dominates the princi-pality from "the Rock." It was built mainly in the 13th century, then enlarged during the Renaissance. Tour the sumptuous *grands apparte-ments* and get a glimpse of the daz-zling red **Throne Room.** To see the 10-minute **Relève de la Garde** (changing of the guard), arrive at

11:55am. In one wing, the **Musée du Palais du Prince** (Souvenirs Napoléoniens et Collection d'Archives) holds a collection of mementos of Napoléon and Monaco. When the royals are in residence, this is the only part of the palace you can visit. ⏱ *1½ hr. Place du Palais.* ☎ *93-25-18-31. www.palais.mc. Admission: combination ticket 8€; 4€ reduced. Palace & museum June–Sept daily 9:30am–6pm; Oct daily 10am–5pm.*

The Prince's Palace, home of the Grimaldi family, rulers of Monaco since the 13th century.

The Café de Paris.

Museum also open Nov 1–11 daily 10am–5pm; Dec 17–May Tues–Sun 10:30am–noon & 2–4:30pm. Palace closed Nov–May; museum closed Nov 12–Dec 16.

2 ★★★ kids **Musée Océanographique.** Albert I founded this museum in 1910 to display exotic specimens he collected during 30 years' worth of expeditions. Some species were unknown before he captured them. The underground aquarium is one of Europe's finest. It contains more than 90 tanks of rare and wonderful species and a shark lagoon. The roof restaurant, La Terasse, is good for a light bite. ⏱ *1hr. Av. St-Martin.* ☎ *93-15-36-00. www.oceano.mc. Admission 13€; 6€ reduced. Free under 6. Apr–Sept daily 9:30am–7pm (til 7:30pm Jul–Aug); Oct–Mar daily 10am–6pm. Closed during Grand Prix.*

Travel Tip

The Azur Express tourist train operates from 10:30am to 6pm (until 5pm, winter). It makes a 30-minute commentated trip around Monaco. Jump on in front of the aquarium. ☎ *92-06-64-38. Closed Jan, mid-Nov–end Dec.*

The Royals Today

When Prince Rainier III died in 2005, his title went to his son Albert II. Albert and his sisters, Caroline and Stephanie, are the children of American film legend Grace Kelly, who died here in a car crash in 1982. Albert has two illegitimate children on record, but he remains unmarried with no official heir. This fact, plus Caroline's failed first marriage and Stephanie's less-than-royal choice of suitors (a trapeze artist, an elephant trainer, and her bodyguard), make them roving targets for the European tabloids.

③ ★★★ The Casino. Built between 1878 and 1910, this ornate Charles Garnier–designed palace is *the* draw for wealthy visitors. An old-fashioned law still prohibits Monégasque citizens and clergymen from entering the gaming rooms. Smart dress (jacket and tie for men) is de rigueur. The minimum bet on roulette tables is 2€. Stakes are higher in the private salons. *Place du Casino.* ☎ *92-16-20-00. www.casino-monte-carlo.com. ID required; must be 18 for entry. Admission min. 15€. Daily from 12pm (private salons from 4pm).*

④ Café de Paris. Along with the casino and the sublimely rococo Hôtel de Paris, this turn-of-the-century cafe is a Monégasque institution. The upstairs salon affords fine views over the coastline. Place du Casino. ☎ *92-16-00-00. $$.*

⑤ Avenue Princesse Grace and Beaches. Most of this seafront stretch is reclaimed land that leads to the **Jardin Japonais** (daily 9am–dusk) and the expensive **Monte-Carlo Beach Club,** 22 av. Princesse-Grace (☎ 04-93-28-66-66). For free sunbathing, head

A specimen from the Jardin Exotique.

just off avenue Princesse-Grace to the **Plage de Larvotto** (☎ 93-30-63-84). At N°17, a charming villa designed by Charles Garnier (creator of the casino and Paris opera house) houses the **Musée National,** a curious museum of dolls and automata (☎ 93-30-91-26; *www.monte-carlo.mc/musee-national; admission 6€, 4€ reduced; Apr–Sept daily 10am–6.30pm;*

Monte Carlo's legendary casino.

Shopping with Billionaires

For glitz, glamor, and designer style, the **Galeries du Metropole** (Ave de la Madone, below the hotel; see "Where to Stay") is unrivaled. **Rue Grimaldi** is the principality's most commercial street, near the fruit, flower, and food market, Place des Armes (daily from 7:30am). **Rue Princesse-Caroline** is also loaded with bakeries and flower shops, and it's the closest thing you'll find to funkiness in Monaco.

The Galeries du Metropole.

Oct–Mar 10am–12:15pm, 2.30–6:30pm).

6 ★ **Collection des Voitures Anciennes.** The late Prince Rainier's private collection of more than 100 vintage cars contains treasures such as a 1903 De Dion Bouton. ⏲ *45 min. Les Terasses de Fontvieille.* ☎ *92-05-28-56. Admission 6€; 3€ reduced. Daily 10am–6pm; closed 25 Dec–1 Jan.*

7 ★★ **kids** **Jardin Exotique.** These gardens, clinging precariously onto cliffs overlooking the principality, are known for their cactus collection. There are also several dolomitic limestone grottoes to explore and the **Musée d'Anthropologie Préhistorique** (☎ 93-15-80-06), with its collection of Stone Age tools and mammoth bones. ⏲ *2 hr. bd. du Jardin-Exotique.* ☎ *93-15-29-80. www.jardin-exotique.mc. Admission (includes museum) 6.90€; 3.60€. Daily 9am–6pm (or sundown). Closed Nov 19, Dec 25.*

The Musée d'Anthropologie Préhistorique.

Where to **Stay** | Where to **Dine**

A waiter at the Café Quai des Artistes.

★★ **Hotel Columbus** FONTVIEILLE This contemporary address with big luxurious leather furnishings is a coveted crash pad, so to speak, for Formula 1 drivers and fans. *123 ave des Papalins.* ☎ *92-05-90-00. www.columbushotels.com. 184 units. Doubles 295€–325€. AE, MC, V.*

★ **Hotel de France** CONDAMINE PORT A small, welcoming hotel, all dressed up in bright yellows and checkered fabrics. *6 rue de la Turbie.* ☎ *93-30-24-64. www.monte-carlo.mc/france. 26 units. Doubles 85€. MC, V.*

★★★ **Métropole** MONTE CARLO CASINO Impeccably discreet, yet utterly luxurious, this timeless palace was entirely revamped by designer Jacques Garcia. Joël Robuchon runs the gourmet restaurant. A pool, solarium, and fabulous luxury spa (ESPA) also encourage relaxation. *4 ave de la Madone.* ☎ *93-15-15-15, www.metropole.com. 169 units. Doubles 385€–1,300€. AE, DC, MC, V.*

★ **Bar et Boeuf** MONTE CARLO *INTERNATIONAL* This upscale Gallic reinvention of a surf-and-turf restaurant is one of the many jewels in the crown of superchef Alain Ducasse. The only fish served is sea bass (bar). *Sporting d'Été, Monte Carlo, av. Princesse-Grace.* ☎ *92-16-60-60. Reservations recommended. Mains 30€–54€. AE, DC, MC, V. Late May–late Sept daily 8pm–1am; closed rest of year.*

kids **Crêperie du Rocher** MONACO-VILLE *CRÊPERIE* Pop by for a quick savory pancake near the Royal Palace. *12 rue Compte Félix Gastaldi.* ☎ *93-30-09-64. Main courses 4€–10€. MC, V. 11am–11pm daily (until 4pm Mon).*

★★★ **Quai des Artistes** CONDAMINE PORT *BRASSERIE* Wonderful, traditional French cuisine in a Parisian-style brasserie. On a warm day, tuck into a giant seafood platter under the arcades overlooking the port. *4 Quai Antoine 1er.* ☎ *97-97-97-77. www.quaidesartistes.com. Menus: lunch 22€; dinner 48€–56€. AE, MC, V. Noon–2:30pm, 7:30–11pm daily.*

Nice

Nightlife
Casa del Sol **32**
Opéra de Nice **29**
Smarties **20**

Shopping
Ave de Suède **27**
Ave Jean Médecin **22**
Fashion Gallery **33**
Molinard **30**
Ombrelle **31**
Rue de Paradis **28**

Where to Stay
Hôtel du Petit Palais **19**
Hôtel Hi **24**
Hôtel Negresco **25**
Hôtel Windsor **26**

Where to Dine
Fenoccio **35**
La Merenda **34**
La Part des Anges **21**
Oliviera **36**
26 Victor Hugo **23**

1 Vieux Nice
2 Promenade des Anglais
3 Musée d'Art Contemporain
4 Musée Matisse
5 Cimiez
6 Musée d'Archéologie
7 Monastère de Cimiez
8 Cathédrale Orthodoxe Russe St-Nicolas
9 Musée National Message Biblique Marc Chagall
10 Palais Lascaris
11 Chez Thérésa
12 Musée des Arts Asiatiques
13 Musée des Beaux-Arts
14 Musée International d'Art Naïf Anatole-Jakovsky
15 The Port
16 Café Borghèse
17 Chapelle de l'Annonciation
18 Cathédrale de St-Réparte

Beach
Information
Post Office
— Railway

0 — 1/4 mi
0 — 0.25 km

Tracing the pebbled shores of the **Baie des Anges** (Angel Bay), and creeping its way up into the surrounding hillside, the capital of the Riviera balances old-world decadence with modern urban energy. Founded by the Greeks in the 4th century B.C., it fell to the Romans, and subsequently the House of Savoy in the Middle Ages, where it remained until Napoleon took it into France in 1860. By the 19th century, the Victorian upper class and tsarist aristocrats were flocking here for the mild winter climate. Nice's spectacular light (averaging 300 days of sunshine a year) also caught the attention of legendary artists such as Marc Chagall and Henri Matisse. Nowadays Nice throbs with activity. With wonderful markets and an age-old cultural respect for good eating, it has become a paradise for foodies. START: **Nice is 21km (13 miles) west of Monaco and 37km (23 miles) east of Cannes.**

Le Grand Tour

The best way to see Nice and get your bearings is to buy a 1- or 2-day pass for the "hop on hop off" Grand Tour bus. It covers 12 sites around the city, and commentary is in seven languages. Buy tickets on board or at the tourist office. ☎ *04-92-29-17-00. www.nicelegrandtour.com.*

① ★★★ **Vieux Nice.** The old town is a maze of narrow streets, teeming with local life and studded with inexpensive restaurants. It begins at the foot of the **Colline du Château**—Nice's former stronghold, which commands

breathtaking vistas (daily 8am–dusk; access via an elevator). It stretches to busy **place Masséna**, recognizable by its sienna-tiled roofs and Italianate facades. The fish market takes place every morning but Monday at **Place St-François** (Tues–Sun 6am–1pm). At the same time, the great **Cours Saleya** market is a flamboyant bustle of bright flowers, fresh fruit, and appetizing vegetables (Tues–Sun 6am–1:30pm). Monday it becomes an antiques market, and by evening it's the focal point of Nice's nightlife. The **Chapelle de la Miséricorde** is also here. One of the world's most beautiful baroque churches, it's a requisite stop.

Nice's Old Town.

The Promenade des Anglais.

2 ★ **Promenade des Anglais.**
This world-famous promenade owes its existence to English aristocrats who, after a bad orange crop in 1822, occupied their idle workers with the construction of this wide boulevard fronting the bay. It's split by islands of palms and flowers. Stretching for about 7km (4 miles) between the pebbled beach and the town, it is lined by rows of grand cafes, famous hotels, the Musée Masséna, and villas, some decaying. Farther east, the promenade becomes **Quai des Etats-Unis,** the original boulevard, lined with more restaurants.

3 ★★★ **Musée d'Art Contemporain.** This modern building— recognizable by its gargantuan cube-head statue near the entrance—is home to exceptional artworks that trace the avant-garde movement from the '60s to the present. U.S. Pop artists and European neo-realists are particularly well represented. The roof affords a fine panorama over the city and surrounding hills. ⏱ *1 hr. Promenade des Arts.* ☎ *04-97-13-42-01. www.mamac-nice.org. Admission 4€; 2.50€ reduced. Tues–Sun 10am–6pm. Closed public holidays.*

4 ★ **Musée Matisse.** In the heart of a public olive tree garden, the 17th-century Italianate villa on Cimiez Hill is a museum in honor of the artist who died in Nice in 1954. The collection contains nude sketches that will make you question how early critics could have denounced them as renderings of "the female animal in all her shame and horror." Other works include *Nude in an Armchair with a Green Plant* (1937), *Nymph in the Forest* (1935–1942), and a chronologically arranged series of paintings from 1890 to 1919. ⏱ *1hr. 164 av. des Arènes-de-Cimiez.* ☎ *04-93-53-40-53, www.musee-matisse-nice.org. Admission 4€; 2.50€ reduced; free under 18. Wed–Mon 10am–6pm;*

Nice's Museum of Modern and Contemporary Art (MAMAC).

The Musée Matisse.

closed Jan 1, May 1, Easter Sunday, and Dec 25.

5 ★★★ **Cimiez.** Five km (3 miles) north of Nice's centre-ville lies the once-aristocratic hilltop quarter of Cimiez. Queen Victoria used to winter here, in the Hôtel Excelsior, with half the English court in tow. The Boulevard de Cimiez still clings to flamboyant remnants of this era. The startling array of magnificent villas ranges in style from Louis XV to Oriental and neo-Gothic. Founded by the Romans, who called it Cemenelum, Cimiez was the capital of the Maritime Alps province. *Drive north, take the Grand Tour, or catch buses 15 or 17 from place Masséna.*

6 ★ **Musée d'Archéologie.** Excavations in Cimiez uncovered the ruins of a Roman town. This museum allows you to wander the dig sites, including old baths and a 5,000-seat amphitheater still used for Nice's **Festival du Jazz** (☎ 04-97-13-36-86; www.nicejazz fest.com) for a week in mid-July. Nice's history is also recounted in the small museum through displays of ceramics, sculpture, coins, and

Mardi Gras of the Riviera

More than a million visitors from around the world flock to the Côte d'Azur for the **Nice Carnaval** (www.nicecarnaval. com). Beginning sometime in February (usually 12 days before Shrove Tuesday), 3 weeks of wild celebration mark the return of spring. Festivities traditionally include spectacularly colorful, bulbous *corsi* (floats), *veglioni* (masked balls), confetti, and glorious battles in which young women toss flowers. The climax is a fireworks display on Shrove Tuesday that lights up the Baie des Anges.

Masked revelers during the Nice Carnival celebrations.

Inside the Palais Lascaris.

tombs. 🕐 1½ hr. 160 av des Arènes. ☎ 04-93-81-59-57. Admission 4€, 2.50€ reduced. Free under 18. Wed–Mon 10am–6pm. Closed some public holidays.

7 ★ Monastère de Cimiez. A handful of Franciscan friars still live in this picturesque monastery, famous for three Louis Bréa altarpieces and the tombs of Henri Matisse and Raoul Dufy, buried in the cemetery. The Musée Franciscain is decorated with 17th-century frescoes. It documents the painful deaths of the Franciscan martyrs. From the magnificent gardens, enjoy the vistas over Nice and the Baie des Anges. 🕐 1 hr. Place du Monastère. ☎ 04-93-81-00-04. Free admission. Museum Mon–Sat 10am–noon and 3–6pm. Church daily 9am–6pm.

8 Cathédrale Orthodoxe Russe St-Nicolas. Ordered and built by Tsar Nicholas II, this cathedral is deemed the most beautiful religious edifice of the Orthodoxy outside Russia. It dates from the Belle Epoque era, when the Romanovs, their entourage, and everyone from grand dukes to ballerinas walked Nice's promenades. Richly decorated with icons, it can be seen from afar thanks to its ornate onion-shaped domes. It's closed to visits during church services. 🕐 30 mins. Av.

Nicolas-II (off bd. du Tzaréwitch). ☎ 04-93-96-88-02. www.acor-nice. com. Admission 2.50€; free under 12s. May–Sept daily 9am–noon & 2:30–6pm; Oct–Apr daily 9:30am–noon & 2:30–5pm.

9 ★ Musée National Message Biblique Marc Chagall. This handsome museum, surrounded by pools and a garden, is devoted to Russian-born Marc Chagall's treatment of biblical themes. It is the most important Chagall collection ever assembled, with some 450 of his oils, gouaches, drawings, pastels, lithographs, sculptures, and ceramics. 🕐 50 min. Av. du Dr.-Ménard. ☎ 04-93-53-87-20. www.musee-chagall.fr. Admission 6.50€; 4.50€ reduced; under 18 free. July–Sept Wed–Mon 10am–6pm; Oct–June Wed–Mon 10am–5pm.

10 ★ Palais Lascaris. Imposing yet almost entirely invisible from the street, the baroque Palais Lascaris in the city's historic core is associated with the Lascaris-Vintimille family, whose recorded history predates the year 1261. Built in the 17th century, it contains elaborately detailed ornaments and ceilings frescoed with mythological scenes. Classified as a historic monument, it retains many of its 18th-century panels and plaster embellishments. A pharmacy, built around 1738, complete with many of

Nice Shopping

Ave Jean Medecin is the main high-street shopping drag, where you'll find the **Galeries Lafayette** department store and the music emporium **FNAC**. For designer labels, target rue Paradis and ave de Suède. Vieux Nice is cluttered with food shops, markets, and clothes creators. **Fashion Gallery**, 5 rue st Suaire (☎ 04-93-80-33-73), brings together several brands in a hip cave-like shop, dressed in chandeliers. **Molinard,** 20 rue st François de Paule (☎ 04-93-62-90-50; www.molinard.com), sells perfume and offers lessons on scent. **Ombrelle,** 17 rue de la Préfecture (☎ 04-93-80-33-13; http://bestagno.exen.fr), has been selling marvelous umbrellas, parasols, and canes since1850.

the original Delftware accessories, is also on the premises. ⏱ *30 min. 15 rue Droite.* ☎ *04-93-62-72-40. Free admission. Wed–Mon 10am–6pm. Closed some public holidays.*

⑪ **★★★ Chez Thérèsa.** Locals can't get enough of Thérèsa's *socca*—a thin, crispy pancake made from chickpea flour, garlic, and olive oil. Along with the pizza-like *pissaladière* (anchovies and caramelized onions), it's the symbol of Niçois street food. *28 rue Droite (Thérèsa also holds a stall on Cours Saleya market).* ☎ *04-93-85-00-04. $.*

⑫ **★ Musée des Arts Asiatiques.** In a swanky minimalist

glass and metal construction near Nice's airport, this museum is a tribute to the sculpture and paintings of Cambodia, China, India, Tibet, and Japan. Inside are some rare ceramics and devotional carvings—many brought back by colonials during the 19th and early 20th centuries. Of special interest are the accoutrements associated with Japanese tea ceremonies, in the tea pavilion, shaded by gingko trees. ⏱ *1 hr. 405 promenade des Anglais.* ☎ *04-92-29-37-00. www.arts-asiatiques.com. Admission 4.50€; 2€ reduced; under 15 free. May–mid-Oct Wed–Mon 10am–6pm; mid-Oct–Apr Wed–Mon 10am–5pm.*

⑬ **★★ Musée des Beaux-Arts.** This fine collection, devoted to the

The Musée Asiatique.

masters of the Second Empire and the Belle Epoque, lives in a Genoese-inspired former residence of a Ukrainian prince. The gallery of sculptures includes works by J. B. Carpeaux, François Rude, and Auguste Rodin. Paintings include treasures by the Dutch Vanloo family dynasty (including Carle Vanloo, Louis XV's premier painter), and 19th- and 20th-century artists Felix Ziem, Jean-Francois Raffaelli, Eugène Boudin, Claude Monet, Armand Guillaumin, and Alfred Sisley. ⏱ *45 min. 33 av. des Baumettes.* ☎ *04-92-15-28-28. www.musee-beaux-arts-nice. org. Admission 4€; 2.50€ reduced; under 18 free. Tues–Sun 10am–6pm.*

⑭ Musée International d'Art Naïf Anatole-Jakovsky (Museum of Naïve Art).

The setting of this unique museum is the dazzling, pink-faceted Château Ste-Hélène—former home to the perfumier Coty. Anatole Jakovsky, one of the world's leading art critics, once owned the collection—some 600 drawings and canvases, and a rare panorama of naïve and primitive art from the 18th century to the present. ⏱ *1hr. Château St-Hélène,*

Nice's harbor.

av. de Fabron. ☎ *04-93-71-78-33. Admission 4€; 2.50€ reduced; under 18 free. Wed–Mon 10am–6pm.*

⑮ The Port.

For 2,000 years, ships anchored in a natural bay at the foot of Chateau Hill. It wasn't until the mid–18th century, under the Duke of Savoy, that it became an official port. In the 19th century, it was deepened and extended, and the surrounding houses ornamented with typical Niçois porticoes. Today ferries, liners, and yachts dwarf the traditional fishing boats. Flea markets are held regularly on the port's Quai Lunel.

⑯ Café Borghèse.

Snug behind the port's old church, this is where locals come for cappuccinos, aperitifs, and copious portions of pasta and meat dishes. *9 brue Fodéré.* ☎ *04-92-04-83-83. $.*

⑰ Chapelle de l'Annonciation.

St. Rita is the patron saint of the terminally ill and the desperate. This, her chapel, is an atmospheric, gilded baroque gem where hopeful visitors light candles for loved ones. *1 rue de la Poissonnerie.* ☎ *04-93-62-13-62. Free admission. Daily 7:30am–noon, 2:30–6:30pm.*

⑱ Cathédrale de St-Réparte.

Set on what is easily Nice's loveliest square, this stucco- and marble-clad cathedral stands out by virtue of its brightly tiled dome. It is named after a young virgin, martyred in the Holy Land, whose body was towed back to Nice by angels (hence the name of Nice's coastline, Baie des Anges, or the Bay of Angels). Frequent classical music concerts take place here—particularly Baroque. *Place Rossetti.* ☎ *04-93-62-34-40. Free admission. Daily 8am–noon, 2–6pm.*

Where to **Stay**

Hotel du Petit Palais CIMIEZ
Sacha Guitry lived in this Belle
Epoque building in the 1930s. The
decor is plain but pretty, with fine
views over Nice and a relaxing garden. *17 av Emile Bieckiert.* ☎ *04-93-
62-19-11. www.petitpalaisnice.com.
25 units. Doubles 85€–170€. AE,
MC, V.*

★★★ Hôtel Hi NEW TOWN   The Hi
is one of the most aggressively avant-
garde hotels in the south of France,
with nine different high-tech room
"concepts." They range from hospital
white-on-white to birch-wood veneer
and acid green. Not always practical,
layouts may include a bathtub tucked
behind a screen of potted plants or a
toilet elevated to a position of theatri-
cal prominence. Organic breakfast
may be taken in the peaceful courtyard. *3 av. des Fleurs.* ☎ *04-97-07-
26-26. www.hi-hotel.net. 38 units.
Doubles 195€–670€. AE, DC, MC, V.
Parking 20€.*

★★ Hôtel Negresco PROME-
NADE DES ANGLAIS   No other
palace hotel on the Riviera can
boast such a wildly kitschy assem-
blage of European art treasures.
Louis XIV portraits hang near
psychedelic Niki de St-Phalle statues,
Rodin sculptures, and, on the fourth
floor, a shoe-shaped copper bathtub
replica where the Revolutionary
Jean-Paul Marat was murdered in his
bath by Charlotte Cordy in 1793.
Honored guests get to meet the
owner's ginger cat, who roams
wherever she pleases. The carousel-
themed breakfast room is a funfair
unto itself, and the restaurant is still
one of the best in town. *37 Promenade des Anglais.* ☎ *04-93-16-64-
00. www.hotel-negresco-nice.com.
145 units. Doubles 280€–650€. AE,
DC, MC, V. Free parking.*

★★ Hôtel Windsor PROMENADE
DES ANGLAIS   One of the most
arts-conscious hotels in Provence is
in a *maison bourgeoise* built by disci-
ples of Gustave Eiffel in 1895. Each
unit is a unique and often wild decorative statement by a different artist.
The fifth floor holds the health club,
steam room, and sauna. The garden
houses scores of tropical and exotic
plants. *11 rue Dalpozzo.* ☎ *04-93-
88-59-35. www.hotelwindsornice.
com. 57 units. Doubles 115€–150€.
MC, V. Parking 10€.*

The Hotel Negresco.

Where to **Dine**

★ **Fenocchio** VIEUX NICE *ICE-CREAM*   Hailing back to its former days as an Italian protectorate, Nice and ice cream go hand in hand. This is the best place in town with around 90 flavors—some rather adventurous (think beer, thyme, tomato, and basil). *2 pl Rossetti.* ☎ *04-93-80-72-52. Scoop 2€. MC, V. Tues–Sun 10am–11:30pm. Closed Dec–Jan.*

★★ **La Merenda** VIEUX NICE *TRADITIONAL NIÇOIS*   Noisy and always bustling, this rustic restaurant wows clients with Niçois classics such as beef with orange polenta, blette tart (made from a sweet cabbage-like leaf), and *petits farcis* (stuffed tomatoes and peppers). *4 rue Raoul Bosio. No phone. Menus 25€. No credit cards. Lunch, dinner Mon–Fri. Closed 1–15 Aug & public holidays.*

★ **La Part des Anges** VIEUX NICE *WINE BAR*   The aroma will lure you from the street into this intimate wine bistro. The sommelier-owner delights his regulars with fine wines and hearty regional cooking. *17 rue Gubernatis.* ☎ *04-93-85-71-53. Menus 25€. AE, MC, V.*

La Part des Anges wine bar.

Mon–Thurs 12–8pm, Fri–Sat 12–2pm, 7–10pm.

★★★ **Oliviera** VIEUX NICE *MEDITERRANEAN*   Olive oil never has, and never will, taste better than in this shop/cafe. Passionate owner

Nice Nightlife

For a special evening, opt for a night at the **Opera de Nice** (4 rue St-Françoise-de-Paule; ☎ 04-92-17-40-40; www.opera-nice.org; tickets from 8€–85€). This sumptuous hall, with red velvet and crystal chandeliers, programs international symphony orchestras, ballets, and operas. **Smarties** (10 rue Défy; ☎ 04-93-62-66-64) is a 70s-themed bar that serves delicious cocktails to a mixed-age crowd. For latino rhythm, head to **Casa del Sol** (12 Cité du Parc; Quai des Etats-Unis; ☎ 04-93-62-87-28) for international cuisine and an after-dinner boogie.

Niçois Cooking School

Rosa Jackson—a respected restaurant critic, author of several cookbooks, and a self-confessed food fanatic—runs a fabulous cooking school, **Les Petits Farcis.** She takes you on a trail of discovery around the Cours Saleya market before teaching you how to prepare an authentic Niçois meal. This is the best cooking school in Nice. *7 rue du Jésus.* ☎ *06-81-67-41-22. www.petitsfarcis.com. Prices start at 200€ per person.*

Rosa Jackson, who runs Les Petits Farcis.

Nadim serves delicious salads and pastas with oils so good you can't stop sopping them up. Even the tiramisu gets a drizzle. *8 bis rue du Collet.* ☎ *04-93-13-06-45. www. oliviera.com. Mains 9€–17€, menu 35€. No credit cards. May–Oct Mon–Sat 10am–10pm, Sun 10am–6pm; Nov–Apr Mon–Sat 10am–8pm, Sun 10am–3pm.*

★★★ **26 Victor Hugo** NEW TOWN *FRENCH* This brand new restaurant, opened by the talented Stéphane Viano, attracts Nice's media crowd with its funky orange and white decor. Elaborate gourmet dishes include fresh cod with crushed potatoes trickled with olive oil. *26 bd Victor Hugo.* ☎ *04-93-82-48-63. Menus 39€–65€. AE, MC, V. Noon–2pm, 7–10:30pm Mon–Sat.*

26 Victor Hugo.

Nîmes

1 Amphithéâtre

2 Maison Carrée

3 Jardin de la Fonataine & Tour Magne

4 Carré d'Art

5 Musée des Beaux Arts

6 Le Mazurier

7 Musée du Vieux Nîmes

8 Musée des Cultures Taurines

9 Musée Archéologique and Musée d'Histoire Naturelle

10 Castellum

11 Rue de la Madeleine

Where to Stay

Hôtel de l'Ampithéâtre 19
Imperator Concorde 12
New Hôtel La Baume 13

Where to Dine

Alexandre 21
Le Chapon Fin 16
Le Wine Bar 20

Shopping

Les Halles 15
Rue de la Madeleine 17
Rue du Général-Perrier 14
Rue de l'Aspic 18
Stade des Costières 22

✝ Church

ⓘ Information

— Railway

FRANCE

Paris ★

Nîmes ●

On the edge of the Camargue plain, the ancient town of Nemausus (Nîmes) grew to prominence during the reign of Caesar Augustus (27 B.C.–A.D. 14). It possesses some of the world's finest Gallo-Roman relics; its pièce de résistance is one of the world's best-preserved Roman amphitheaters, where bullfights now take place. An honorary part of Provence, due to its Provençal atmosphere and culture, it's technically in the nearby Languedoc. Spain's influence is also palpable—especially when cafes serving paella and sangria spill onto the streets at night, and during the Camargue running of the bulls through the streets. And its influence on the U.S. is indisputable, though little known: It was here that Levi-Strauss invented his durable cloth de Nîmes—also known as denim. START: **Nîmes is 51km (32 miles) west of Avignon and 31km (19 miles) northwest of Arles.**

1 ★★★ kids **Amphithéâtre (Arènes).** With its perfect classical proportions, Nîmes' Roman arena is a better-preserved twin of the one in Arles, and it's more complete than Rome's. It has two stories, each with 60 arches, and it was built of huge stones painstakingly fitted together without mortar. Concerts, ballets, and bullfights now take place where the Romans staged gladiatorial combat, wolf or boar hunts, and even mock sea battles during which the ring was filled with water. 🕐 *45 min. Amphithéâtre Romain de Nîmes. ☎ 04-66-76-72-77. Admission 7.70€, 5.80€ reduced. Free under 7. Daily 9am–7pm*

Jun–Aug; until 6pm Mar, Oct; until 6:30pm Apr–May, Sept; 9:30am–5pm Dec–Feb, Nov.

2 ★★★ **Maison Carée.** Built during the reign of Caesar Augustus, this temple is the pride of Nîmes. Consisting of a raised platform with tall, finely fluted Corinthian columns and friezes of acanthus leaves, it's one of Europe's most beautiful, best-preserved Roman temples. It inspired the builders of La Madeleine in Paris as well as Thomas Jefferson. It shows cultural and art exhibits, presented beneath an authentically preserved roof. 🕐 *45 min. place de la Maison*

Nîmes' Roman ampitheater.

The ancient Maison Carée.

Carée. ☎ 04-66-36-26-76. Admission 4.50€; 3.60€ reduced; under 7 free. Daily 10am–7:30pm Jun–Aug; Apr–May, Sept until 7pm; Mar, Oct until 6:30pm; Dec–Feb, Nov 10am–1pm, 2–5pm.

3 ★★★ kids Jardin de la Fontaine and Tour Magne. This oasis of greenery, laid out in the 18th century, surrounds the ruins of a Roman shrine. It's one of France's most beautiful parks, planted with rows of chestnuts and elms, adorned with statues, and intersected by grottoes, canals, and a natural spring that inspired Nimes' ancient name—Nemausus, after the Roman river god. The grounds encompass the ruined **Temple de Diane,** Roman baths, and the sturdy bulk of the **★ Tour Magne,** the city's oldest Roman monument. The tower is on a low, rocky hill called **Mont Cavalier,**

Musée des Beaux Arts.

a 10-minute walk north through the park. Climb 140 steps for views over Les Alpilles mountains. *Admission 2.70€; 2.30€ reduced. Gardens daily Oct–Mar 7:30am–6:30pm, until 10pm Mar–Oct.*

Tip

Buy a combined ticket for the Arena, Maison Carrée, and Tour Magne for 9.80€ (7.40€ reduced).

4 ★ Carré d'Art. Opposite the Maison Carée stands its glass-and-metal modern-day twin. Inside is a research center and exhibition space with a library and newspaper kiosk. The **Musée d'Art Contemporain** displays French art from the 1960s to the present. The terrace affords a panorama of most of Nimes' ancient monuments and medieval churches. ⏱ *45 min. Place de la Maison Carrée.* ☎ *04-66-76-35-70. www.nimes.fr. Admission 5€; 3.70€ reduced. Tues–Sun 10am–6pm.*

5 ★ Musée des Beaux Arts. This early-20th-century building exhibits French paintings and sculptures from the 17th to the 20th centuries, as well as Flemish, Dutch, and Italian works from the 15th to the 18th centuries. Seek out the G. B. Moroni masterpiece, *La Calomnie d'Apelle,* and the well-preserved Gallo-Roman mosaic. ⏱ *45 min. Rue de la Cité-Foulc.* ☎ *04-66-67-38-21. www.nimes.fr. Admission 4.90€; 3.60€ reduced. Under 10 free. Tues–Sun 10am–6pm (until 8pm Thurs).*

Take a Break

6 Le Mazurier. This tasteful Belle Epoque brasserie makes a fine spot for a relaxing coffee, a quick bite on the terrace, or an aperitif at the zinc bar. *9 bd Am Courbet.* ☎ *04-66-67-27-48. $.*

The Maison Carée's modern counterpont, the Carré d'Art.

7 Musée du Vieux Nîmes.
Housed in an Episcopal palace from the 1700s, this museum opened in the 1920s to preserve regional antiques, workday objects from the 18th and 19th centuries, and industrial artifacts. Most of the rooms are mock-up interiors illustrating daily life in Nîmes. ⏱ *40 min. Place aux Herbes.* ☎ *04-66-76-73-70. Free admission. Tues–Sun 10am–6pm.*

8 Musée des Cultures Taurines. This small museum, in an annex of the Musée du Vieux Nîmes, is devoted to *tauromachy* (bullfighting) and the role it plays in Nîmes. ⏱ *30 min. 6 rue Alexandre Ducros.* ☎ *04-66-36-83-77. Admission 4.90€; 3.60€ concession. Tues–Sun 10am–6pm.*

9 kids Musée Archéologique and Musée d'Histoire Naturelle. Within the former Jesuit college, two museums showcase complimentary collections. The archaeology museum houses Roman statues, coins, pottery mosaics, and statues. The Natural History museum is a taxidermist's dream, with numerous stuffed animals, an interesting anthropological section, and some Iron Age menhirs. ⏱ *1hr. 13 bis bd Amiral Courbet.* ☎ *04-66-76-74-80/ 04-66-76-73-45. Free admission. Tues–Sun 10am–6pm.*

10 Castellum. In rue Lampèze, to the north of the center, archaeologists recently unearthed these remnants of a Roman water tower, which received water from the Pont du Gard aqueduct. Huge lead pipes, the holes for which are still visible, distributed the water across town.

11 ★ Rue de la Madeleine. Locals go about their daily business on this shopping thoroughfare. **Maison Villaret,** N°13 (☎ 04-66-67-41-79), bakes and sells Nîmes specialty cookies *(croquants)*, and the Romanesque façade at N°1 belongs to the oldest house in Nîmes. Grab a seat at one of the many terrace-cafes on **Place aux Herbes,** just off Madeleine.

Inside the Musée du Vieux Nîmes.

Where to **Stay**

Hôtel de l'Amphithéâtre The core of this hotel dates from the 18th century, when it was built as a private home. A stay here involves trekking to your room up steep flights of creaking stairs and navigating a labyrinth of corridors. Everything is old, the beds squeak, and the staff long ago grew jaded to the fact that the hotel is less than perfect. But at these prices, who's complaining? *4 rue des Arènes.* ☎ *04-66-67-28-51. http://perso.orange.fr/hotel-amphitheatre/index.htm. 15 units. Doubles 50€–80€. MC, V. Parking 10€. Closed Jan 2–20.*

★★ Imperator Concorde This hotel, the largest and finest in town, is adjacent to Les Jardins de la Fontaine. The artful and cozy but ample rooms have traditional or French furniture, with fluted or cabriole legs in one or another of the Louis styles. Order a meal in the hotel's verdant rear gardens or in a high-ceilinged dining room. *L'Enclos de la Fontaine. Quai de la Fontaine.* ☎ *04-66-21-90-30. www.hotel-imperator.com. 62 units. Doubles 119€–235€. AE, DC, MC, V. Parking 13€.*

★ New Hôtel La Baume One of my favorite nests in Nîmes bears the name of the Marquis de la Baume, whose family built this 17th-century mansion. A magnificent staircase ornaments the interior courtyard and lends the place a sense of grandeur. In contrast to the stately exterior, the guest rooms are hyper-contemporary, usually in tones of soft reds, oranges, and ochers. *21 rue Nationale.* ☎ *04-66-76-28-42. www.new-hotel.com. 34 units. Doubles 130€—230€. AE, DC, MC, V. Parking 9€.*

Bridge to the Past

Dating to 19 B.C., the Pont du Gard aqueduct stands strong, spanning the Gard River, 23km (14 miles) northeast of Nîmes. Its huge stones, fitted together without mortar, form three tiers of arches arranged gracefully into symmetrical patterns. One of the region's

most vivid Roman achievements, it is now a UNESCO World Heritage site. Frédéric Mistral, national poet of Provence and Languedoc, recorded a legend touting that the devil himself constructed the bridge with the promise that he could claim the soul of the first person to cross it. From Nîmes, take N86 to a point 3km (2 miles) from the village of Remoulins, and follow signs.

The Ponte du Garde.

Where to **Dine**

★★★ Alexandre (Michel Kayser) OUTSKIRTS TRADITIONAL FRENCH

The most charming restaurant around is 8km (5 miles) south of Nîmes in an elegantly rustic setting. Chef Michel Kayser amuses and satisfies the palate with dishes such as *île flottante*—a playful savory variation on the French dessert, with truffles and *velouté* of cèpe mushrooms. The dessert trolley and wine list are irresistible. *Rte. de l'Aéroport de Garons.* ☎ *04-66-70-08-99. www.michelkayser.com. Reservations recommended. Mains 28€–54€; lunch menus 38€; dinner menus 42€–95€. AE, DC, MC, V. Tues–Sat 12:30–2:30pm, 7pm–10pm; closed 2 weeks in Feb. From town center, take rue de la République southwest to av Jean-Jaurès; then head south and follow signs to the airport (toward Garons).*

★★ Le Chapon Fin CENTER

TRADITIONAL NÎMES This tavern-restaurant is an institution in Nîmes. Specialties include foie gras with truffles, casserole of roasted lamb and eggplant, sauerkraut, and brandade of codfish. *3 rue du Château-Fadaise.* ☎ *04-66-67-34-73. Reservations required. Mains 16€ menus 22€–30€. MC, V. Noon–2:30pm, 7–10:30pm Mon–Fri; 7–10:30pm Sat.*

The Café Mazurier (see p 176).

★ Le Wine Bar ARENA TRADITIONAL FRENCH

This mahogany-paneled place has leather banquettes evocative of a California saloon from the early 1900s. A restaurateur extraordinaire, Michel Hermet makes his own wine at vineyards that have been associated with his family for many generations. More than 300 varieties of wine are in stock. Typical dishes are magret of duckling, top-notch beefsteaks, and fresh fish, usually grilled. *1 place des Arènes.* ☎ *04-66-76-19-59. Main courses 8.50€–25€; menus lunch 12€–21€; dinner 18€–25€. AE, MC, V. Noon–2pm Tues–Fri; 7–10pm Mon–Sat.*

Shopping in Nîmes

Most of Nîmes' shops are in the center of town, on **rue du Général-Perrier, rue des Marchands, rue du Chapître,** and the pedestrian **rue de l'Aspic** and **rue de la Madeleine.** A Sunday market runs from 8am until 1pm in the parking lot of the **Stade des Costières**—site of most of the town's football (soccer) matches, adjacent to the southern edge of the boulevard *périphérique* that encircles Nîmes. The covered market in **Les Halles** (rue des Halles) is open daily from 7am until 1pm.

St-Rémy

LES MAGNANARELLES

SANS SOUCI

LE ROUGADOU

ST-JOSEPH

QUATRE CANTONS

Office de Tourisme

Cimetière

Canal des Alpilles

To Ruins de Glanum

Church   ✝
Information   ⓘ
Parking   🅿

① Circular Boulevards
② Collégiale St-Martin
③ Maison Natale de Nostradamus
④ Hôtel de Sade–Musée Archéologique
⑤ Hôtel Estrine–Centre d'Art
    Présence Van Gogh
6🅿 Café des Arts
⑦ Musée des Alpilles
⑧ Musée des Arômes et des Parfums
⑨ Monastère St-Paul-de-Mausolée
⑩ Ruines de Glanum

Where to Stay
Château de Roussan 13
Hôtel Les Ateliers de l'Image 15
Le Mas des Carassins 16

Where to Dine
La Cassolette 12
La Maison Jaune 11
Le Jardin de Frédéric 14

At the foot of the mysterious Alpilles hills, elegant St-Rémy is the archetypal Provençal town, with tree-lined boulevards, bubbling fountains, lively squares, atmospheric alleys, and chic residents who have made an art form of posing in cafes. Nostradamus, the physician and astrologer, was born here in 1503. Now it is more closely associated with Dutchman Vincent van Gogh, who committed himself to an asylum just outside town in 1889. Just south of the center, don't miss the ancient ruins of the city of Glanum, which date to the 1st century. START: **St-Rémy is 21km (13 mile) south of Avignon and 75km (47 mile) northwest of Aix-en-Provence.**

❶ ★★ Circular Boulevards. The most vibrant parts of town are the boulevards **Victor Hugo, Mirabeau, Gambetta,** and **Marceau,** which follow St-Rémy's old ramparts and positively burst with cafes, restaurants, and boutiques. **Place de la République** seals the loop with yet more activity and bustling cafe terraces. On Wednesday morning on the streets of the old town, vendors spread out their wares, including spices, olives, fabrics, and crafts. On Saturday morning, a small vegetable market is held near the Eglise St-Martin on Boulevard Marceau.

❷ ★ Collégiale St-Martin. The 14th-century vestiges of this collegiate church line rue Hoche. The rest—aside from the bell tower, which also dates from the 14th century—had to be rebuilt around 1820, when the building caved in. The 5,000-pipe organ, renowned throughout France, is used for summer concerts. ⏲ 30 min. Bd Marceau. ☎ 04-90-92-10-51. Admission free. 9–11am, 3–5pm, but check with tourist office.

❸ Maison Natale de Nostradamus. On December 14, 1503, Nostradamus was born to a wealthy family of merchants in this 15th-century house (no visits—seen from the street only). A doctor adept in astrology, astronomy, and clairvoyance, he

wrote a collection of prophecies (Les Propheties, 1555) construed to have predicted some of history's most pivotal events: the Great Fire of London (1666), the French Revolution (1789), Hitler's birth and rise to power, the assassination of John F. Kennedy, and even the destruction of the space shuttle Challenger. This abode, where he resided for 20 years before studying medicine in Avignon and Montpellier, would have been much larger than what remains today. The surrounding squares, narrow passages, and Renaissance mansions still convey a sense of St-Rémy's famously wealthy past. Rue Hoche.

A shop in St-Rémy.

④ ★★ Hôtel de Sade–Musée Archéologique. This stunning Renaissance mansion belonged to the family of the Marquis de Sade (1740–1814), France's infamous Libertine writer, imprisoned on several occasions for sexual debaucheries. Built on the site of Roman baths, it shows fragments found at Glanum, an impressive array of pre-Roman sculpture, and a stone lintel with grooves once used to display the severed heads of enemies. *Closed until late 2008 for renovations. Rue du Parage.* ☎ *04-90-92-64-04. Check with tourist office for new opening times and admission prices.*

⑤ Hôtel Estrine–Centre d'Art Présence van Gogh. Joseph de Pistoye, judge to the Prince of Monaco, built this handsome mansion in 1748. It takes its name from Louis Estrine, a master rope maker from Marseille who resided here. Built from ashlar masonry, over three stories tall, it pays homage to Vincent van Gogh with permanent temporary exhibitions of his works, reproductions, and letters from Vincent to his brother Theo. *Rue Estrine.* ☎ *04-90-92-34-72. Admission 3.20€; 2.30€ reduced. Late Mar–mid-Oct Tues–Sun 10am–1pm, 3–7pm; mid-Oct–Dec 10:30am–12:30pm, 2–6pm. Closed Jan–late Mar.*

⑥ Café des Arts. The terrace of this cafe has been a center for people-watching since the 1950s. Soak up the hustle and bustle over a cool pastis or a glass of wine (no food is served). *30 bd Victor Hugo.* ☎ *04-90-92-08-50. $.*

⑦ ★ Musée des Alpilles. The former Mistral de Montdragon family mansion is devoted to the arts and traditions of the Alpilles area, with permanent collections on the

The asylum in the monastery of St-Paul-de-Mausolée, where van Gogh convalesced.

landscape, flora and fauna, and tauromachy. The 16th-century galleried courtyard, embellished with a turreted staircase and a 20th-century bust of van Gogh by Ossip Zadkine, is a masterpiece unto itself. 🕐 *45 min. 1 place Flavier.* ☎ *04-90-92-68-24. Admission 3€; 2€ reduced. Tues–Sat & 1st Sun each month 2pm–5pm Nov–Feb, 10am–12pm, 2–6pm Mar–Jun, Sept–Oct (until 7pm Jul–Aug).*

⑧ Musée des Arômes et des Parfums. For thousands of years, Provence has been a center for fragrance and aromatherapy. This unexpected museum recounts that history with a vast collection of perfume bottles and stills, and some heady essential oils. 🕐 *40 min. 34 bd Mirabeau.* ☎ *04-90-92-48-70. Free admission. Daily 10:30am–12:30pm, 2:30–7pm. Sept–Easter closed Sun.*

⑨ ★★★ Monastère St-Paul-de-Mausolée. Van Gogh rendered this asylum's 12th-century cloisters famous when he admitted himself as a patient in 1889, commencing a period of creative fury. Between treatments and moods of despair, he produced some 150 paintings in 1 year here, including *Starry Night*, *Olive Trees,* and *Cypresses*. The complex is a former Augustinian and Franciscan monastery that became a convalescent hospital in the 18th century. A self-guided walking tour leads visitors through van Gogh's daily paces, through the cloisters and surrounding gardens, indicating various spots that are still recognizable in his paintings. ⏱ *1 hr. Av. Van Gogh.* ☎ *04-90-92-77-00. Admission 4€, 3€ reduced; under 12 free. Apr–Oct daily 9:30am–6:45pm; Nov–Mar daily 10:30am–4:45pm.*

🔟 ★★★ **Ruines de Glanum.** In a bucolic spot, with rolling panoramas across the Durance Valley to Mont Ventoux, lie the mishmash vestiges of a Gallo-Roman settlement. Ruins include a triumphal arch from the time of Julius Caesar; the oldest cenotaph in Provence, called the Mausolée des Jules (a mausoleum raised to honor the grandsons of Augustus); and some impressive remains from a Gallo-Greek town of the 2nd century

A statue of van Gogh at St-Paul-de-Mausdée.

B.C. Some parts are undergoing renovation work until late 2008. ⏱ *1½ hr. Ave Van Gogh/Rte des Baux. From St-Rémy, take D5 1.5km (1 mile) south, following signs to les antiques* ☎ *04-90-92-23-79. Admission 6.50€; 4.50€ reduced. Apr–Sept daily 10am–6:30pm; Oct–Mar Tues–Sun 10:30am–5pm.*

A fountain in St-Rémy.

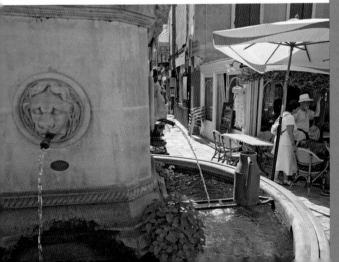

Where to **Stay**

★★ Château de Roussan

You'll be pressed to find more breathtakingly romantic lodgings than this château, Notstradamus's ancestral home, just outside St-Rémy. It's set in 15 acres of parkland, where swans swim in the lake, budgies fly around the greenhouse, and streams gurgle over rounded pebbles. Furnished with antiques, rooms are an excellent value—even if some bathrooms are sparse. *Route de Tarascon.* 📷 *04-90-92-11-63. www.chateau-de-roussan.com. 22 units. Doubles 60€–125€. MC, V.*

★★★ Hôtel Les Ateliers de l'Image

This radical photography-themed hotel, in a cinema converted by Roland Paillat, is an absolute treat. Rooms strike an ideal balance between comfort and

The Hotel Les Ateliers de l'Image.

Inside the Hôtel Les Ateliers.

concept—the tree-house suite, for instance, has its own private tree-house. The gardens are beautifully landscaped, with pools and even a sushi bar. *36 bd Victor Hugo.* 📷 *04-90-92-51-50. www.hotelphoto.com. 32 units. Doubles 165€–305€. AE, MC, V.*

★★★ Le Mas des Carassins

CENTER/GLANUM This converted 19th-century farmhouse is an oasis of calm, with views onto the Alpilles; a magnificent, lavender-filled garden, shaded by century-old olive trees; a pool; an excellent restaurant; and individually decorated, rustic rooms that leave you feeling pampered. *1 chemin Gaulois.* 📷 *04-90-92-15-48. www.masdescarassins.com. 14 units. Doubles 99€–188€ w/breakfast. AE, MC, V.*

Where to **Dine**

★ **La Cassolette** OLD QUARTER
REGIONAL Hidden away in the
heart of St-Rémy's old quarter, this
little old house serves decadent
regional cuisine, fresh from the
market. *53 rue Carnot.* ☎ *04-90-92-
40-50. Mains 14€–20€. No credit
cards. Noon–2pm, 7–10pm Tues–Sun.
Closed Nov–1 Feb & public holidays.*

★★ **La Maison Jaune** CENTER
PROVENCAL This local haunt
charms with its yellow façade and
two-story shaded terrace. Food is
fresh, flavorful, and inventive, with
dishes such as sardines roasted
with fennel, or roast pigeon on a
bed of red cabbage, drizzled with
hazelnut oil. *15 rue Carnot.* ☎ *04-
90-92-56-14. Mains 14€–25€. MC, V.
Wed–Sat noon–2pm, 7–10pm; Tues
7–10pm. Closed some evenings in
winter; closed Jan–Mar.*

The chef at La Maison Jaune.

Le Jardin de Frédéric CENTER
FRENCH Diners tuck into inventive
delights such as lamb in garlic sauce
and saffron flavored cod soufflé
here at this pretty green-painted

villa. *8 bd Gambetta.* ☎ *04-90-92-
27-76. A la Carte 25€–30€. MC,
V. 7–10:30pm Thurs; noon–2pm,
7–10:30pm Fri–Wed.*

Outdoor seating at La Maison Jaune.

St-Tropez

1 The Port

2 Café Sénéquier

3 The Beaches

4 La Ponche Quarter

5 Château Suffran

6 Môle Jean-Réveille

7 La Tarte Tropézienne

8 Place des Lices

9 Musée de l'Annonciade

10 Maison des Papillons

11 Citadelle

Where to Stay

Bastide de St-Tropez 24

Hôtel La Ponche 12

Hôtel Sube 16

Where to Dine

Le Café 23

Le Girelier 13

Spoon Byblos 25

Shopping

Autour des Oliviers 19

Galeries Tropéziennes 20

Jacqueline Thienot 21

Le Dépôt 22

Nightlife

Café de Paris 14

Le Bar du Port 15

Le Papagayo 18

Le VIP Room 17

Les Caves du Roy 26

At its most **Bacchanalian,** between May and September, St-Tropez is as steamy and sun-kissed as ever. The Brigitte Bardot vehicle, *And God Created Woman,* may have put St-Tropez on the tourist map, but Colette also lived here, and Anaïs Nin famously posed for a little cheesecake on the beach in 1939 in a Dorothy Lamour–style bathing suit. In summer, artists, composers, novelists, and the film colony still drop anchor here in extortionately expensive yachts. The rest of the year, however, St-Tropez goes back to doing what it knows best: being a simple port, for simple (if not monied) folk, with a darling old historic center. **START: St-Tropez is 37km (23 miles) southwest of Fréjus and 50km (31 miles) east of Hyères.**

St-Tropez's lively harbor.

1 ★★★ **The Port.** Fishing boats, commercial vessels, and luxury yachts moor in this harbor while their owners disappear into St-Tropez's narrow streets lined with pink and yellow houses. Every year the port fills with more than 800 boats and 10,000 crew members for the annual Mediterranean regatta. Behind the tourist office, the **Porte de la Poissonnerie**—with its tiny fish market dressed in colorful mosaics and marble slabs—is the entrance to the old town and the Place aux Herbes miniature fruit, vegetable, and flower market.

2 **Café Sénéquier.** This legendary cafe is historic, venerable, snobbish, and, at its worst, dauntingly stylish.

But no trip to St-Trop' is complete without a stop here. *Quai Jean-Jaurès.* ☎ 04-94-97-00-90. $.

3 ★★ **kids** **The Beaches.** St-Tropez has the hottest Riviera beaches. The best for families are closest to the center, including the **Plage de la Bouillabaisse** and **Plage des Graniers.** More daring are the 9.5km (6 miles) crescents at **Plage des Salins** and at **Plage de Pampelonne,** with its riotous cash-only club **La Voile Rouge** (☎ 04-94-79-84-34)—the most outrageous, sexiest, and exhibitionist of the beaches (leave the kids at home). **Plage des Jumeaux** (☎ 04-94-55-21-80) is another active beach, drawing in families

The beach in St-Tropez.

with its playground equipment. Notoriously decadent **Plage de Tahiti,** a strip of golden sand long favored by exhibitionists, occupies the north end of the 5.5km (3 mile)-long Pampelonne. Gay men tend to gravitate to **Coco Beach** in Ramatuelle, about 6.5km (4 miles) from the center of St-Tropez.

④ ★★★ **La Ponche Quarter.** *Ponche*—or *pouncho* in Provençal—means point or extremity. Tucked between the port and the citadel, this district is the oldest and prettiest part of town, once inhabited by fishermen and artists.

A sunbather.

⑤ **Château Suffran.** On Place de l'Hôtel de Ville (City Hall), the massive 16th-century tower is all that remains of the Château Suffran, home to the seigneurs of St-Tropez. It houses occasional art and photography exhibitions.

⑥ ★ **Môle Jean-Réveille.** For sweeping vistas along the coastline, head to this stone jetty. It was destroyed during the Allied landings in 1944, rebuilt in 1950, and extended in 1966. The beacon at the end is an exact replica of the original, dating from 1837.

⑦ ★★ **La Tarte Tropézienne.** St-Tropez's famous eponymous cake was invented here by Polish baker Alexandre Micka. It is a sponge-like cake, flavored with orange-blossom, filled with cream-custard, and sprinkled with icing sugar. Delightful! *Place des Lices.* ☎ *04-94-97-71-42. www.tarte-tropezienne-traiteur.com. Daily 6:30am–10pm.*

⑧ ★★ **Place des Lices.** After the port, this is St-Tropez's second hub—a favorite local meeting place, lined with restaurants, plane trees, and sandy patches for playing *boules.* A market is held here every Tuesday and Saturday morning.

Lively Place des Lices.

9 ★★★ **Musée de l'Annonciade.** Near the harbor, this museum occupies the former chapel of the Annonciade. It houses one of the Riviera's finest collections of post-Impressionist masters, many of whom depicted the port of St-Tropez. The collection includes works such as Van Dongen's *Women of the Balustrade*, as well as paintings and sculpture by Pierre Bonnard, Henri Matisse, Georges Braque, Raoul Dufy, Maurice Utrillo, Georges Seurat, André Derain, and Aristide Maillol. ⏱ *45 min. Place Grammont.* ☎ *04-94-17-84-10. 6€; 4€ 12–18 yrs; under 12 free. Wed–Mon 10am–noon, 2–6pm. Closed Nov & public holidays.*

10 ★ **Maison des Papillons.** Hidden down a narrow alley, this Provençal house is filled with mounted butterflies. Entomologist

The *Bravades* of St-Tropez

Every year from May 16th to 18th, St-Tropez becomes a sea of red and white—the colors of the Corsairs—as locals celebrate the bravery *(bravade)* of their patron Saint Tropez. St. Paul converted the Roman citizen Tropes to Christianity. Refusing to renounce his faith before the Romans, he was decapitated, and his body set to sea. It washed up on the shores of St-Tropez, where the residents worshiped him as a martyr. Twenty-one shots of gunpowder mark the beginning of the celebrations, including a religious parade, conducted in traditional dress, with much merrymaking.

Where to Drop Euros in St-Trop

Most shops in St-Tropez are tucked in out-of-the-way corners of the old town. Big names include Hermès, Sonia Rykiel, and Dior. For discounts, **Le Dépot** (Boulevard Louis-Blanc; ☎ 04-94-97-80-10) sells secondhand designer clothes, some still with original tags. **Galeries Tropéziennes** (56 rue Gambetta; ☎ 04-94-97-02-21) crowds hundreds of gift items—some worthwhile, some silly—into its showrooms near Place des Lices. **Jacqueline Thienot** (12 rue Georges-Clemenceau; ☎ 04-94-97-05-70) maintains an inventory of Provençal antiques prized by dealers from as far away as Paris. For wooden carvings, head to **Autour des Oliviers** (2 Place de l'Ormeau; ☎ 04-94-97-64-31), which stocks large inventories of kitchen utensils, pottery, and gift items carved from yellow-and-brown wood.

Dany Lartigue (son of the photographer J. H. Lartigue) has collected more than 25,000 specimens from all four corners of the earth—all displayed in an informative and artistic manner. ⏱ *30 min. 9 rue Etienne-Berny.* ☎ *04-94-97-63-45. http:// maisondespapillons.ifrance.com. Admission 3.05€. Wed–Mon 10am–12pm, 2–6pm (until 7pm Jun–Aug).*

⑪ kids Citadelle. At the top of a steep, touristy street, the citadel is a fine example of 16th- and 17th-century military architecture. Today it houses a somewhat forlorn marine museum, but it's worth a visit for the spectacular views from the ramparts over the Bay of St-Tropez, Ste-Maxime, and the Maure hills. ⏱ *30 min. La Citadelle.* ☎ *04-94-97-59-43. Museum admission 4€; free under 8. Wed–Sun 10am–12:30pm, 1:30–6:30pm.*

*Mounted butterfly specimens at the **Maison des Papillons**.*

Where to **Stay**

★★★ Bastide de St-Tropez

NORTH This pink *mas* (country house) is an elegant, friendly oasis for those who can afford to splurge here, north of Place des Lices, in an exotic garden that overlooks a swimming pool. Rooms are smothered in plush fabrics, many have a private terrace, and the restaurant (dine by the pool or in the beautiful glass veranda) serves fine Provençal cuisine. *Route des Carles.* ☎ *04-94-55-82-55. www. bastide-saint-tropez.com. 26 units. Double 360€. AE, MC, V.*

★ Hôtel La Ponche

PORT This family-run hotel is the most discreet and charming establishment in town, with the least celebrity ostentatiousness. Filled with the original airy paintings of Jacques Cordier, who died in 1978, the redecorated rooms are well equipped and open onto sea views. Sun-colored walls with subtle lighting lend a homey feel. *Port des Pécheurs.* ☎ *04-94-97-02-53. www.laponche.com. 18 units. Doubles 150€–555€. AE, MC, V. Parking 21€. Closed Nov–mid-Feb.*

The pool at the Bastide de St-Tropez.

★★ Hôtel Sube

PORT If you want to be right on the port, in an ideal location for ship- and celebrity-watching, this might be your first choice. It's directly over the Café de Paris bar, in the center of a shopping arcade. Rooms are small but comfortable. *15 Quai Suffren.* ☎ *04-94-97-30-04. www.hotel-sube.com. 28 units. Doubles 115€–290€. AE, MC, V. Parking nearby 30€.*

Where to Party

On the lobby level of the Hôtel Byblos, **Les Caves du Roy,** avenue Paul-Signac (☎ 04-94-97-16-02, www.byblos.com), is the most self-consciously chic nightclub in St-Tropez. Entrance is free, but drink prices begin at a whopping 18€. **Le Papagayo,** in the Résidence du Nouveau-Port, rue Gambetta (☎ 04-94-97-76-70), is one of the largest nightclubs in town with psychedelic 1960s-inspired decor. Adjacent is the all steeled, chromed, and mirrored **Le VIP Room** (☎ 04-94-97-78-92). On the port, the **Café de Paris's** long zinc bar (☎ 04-94-97-00-56) is frequently propped up by joyous locals; and **Le Bar du Port,** adjacent to the Café de Paris (☎ **04-94-97-00-54**), is breezy, airy, and almost obsessively hip and self-consciously trendy.

The Best Cities & Towns

Where to **Dine**

★★ **Le Café** LICES *FRENCH* The terrace of this trendy restaurant, with its famous zinc bar, doubles as a sports ground for watching the endless matches of *boules* played on the sand in front. The blackboard menu is the best value, with plenty of well-cooked fish. The desserts never fail here either. *5 Place des Lices.* ☎ *04-94-97-44-69. www. lecafe.fr. Menus 26€–45€. AE, MC, V. Daily noon–2:30pm, 7–10pm.*

★ **Le Girelier** PORT *PROVENÇAL* The blue-and-white color scheme has become the trademark of this coveted restaurant. They serve many versions of grilled fish, as well as bouillabaisse (for two). Also on the menu are brochette of monkfish, a kettle of spicy mussels, and *pipérade* (a Basque omelette with pimientos, garlic, and tomatoes). *Quai Jean-Jaurès.* ☎ *04-94-97-03-87. Mains 28€–82€; menus 42€. AE, DC, MC, V. Daily* noon–2pm, 7:30–10:30pm. Closed Nov–Feb 15.

★★★ **Spoon Byblos** PORT *FRENCH/INTERNATIONAL* This is one of many entrepreneurial statements by Alain Ducasse, widely considered the world's greatest chef—or at least the most acclaimed. Originally launched in Paris, Spoon draws special inspiration from the food of Catalonia, Andalusia, and Morocco, and offers more than 300 wines. Dig into shrimp and squid consommé with a hint of jasmine and orange, then try delectable lamb couscous or spit-roasted John Dory. The chef's favorite cheesecake is to die for. *Hôtel Byblos, av. Paul-Signac.* ☎ *04-94-56-68-00. www.byblos.com/spoon byblos. Reservations required. Mains 30€–40€. AE, DC, MC, V. 8–11:30pm Thur–Tues. Closed lunchtime & mid-Oct–mid-Apr.* ●

Le Café waiter.

The
Savvy Traveler

Before You Go

Government Tourist Offices

AIGUES-MORTES pl St Louis 30220; ☎ 04-66-53-73-00; www.ot-aigues mortes.fr

AIX-EN-PROVENCE 2 pl Gén de Gaulle 13100; ☎ 04-42-16-11-61; www.aixenprovencetourism.com

ANSOUIS pl Château 84240; ☎ 04-90-09-86-98; www.ansouis.fr

ANTIBES 11 pl Gén de Gaulle 06600; ☎ 04-97-23-11-11; www.antibesjuanlespins.com

ARLES esplanade Charles de Gaulle/bd Craponne 13200; ☎ 04-90-18-41-20; www.tourisme.ville-arles.fr

AVIGNON 41 cours Jean Jaures 84000; ☎ 04-32-74-32-74; www.ot-avignon.fr.

BANDOL allée Alfred Vivien 83150; ☎ 04-94-29-41-35; www.bandol.org

LES BAUX DE PROVENCE rue Porte Mage 13520; ☎ 04-90-54-34-39; www.lesbauxdeprovence.com

BIOT: 46 rue St Sébastien 06410; ☎ 04-93-65-78-00; www.biot.fr

BORMES LES MIMOSAS 1 pl Gambetta 83230; ☎ 04-94-01-38-38; www.bormeslesmimosas.com

BRIGNOLES carrefour Europe 83170; ☎ 04-94-72-04-21; www.officedetourisme-brignoles.com

CAGNES Place du Dr Maurel 06800; ☎ 04-92-02-85-05; www.cagnes-tourisme.com

CANNES Bureau Palais des Festivals La Croisette; ☎ 04-92-99-84-22; www.palaisdesfestivals.com

CARPENTRAS pl Aristide Briand 84200; ☎ 04-90-63-00-78; www.carpentras-ventoux.com

CASSIS quai des Moulins 13260; ☎ 08-92-25-98-92; www.ot-cassis.com

Idling outside the Monte Carlo Casino.

LA CASTELLET Hôtel de Ville 83330; ☎ 04-94-98-57-90; www.tourisme83.com

CAVAILLON 79 pl François Tourel 84300; ☎ 04-90-71-32-01; www.cavaillon-luberon.fr

CHATEAUNEUF-DU-PAPE pl Portail 84230; ☎ **04-90-83-50-34**

DRAGUIGNAN Av. Lazare Carnot 83300; ☎ 04-98-10-51 -05; www.dracenie.com

EZE pl Gén de Gaulle 06360; ☎ 04-93-41-26-00; www.eze-riviera.com

FONTAINE DE VAUCLUSE chemin Fontaine 84800; ☎ 04-90-20-32-22; www.oti-delasorgue.fr

FRÉJUS 325 r Jean Jaurès 83600; ☎ 04-94-51-83-83; www.frejus.fr

GORDES pl Château 84220; ☎ 04-90-72-02-75; www.gordes-village.com

GRASSE 22 cours Honoré Cresp 06130; ☎ 04-93-36-66-66; www.grasse.fr

HYÈRES av Ambroise Thomas 83400; ☎ 04-94-01-84-50; www.hyeres-tourisme.com

L'ISLE-SUR-LA-SORGUES pl Liberté 84800; ☎ 04-90-38-04-78; www.oti-delasorgue.fr

LORGUES 1 bd République 83510; ☎ **04-94-73-92-37**

MALAUCÈNE Place de la Mairie 84340; ☎ **04-90-65-22-59**

MARSEILLE 4 La Canebière 13001; ☎ 04-91-13-89-00; www.marseille-tourisme.com

MENTON 8 av Boyer 06500; ☎ 04-92-41-76-76; www.menton.fr

MONACO 2 a bd Moulins 98000; ☎ **04-93-75-87 -67;** www.visit monaco.com

MOUGINS 96 av Moulin de la Croix 06250; ☎ 04-93-75-87-67; www.mougins-coteazur.org

NICE 5 promenade des Anglais 06302; ☎ 08-92-70-74-07; www.nicetourisme.biz

Nîmes 6 r Auguste 30000;
☎ 04-66-58-38-00; **www.ot-nimes.fr**

La Rayol pl Michel Goy 83820;
☎ 04-94-05-65-69; **www.tourismevar.com**

Roussillon pl Poste 84220; ☎ 04-90-05-60-25; **www.roussillon-provence.com**

St-Jean-Cap-Ferrat av Denis Semeria 06230; ☎ 04-93-76-08-90; **http://saintjean-capferrat.com**

Stes-Maries-de-la-Mer 5 av Van Gogh 13460; ☎ 04-90-97-82-55; **www.saintesmaries.com**

St-Paul de Vence 2 r Grande 06570; ☎ 04-93-32-86-95; **www.saint-pauldevence.com**

Salon de Provence 56 cours Gimon 13300; ☎ 04-90-56-27-60; **www.visitsalondeprovence.com**

St-Raphaël Quai Albert 1er 83702; ☎ 04-94-19-52-52; **www.saint-raphael.com**

St-Rémy pl Jean Jaurès 13210; ☎ 04-90-92-05-22; **www.saintremy-de-provence.com**

St-Tropez Quai Jean Jaurès 83990; ☎ 08-92-68-48-28; **www.ot-saint-tropez.com**

Sault en Provence av Promenade 84390; ☎ 04-90-64-01-21; **www.saultenprovence.com**

Taradeau 1 av St Joseph 83460; ☎ **04-94-73-01-07**

Toulon pl Raimu 83000; ☎ 04-94-18-53-00; **www.toulontourisme.com**

La Turbie Place Detras; ☎ 04-93-41-21-15; **www.ville-la-turbie.fr**

Vaison-la-Romaine av Chanoine Sautel 84110; ☎ 04-90-36-02-11; **www.vaison-la-romaine.com**

Vallauris av Frères Roustan 06220; ☎ 04-93-63-21 07; **www.vallauris-golfe-juan.com**

Venasque Grande Rue 84210; ☎ 04-90-66-11-66; **www.venasque.fr**

Vence 8 pl Grand Jardin 06140; ☎ 04-93-58-06-38; **www.vence.fr**

When to Go

In terms of weather, the most idyllic months for visiting the south of France are May and June. Though the sun is intense, it's not uncomfortable. Coastal waters have warmed up by then, so swimming is possible. The resorts have come alive after a winter slumber but aren't yet overrun. The flowers and herbs in the countryside are at their peak, and driving conditions are ideal. In June, it remains light until around 10:30pm.

The hottest, most overcrowded times are July and August, when seemingly half of Paris shows up in the briefest of bikinis. Reservations are difficult to get, discos are blasting, and space is tight on the popular beaches. The worst traffic jams on the coast occur all the way from St-Tropez to Menton.

Aside from May and June, our favorite time is September and even early October, when the sun is still hot and the great hordes have headed back north.

In November, the weather is often pleasant, especially at midday, though some of the restaurants and inns you'll want to visit might take a sudden vacation: It's the month when many chefs and hoteliers elect to go on their own vacations after a summer of hard work.

Winter on the Riviera is being rediscovered, and many visitors (particularly retired people or those with leisure time) elect to visit then. If you don't mind the absence of sunbathing and beach life, this could be a good time to show up. However, some resorts, like St-Tropez, become ghost towns when the cold weather comes, though Cannes, Nice, Monaco, and Menton remain active year-round.

The Mediterranean coast has the driest climate in France. Most rain falls in spring and autumn. Summers

AVERAGE TEMPERATURE & RAINFALL IN PROVENCE & THE RIVIERA

MARSEILLE	JAN	FEB	MAR	APR	MAY	JUNE
Temp. (°F)	44	46	50	55	62	70
Temp. (°C)	6.7	7.8	10	13	17	21
Rainfall (in.)	1.9	1.6	1.8	1.8	1.8	1.0
Rainfall (cm)	4.8	4.1	4.6	4.6	4.6	2.5
	JULY	AUG	SEPT	OCT	NOV	DEC
Temp. (°F)	75	74	69	60	51	46
Temp. (°C)	24	23	21	16	11	7.8
Rainfall (in.)	0.6	1.0	2.5	3.7	3.0	2.3
Rainfall (cm)	1.5	2.5	6.4	9.4	7.6	5.8

NICE	JAN	FEB	MAR	APR	MAY	JUNE
Temp. (°F)	48	49	52	55	62	68
Temp. (°C)	8.9	9.4	11	13	17	20
Rainfall (in.)	3.0	2.9	2.9	2.5	1.9	1.5
Rainfall (cm)	7.6	7.4	7.4	6.4	4.8	3.8
	JULY	AUG	SEPT	OCT	NOV	DEC
Temp. (°F)	74	74	70	62	54	50
Temp. (°C)	23	23	21	17	12	10
Rainfall (in.)	0.7	1.2	2.6	4.4	4.6	3.5
Rainfall (cm)	1.8	3	6.6	11.2	11.7	8.9

are comfortably dry—beneficial to humans but deadly to vegetation, which (unless it's irrigated) often dries and burns up in the parched months.

Provence dreads *le mistral* (a cold, violent wind from the French and Swiss Alps that roars south down the Rhône Valley). It most often blows in winter, sometimes for up to 2 weeks.

Festivals, Special Events & Public Holidays

In France, holidays are known as *jours fériés*. Shops and many businesses close, but hotels and emergency services remain open.

The main holidays—a mix of secular and religious—include New Year's Day (Jan 1), Easter Sunday and Monday (early Apr), Labor Day (May 1), V-E Day in Europe (May 8), Whit Monday (mid-May), Ascension Thursday (40 days after Easter), Bastille Day (July 14), Assumption of the Blessed Virgin (Aug 15), All

Saints' Day (Nov 1), Armistice Day (Nov 11), and Christmas (Dec 25).

For more information on the following, call the local tourist office, listed above.

JAN. Monte Carlo Motor Rally. The world's most venerable car race.

Fête de Citron. Menton's fun and famous lemon festival.

Fête du Mimosa. See the pretty yellow flowers adorn floats and people alike in Bormes-les-Mimosas.

FEB. Carnival of Nice. Float processions, parades, confetti battles, boat races, street music and food, masked balls, and fireworks are part of this ancient celebration. Come armed with a hotel reservation. Mid-February to early March.

MAR. Féria Pascale (Easter Bullfighting Festival), Arles. This is a major bullfighting event that includes not only appearances by the greatest matadors, but also *abrivados* and *bodegas* (wine stalls).

APR. **La Fête des Gardians** (Camargue Cowboys' Festival), Arles. This event features a procession of Camargue cowboys through the streets of town. Activities feature various games involving bulls, including Courses Camarguaises, in which competitors have to snatch a rosette from the horns of a bull. On the last Sunday in April and in May.

MAY. **Cannes Film Festival.** Movie madness transforms this city into the kingdom of the media deal, with daily melodramas acted out in cafes, on sidewalks, and in hotel lobbies. It's great for voyeurs. Reserve early and make a deposit. Getting a table on the Carlton terrace is even more difficult than procuring a room. Admission to some of the prestigious films is by invitation only. There are box-office tickets for the less important films, which play 24 hours. For information, contact the **Association Française du Festival International du Film,** 3 rue Amélie, 75007 Paris ☎ **01-53-59-61-00;** www. festival-cannes.org. Mid-May.

Festival des Musiques d'Aujourd'hui, Marseille. This festival presents the works of young French and European composers in music and dance. For more information, call **Experimental Music Groups of Marseille** at ☎ **04-96-20-60-10;** www.gmem.org. Mid-May.

Monaco Grand Prix de Formule. Hundreds of cars race through the narrow streets and winding roads in a surreal blend of high-tech machinery and medieval architecture. For more information, call ☎ **377-93-15-26-00;** www.acm.mc. Late May.

JUNE. **Festival Aix en Musique,** Aix-en-Provence. Concerts of classical music and choral singing are held in historic buildings, such as the Théâtre de l'Archevêché and the Hôtel Maynier d'Oppède. For more information, call ☎ **04-42-17-34-34;** www.festival-aix.com. Late June to late July.

Festival de Marseille Méditerranée. This festival features concerts and recitals of music and song from the entire Mediterranean region. Theater and dance are also presented, along with special exhibitions in the city's main museums. For more information, call ☎ **04-91-13-89-00** or 04-91-99-00-20. Late June to late July.

JULY. **Bastille Day.** Celebrating the birth of modern-day France, the festivities in the south reach their peak in Nice with street fairs, pageants, fireworks, and feasts. The day begins with a parade down the promenade des Anglais and ends with fireworks in the Vieille Ville. No matter where you are, by the end of the day you'll hear Piaf warbling "La Foule" (The Crowd), the song that celebrated her passion for the stranger she met and later lost in a crowd on Bastille Day. Similar celebrations also take place in Cannes, Arles, Aix, Marseille, and Avignon. July 14.

Nuit Taurine (Nocturnal Bull Festival), St-Rémy. At this festival, the focus is on the age-old allure of bulls and their primeval appeal to roaring crowds. *Abrivados* involve bulls in the town square as "chaperoned" by trained herders on horseback; *encierros* highlight a Pamplona-style stampeding of bulls through the streets. Music from local guitarists and flaming torches add drama. For more information, call ☎ **04-90-92-05-22.** Mid-July.

Nice Jazz Festival. This is the biggest, flashiest, and most prestigious jazz festival in Europe, with world-class entertainers. Concerts begin in early afternoon and go on until late at night (sometimes all night in the clubs) on the Arènes de Cimiez, a picturesque hill above the city. Reserve hotel rooms way in advance. For information, contact the Grand Parade du Jazz, c/o the tourist office of Nice ☎ **08-92-70-74-07;** www.nicejazzfest.com. Mid-July.

Les Chorégies d'Orange, Orange. One of southern France's most important lyric festivals presents oratorios and choral works by master performers whose voices are amplified by the ancient acoustics of France's best-preserved Roman amphitheater. For more information, call ☎ **04-90-34-24-24;** www.choregies.asso.fr. Early July to early August.

Festival d'Avignon. One of France's most prestigious theater events, this world-class festival has a reputation for exposing new talent to critical acclaim. The focus is usually on avant-garde works in theater, dance, and music by groups from around the world. Make hotel reservations early. For information, call ☎ **04-90-27-66-50;** www.festival-avignon.com. Last 3 weeks of July.

AUG. **Féria de St-Rémy,** St-Rémy. This event features a 4-day celebration of bulls with *abrivado* and *encierro* (see the Nuit Taurine entry, above), branding, and Portuguese bull fighting (matadors on horseback). For more information, call ☎ **04-90-92-05-22.** Mid-August.

SEPT. **Féria des Prémices du Riz** (Rice Harvest Festival), Arles.

Bullfights are held in the amphitheater with leading matadors, and a procession of floats makes its way along the boulevard des Lices; there are also traditional events with cowboys and women in regional costume. For more information, call ☎ **04-90-18-41-20.** Early September.

OCT. **Foire Internationale de Marseille.** Join the throngs who flock to see this annual fair—a jamboree of music, crafts, sport, and entertainment from all over the world. Late September to late October.

NOV. **Fête du Prince,** Monaco. Fabulous fireworks over the harbor mark the end of Monaco's National day on the 19th November.

DEC. **Foire de Noël,** Mougins. Hundreds of merchants, selling all manner of Christmas ornaments and gifts, descend on Mougins in Provence, to herald in the Christmas spirit. For more information, call ☎ **04-93-75-87-67.** Mid- to late December.

Fête de St-Sylvestre (New Year's Eve), nationwide. Along the Riviera, it's most boisterously celebrated in Nice's Vieille Ville around place Garibaldi. At midnight, the city explodes. Strangers kiss strangers, and place Masséna and the promenade des Anglais become virtual pedestrian malls. December 31.

Getting **There**

By Plane
From Paris, if you're heading for the French Riviera, your connecting flight will probably land you in Nice's international airport, **Aéroport Nice–Côte d'Azur.** There are also small airports in Avignon, Marseille, Montpellier, Nîmes, and Toulouse.

All major airlines fly to Paris from the U.S. cities listed below. Once you fly into **Orly** or **Charles de Gaulle,** you must take **Air France** (☎ **800/237-2747;** www.airfrance.com) to reach your destination in Provence or the Riviera. From Orly and Charles de Gaulle, there are 20 flights per day to Marseille and to Nice, 16 to Toulouse, and 4 from Monday to Friday and 2 Saturday and Sunday to Avignon.

American Airlines (☎ **800/433-7300;** www.aa.com) offers daily flights to Paris from Dallas–Fort Worth, Chicago, Miami, Boston, and New York. **Delta Airlines** (☎ **800/241-4141;** www.delta.com) flies nonstop to Paris from Atlanta, Cincinnati, and New York. All these flights depart late enough in the day to permit transfers from much of Delta's vast North American network. Note that Delta is the only American airline offering nonstop service from New York to Nice.

Continental Airlines (☎ **800/231-0856;** www.continental.com) flies nonstop to Paris daily from Newark and four to seven times a week, depending on the season, from Houston. **US Airways** (☎ **800/428-4322;** www.usairways. com) offers daily nonstop service from Philadelphia to Paris.

Air France (☎ **800/237-2747;** www.airfrance.com) offers a daily nonstop flight between New York and Nice and also offers regular flights between Paris and such North American cities as Newark; Washington, D.C.; Miami; Atlanta; Boston; Cincinnati; Chicago; New York; Houston; San Francisco; Los Angeles; Montréal; Toronto; and Mexico City.

Canadians usually choose the **Air Canada** (☎ **888/247-2262** in the U.S. and Canada; www.air canada.com) flights to Paris from Toronto and Montréal that depart every evening. Two of Air Canada's flights from Toronto are shared with Air France and feature Air France aircraft.

By Train
The world's fastest trains link some 50 French cities, allowing you to get from Paris to just about anywhere else in the country in hours. With 39,000km (24,233 miles) of track and about 3,000 stations, **SNCF** (French National Railroads; www.voyages-sncf.com) is fabled for its on-time performance. You can travel in first or second class by day and in couchette by night. Many trains have dining facilities.

INFORMATION If you plan to travel a lot on European railroads, get the latest copy of the **Thomas Cook Timetable of European Passenger Railroads.** This 500-plus-page book documents all of Europe's main passenger rail services with detail and accuracy. It's available online at www.thomas cookpublishing.com.

In the United States: For more information and to purchase rail passes before you leave, contact **Rail Europe** (☎ **877/272-RAIL;** www.raileurope.com).

In Canada: Call Rail Europe at ☎ **800/361-RAIL.**

In London: SNCF has offices at Rail Europe, 179 Piccadilly, London W1V 0BA (☎ **0870/584-8848**).

In Paris: For information or reservations, go online (www. voyages-sncf.fr) or call ☎ **36-35.** You can also go to any local travel agency. A simpler way to buy tickets is to use the *billetterie* (ticket machine) in every train station. If you know your PIN, you can use a credit card to buy your ticket.

FRANCE RAIL PASSES Working cooperatively with SNCF, Air Inter Europe, and Avis, Rail Europe offers three flexible rail passes that can reduce travel costs considerably.

The **France Railpass** provides unlimited rail transport in France for any 3 days within 1 month, at $267 in first class and $227 in second. You can purchase up to 6 more days for an extra $34 to $39 per person per day. Children 4 to 11 travel for half price.

Have a Seat

Remember that a train ticket does not guarantee you a seat; it merely gets you from one place to another. On crowded trains during peak times, you'll have to make a **seat reservation** (and pay for the privilege) if you want to guarantee a seat somewhere other than atop your luggage. Seat reservations cost 10€ ($13) per person.

The **France Rail 'n' Drive Pass,** available only in North America, combines good value on both rail travel and Avis car rentals, and is best used by arriving at a major rail depot and then striking out to explore the countryside by car. It includes the France Railpass (see above) and use of a rental car. You have 1 month to complete your travel on this pass that grants 2 days of unlimited train travel and 2 days of car rental with unlimited mileage in France. Prices for an economy car begin at $325.

The best deal if you're traveling in France with a friend—or even 3 or 4 friends—is the **France Saverpass,** granting 3 days of unlimited travel in a 1-month period. The cost is $228 per person first class or $195 second class. For travelers age 60 and over there is the **France Senior Pass,** which allows 3 days

of unlimited first-class travel within 1 month for $243. Up to 6 more additional days may be purchased at $35 per day. There's also a **France Youthpass** for travelers 25 or under, granting 3 days of unlimited train travel within a month. The cost is $198 in first class or $167 in second class.

EURAILPASS   The Eurailpass permits unlimited first-class rail travel in any country in western Europe except the British Isles (good in Ireland). Passes are available for purchase online (www.eurail.com) and at various offices/agents around the world. It is strongly recommended that you purchase passes before you leave home as not all passes are available in Europe; also, passes purchased in Europe will cost about 20% more. Numerous options are available for travel in France. See the website for details and options.

Getting **Around**

The most charming Provençal villages and best country hotels always seem to lie away from the main cities and train stations. Renting a car is usually the best way to travel once you reach the south of France, especially if you plan to explore in depth and not stick to the standard route along the coast.

However, the south of France also has one of the most reliable bus and rail transportation systems in Europe. Trains connect all the major cities and towns, such as Nice and Avignon. Where the train leaves off, you can most often rely on local bus service.

By Car

Driving time in Europe is largely a matter of conjecture, urgency, and how much sightseeing you do along the way. The driving time from Marseille to Paris is a matter of national pride, and tall tales abound about how rapidly the French can do it. With the accelerator pressed to the floor, you might conceivably make it in 7 hours, but we always make a 2-day journey of it.

CAR RENTALS   To rent a car, you'll need to present a passport, a driver's license, and a credit card. You'll also have to meet the minimum-age requirement of the company. (For the least expensive cars, this is 21 at Hertz, 23 at Avis, and 25 at Budget. More expensive cars might require that you be at least 25.) It usually isn't obligatory within France, but certain companies have at times asked for the presentation of an International Driver's License, even though this is becoming increasingly superfluous in western Europe.

For rentals of more than 7 days, in most cases cars can be picked up in one French city and dropped off in another, but there are additional charges. Still, Budget's rates are among the most competitive, and its cars are well maintained. **Budget** (www.budget.com) has numerous locations in southern France, including those in **Avignon** at the airport (☎ 04-90-87-17-75); in **Marseille** at the airport (☎ 04-42-14-24-55), and at 40 bd. De Plombières (☎ 04-91-64-40-03); in **Nice** at the airport (☎ 04-93-21-36-50); and in **Toulouse** at the airport (☎ 05-61-71-85-80).

Hertz (www.hertz.com) is also well represented, with offices in **Avignon** at the airport (☎ 04-90-84-19-50) and at the train station (☎ 04-32-74-62-80); in **Marseille** at the airport (☎ 08-25-09-13-13) and at 15 bd. Maurice-Bourdet (☎ 04-91-14-04-24); in **Montpellier** at the airport (☎ 04-67-20-04-64); in **Nice** at the airport (☎ 08-25-34-23-43); and in **Toulouse** at the airport (☎ 05-61-71-27-09) and at the rail station (☎ 05-62-73-39-47). When making inquiries, be sure to ask about promotional discounts.

Avis (www.avis.com) has offices in **Avignon** at the airport (☎ 04-90-87-17-75) and at the railway station (☎ 04-90-27-96-10); in **Marseille** at the airport (☎ 04-42-14-21-67) and at 267 bd. National (☎ 04-91-50-70-11); in **Montpellier** at the airport (☎ 04-67-20-14-95) and at the railway station (☎ 04-67-92-92-00); in **Nice** at the airport (☎ 04-93-21-36-33) and at Place Massena, 2 av. des Phocéens (☎ 04-93-80-63-52); and in **Toulouse** at the airport (☎ 05-34-60-46-50) and at the train station (☎ 05-61-62-50-40).

National (www.nationalcar.com) is represented in France by Europcar, with locations in **Avignon** at the train station (☎ 04-90-27-30-07); in **Marseille** at the airport (☎ 04-42-14-24-90) and at the St-Charles train station, 96 blvd. Rabatau (☎ 04-91-83-05-05); in **Montpellier** at the airport (☎ 04-67-15-13-47); in **Nice** at the airport (☎ 04-93-21-80-90); and in **Toulouse** at the airport (☎ 05-61-30-00-01). You can rent a car on the spot at any of these offices, but lower rates are available by making advance reservations from North America.

Two United States–based agencies that don't have France offices but act as booking agents for France-based agencies are **Kemwel Drive Group** (☎ 877/820-0668 or 207/842-2285; www.kemwel.com) and **Auto Europe** (☎ 888/223-5555; www.autoeurope.com). These can make bookings in the United States only, so call before your trip.

Driving in Provence

- **On the road, routes are designated by destinations,** even though they're numbered on most maps. If you're planning to take the D22 to St-Rémy, for instance, don't look for signs for the D22; you won't find them. Follow signs for St-Rémy instead.
- **Directionals appear then disappear for long distances.** But rest assured: Once you've followed a signpost toward your destination, you can follow that road until further notice—even if it means covering several kilometers without seeing another directional. It's easy to feel like you've taken a wrong turn, but your destination will reappear—provided you were on the right track to start with!
- **Be prepared for many turnabouts,** or rotaries, on the roads. You'll get used to driving them after a few turns, but the first time can be harrowing as you're looking for directionals and oncoming traffic at once.

GASOLINE Known in France as *essence*, gas is expensive for those accustomed to North American prices. All but the least expensive cars usually require an octane rating that the French classify as *essence super*, the most expensive variety. Depending on your car, you'll need either leaded *(avec plomb)* or unleaded *(sans plomb)*.

Beware the mixture of gasoline and oil called *mélange* or *gasoil* sold in some rural communities; this mixture is for very old two-cycle engines.

Note: Sometimes you can drive for miles in rural France without encountering a gas station, so don't let your tank get dangerously low.

DRIVING RULES Everyone in the car, in both the front and the back seats, must wear seat belts. Children under 12 must ride in the back seat. Drivers are supposed to yield to the car on their right, except where signs indicate otherwise, as at traffic circles.

If you violate the speed limit, expect a big fine. Those limits are about 130kmph (81 mph) on

expressways, about 100kmph (62 mph) on major national highways, and 90kmph (56 mph) on country roads. In towns, don't exceed 60kmph (37 mph).

MAPS For France as a whole, most motorists opt for Michelin map 989. For regions, Michelin publishes a series of yellow maps that are quite good. Big travel-book stores in North America carry these maps, and they're commonly available in France (at lower prices). In this age of congested traffic, one useful feature of the Michelin map is its designations of alternative *routes de dégagement,* which let you skirt big cities and avoid traffic-clogged highways. They also highlight routes in green, which are recommended for tourists.

Another recommended option is *Frommer's Road Atlas Europe.*

BREAKDOWNS/ASSISTANCE A breakdown is called *une panne* in France. Call the police at ☎ **17** anywhere in France to be put in touch with the nearest garage. If the breakdown occurs on an expressway, find the nearest roadside emergency phone box, pick up the phone, and put a call through. You'll be connected to the nearest breakdown service facility.

By Train

Rail services between the large cities of Languedoc-Roussillon and Provence and the French Riviera are excellent. If you don't have a car, you can tour all the major hot spots by train. Of course, with a car you can also explore the hidden villages, such as the little Riviera hill towns; but for short visits with only major stopovers on your itinerary, such as Nice and Avignon, the train should suffice. Service is fast and frequent.

The ancient city of Nîmes, one of the most visited in the area, is a major rail terminus, a stop on the rail link between Bordeaux and Marseille. Marseille, the largest city in the south of France, has rail connections with all major towns on the Riviera as well as with the rest of France. Seventeen high-speed TGVs arrive from Paris daily (trip time: 3 hr. 15 min.). The major rail transportation hub along the French Riviera is Nice, although Cannes also enjoys good train connections. Nice and Monaco are linked by frequent service, and in summer about eight trains per day connect Nice with the rapid TGV train from Paris to Marseille. In winter, the schedule is curtailed depending on demand. The most visited Riviera destination in the east, Monaco also has excellent rail links along the Riviera.

The website for the national rail service is **www.voyages-sncf.com**. Otherwise, call ☎ **36-35**, or **08-92-35-35-35** when outside France.

By Bus

While the trains are faster and more efficient if you are traveling between major cities, both the towns and villages of Provence, including the French Riviera, are linked by frequent bus service. You can use the network of buses that link the villages and hamlets with each other and the major cities to get off the beaten path.

Plan to take advantage of the bus services from Monday to Saturday when they run frequently; very few buses run on Sunday.

Sodetrav (☎ **08-25-00-06-50** or 04-94-12-55-12; www.sodetrav.fr) has some of the best bus routes, and is especially strong in the western Riviera, taking in stopovers at such destinations as St-Raphaël, St-Tropez, Arles, Grasse, Avignon, Marseille, Nimes, and Hyères. One of its most popular routes is the run between Toulon and St-Tropez, with 20 buses daily.

Fast **Facts**

AUTO CLUB An organization designed to help motorists navigate their way through breakdowns and motoring problems is **Club Automobile de Provence,** 149 bd. Rabatau, 13010 Marseille (☎ **04-91-78-83-00;** www.automobileclub provence.com).

BUSINESS HOURS Business hours here are erratic. Most banks are open Monday to Friday from 9:30am to 4:30pm. Many, particularly in smaller towns or villages, take a lunch break at varying times. Hours are usually posted on the door. Most museums close 1 day a week (often Tues), and they're generally closed on national holidays. Usual hours are from 9:30am to 5pm. Some museums, particularly the smaller and less-staffed ones, close for lunch from noon to 2pm. Most French museums are open on Saturday; many are closed Sunday morning but open Sunday afternoon. Again, refer to the individual museum listings.

Generally, offices are open Monday to Friday from 9am to 5pm, but always call first. In larger cities, stores are open from 9 or 9:30am (often 10am) to 6 or 7pm without a break for lunch. Some shops, particularly those operated by foreigners, open at 8am and close at 8 or 9pm. In some small stores, the lunch break can last 3 hours, beginning at 1pm.

CUSTOMS Customs restrictions for visitors entering France differ for citizens of the European Union and for citizens of non-E.U. countries.

FOR U.S. CITIZENS For specifics on what you can bring back, download the invaluable free pamphlet *Know Before You Go* online at **www. cbp.gov,** or contact the **U.S. Customs Border Protection (CBP),** 1300 Pennsylvania Ave. NW, Washington, DC 20229 (☎ **877/ 287-8867),** and request the pamphlet.

FOR CANADIAN CITIZENS For a clear summary of **Canadian** rules, write for the booklet *I Declare,* issued by the **Canada Customs and Revenue Agency** (☎ **800/461-9999** in Canada, or 204/983-3500; www. cbsa-asfc.gc.ca).

FOR U.K. CITIZENS For more information, contact HM Revenue & Customs at ☎ **0845/010-9000** (from outside the United Kingdom, 02920/ 501-261), or consult the website www.hmrc.gov.uk.

FOR AUSTRALIAN CITIZENS A helpful brochure available from Australian consulates or Customs offices is *Know Before You Go.* For more information, call the **Australian Customs Service** at ☎ **1300/363-263,** or log on to www.customs.gov.au.

FOR NEW ZEALAND CITIZENS Request the free pamphlet *New Zealand Customs Guide for Travellers, Notice no. 4* from **New Zealand Customs Service,** The Customhouse, 17–21 Whitmore St., Box 2218, Wellington (☎ **04/473-6099** or 0800/428-786; www.customs.govt.nz).

CELLPHONES If your phone has GSM (Global System for Mobiles) capability, and you have a world-compatible phone, you should be able to make and receive calls in Provence and the Riviera. Check with your service operator first to see if your phone has this capability. Call charges can be high. Alternatively, you can rent a phone through **Cellhire** (www.cell hire.com, www.cellhire.co.uk, and www.cellhire.com.au). After a simple online registration, they will ship a phone (usually with a U.K. number) to your home or office. Usage charges can be astronomical, so read the fine print. U.K. mobiles work in France; call your service provider before departing your home country to ensure that the international call bar has been switched off and to check call charges, which can be extremely high. Also remember that you are charged for calls you receive on a U.K. mobile used abroad.

DRUGSTORES In France they are called *pharmacie.* Pharmacies take turns staying open at night and on Sunday; the local Commissariat de Police will tell you the location of the nearest one.

ELECTRICITY In general, expect 200 volts, 50 cycles, though you'll encounter 110 and 115 volts in some older hotels. Adapters are needed to fit sockets.

EMBASSIES & CONSULATES All embassies are in Paris. The Embassy and Consulate of the **United States** are at 2 av. Gabriel (☎ 01-43-12-22-22; Métro: Concorde). The United States also maintains a consulate in Marseille at Place Varian Fry, 13286 Marseille (☎ 04-91-54-92-00).The Embassy of **Canada** is at 35 av. Montaigne (☎ 01-44-43-29-00; Métro: Franklin-D-Roosevelt). The Embassy of the United Kingdom is at 35 rue du Faubourg St-Honoré (☎ 01-44-51-31-00; Métro: Concorde), open Monday through Friday from 9:30am to 1pm and 2:30 to 5pm; the U.K. consulate, 18 bis rue d'Anjou (☎ 01-44-51-31-02; Métro: Concorde), is open Monday through Friday from 9am to noon and 2 to 5pm.

EMERGENCIES   In an emergency while at a hotel, contact the front desk to summon an ambulance or do whatever is necessary. But for something like a stolen wallet, go to the police station in person. Otherwise, you can get help anywhere in France by calling ☎ 17 for the police or ☎ 18 for the fire department *(pompiers)*. For roadside emergencies, see "Getting Around," earlier in this chapter.

LEGAL AID   The French government advises foreigners to consult their embassy or consulate (see above) in case of an arrest or similar problem. The staff can generally offer advice on how you can obtain help locally and can furnish you with a list of local attorneys. If you are arrested for illegal possession of drugs, the U.S. embassy and consular officials cannot interfere with the French judicial system. A consulate can advise you only of your rights.

LOST & FOUND   Use the following numbers in France to report your lost or stolen credit card: **American Express** (call collect), ☎ 336/393-1111; www.americanexpress.com; **MasterCard,** ☎ 08-00-90-13-87; www.mastercard.com; **Visa,** ☎ 08-00-90-11-79; www.visaeurope.com.

Your credit card company may be able to wire you a cash advance immediately or deliver an emergency card in a day or two.

MAIL   Most post offices in France are open Monday through Friday from 8am to 7pm, and Saturday from 8am to noon. Allow 5 to 8 days to send or receive mail from your home. Airmail letters to North America cost .85€ for 20 grams. Letters to the U.K. cost .54€ for up to 20 grams. An airmail postcard to North America or Europe (outside France) costs .85€.

You can exchange money at post offices. Many hotels sell stamps, as do local post offices and cafes displaying a red TABAC sign outside.

POLICE   Call ☎ 17 anywhere in France.

RESTROOMS   If you're in dire need, duck into a cafe or brasserie. It's customary to make some small purchase if you do so. France still has many "hole-in-the-ground" toilets, so be forewarned.

TAXES   As a member of the European Union, France imposes a value-added tax (VAT) on many goods and services. The standard VAT on merchandise is 19.6%. Refunds are made for the tax on certain goods, but not on services. The minimum purchase is 175€ for nationals or residents of countries outside the E.U.

TELEPHONE   The French use a **télécarte,** a phone debit card, which you can purchase at rail stations, post offices, and other places. Sold in two versions, it allows you to use either 50 or 120 charge units by inserting the card into the slot of most public phones. Depending on the type of card you buy, the cost starts at 10€ and goes up from there.

If possible, avoid making calls from your hotel; some French establishments double or triple the charges.

TIME The French equivalent of daylight saving time lasts from around April to September, which puts it 1 hour ahead of French winter time. Depending on the time of year, France is 6 or 7 hours ahead of U.S. Eastern Standard Time.

TIPPING All bills, as required by law, are supposed to say *service compris*, which means that the tip has been included. Here are some general guidelines: For **hotel staff,** tip 1.05€ to 1.50€ for every item of baggage the porter carries on arrival and departure, and 1.50€ per day for the chambermaid. You're not obligated to tip the concierge, doorperson, or anyone else—unless you use his or her services. In cafes, **waiter** service is usually included. For **porters,** there's no real need to tip extra after their bill is presented, unless they've performed some special service. Tip **taxi drivers** 10% to 15% of the amount on the meter. In theaters and restaurants, give **cloakroom attendants** at least .75€ per item. Give **restroom attendants** about .30€ in nightclubs and such places. Give **cinema and theater ushers** about .30€. Tip the **hairdresser** about 15%, and don't forget to tip the person who gives you a shampoo or manicure 2€. For **guides** of group visits to sights, 1€ to 1.50€ per person is reasonable.

Survival **French**

Basic French Vocabulary & Phrases

ENGLISH	FRENCH	PRONUNCIATION
Yes/No	Oui/Non	wee/nohn
Okay	D'accord	*dah*-core
Please	S'il vous plait	seel voo play
Thank you	Merci	*mair*-see
You're welcome	De rien	duh ree-*ehn*
Hello (during daylight)	Bonjour	bohn-*jhoor*
Good evening	Bonsoir	bohn-*swahr*
Goodbye	Au revoir	o ruh-*vwahr*
What's your name?	Comment vous appellez-vous?	ko-*mahn*-voo-za-pell-ay-*voo*?
My name is	Je m'appelle	*jhuh* ma-pell
How are you?	Comment allez-vous?	kuh-mahn-tahl-ay-*voo*?
So-so	Comme ci, comme ça	kum-*see*, kum-*sah*
I'm sorry/excuse me	Pardon	pahr-*dohn*

Getting Around/Street Smarts

ENGLISH	FRENCH	PRONUNCIATION
Do you speak English?	Parlez-vous anglais?	par-lay-voo-ahn-*glay*?
I don't speak French	Je ne parle pas français	jhuh ne parl pah frahn-*say*

ENGLISH	FRENCH	PRONUNCIACION
I don't understand	Je ne comprends pas	jhuh ne kohm-*prahn* pas
Could you speak more loudly/more slowly?	Pouvez-vous parler plus fort/plus lentement?	Poo-*vay* voo par-lay ploo for/ploo lan-te-*ment?*
What is it?	Qu'est-ce que c'est?	kess-kuh-*say?*
What time is it?	Qu'elle heure est-il?	kel uhr eh-*teel?*
What?	Quoi?	kwah?
How? or What did you say?	Comment?	ko-*mahn?*
When?	Quand?	kahn?
Where is?	Où est?	oo eh?
Who?	Qui?	kee?
Why?	Pourquoi?	poor-*kwah?*
here/there	ici/là	ee-*see*/lah
left/right	à gauche/à droite	a goash/a drwaht
straight ahead	tout droit	too-*drwah*
Fill the tank (of a car), please	Le plein, s'il vous plaît	luh plan, seel-voo-*play*
I want to get off at	Je voudrais descendre à	jhe voo-*dray* day-son drah-ah
airport	l'aéroport	lair-o-*por*
bank	la banque	lah bahnk
bridge	le pont	luh pohn
bus station	la gare routière	lah *gar* roo-tee-*air*
bus stop	l'arrêt de bus	lah-*ray* duh boohss
by means of a car	en voiture	ahn vwa-*toor*
cashier	la caisse	lah kess
cathedral	le cathedral	luh ka-tay-*dral*
church	l'église	lay-*gleez*
driver's license	le permis de conduire	luh per-*mee* duh con-*dweer*
elevator	l'ascenseur	lah sahn *seuhr*
entrance (to a building or a city)	une porte	ewn port
exit (from a building or a freeway)	une sortie	ewn sor-*tee*
gasoline	du pétrol/ de l'essence	duh pay-*troll*/ de lay-*sahns*
hospital	l'hôpital	low-pee-*tahl*
luggage storage	la consigne	lah kohn-*seen*-yuh
museum	le musée	luh mew-*zay*
no smoking	défense de fumer	day-*fahns* de fu-may
one-day pass	le ticket journalier	luh tee-*kay* jhoor-nall-ee-*ay*
one-way ticket	l'aller simple	lah-*lay* sam-pluh

The Savvy Traveler

ENGLISH	FRENCH	PRONUNCIATION
police	la police	lah po-lees
round-trip ticket	l'aller-retour	lah-lay re-toor
second floor	le premier étage	luh prem-ee-ehr ay-taj
slow down	ralentir	rah-lahn-teer
store	le magasin	luh ma-ga-zehn
street	la rue	lah roo
subway/ underground/ Tube	le Métro	le may-tro
telephone	le téléphone	luh tay-lay-phone
ticket	un billet	uh bee-yay
toilets	les toilettes/les WC	lay twa-lets/les vay-say

Necessities

ENGLISH	FRENCH	PRONUNCIATION
I'd like	Je voudrais	jhe voo-dray
a room	une chambre	ewn shahm-bruh
the key	la clé (la clef)	la clay
How much does it cost?	C'est combien?/ Ça coûte combien?	say comb-bee-ehn?/ sah coot comb-bee-ehn?
That's expensive	C'est cher/chère	say share
Do you take credit cards?	Est-ce que vous acceptez les cartes de credit?	es-kuh voo zaksep-tay lay kart duh creh-dee?
I'd like to buy	Je voudrais acheter	jhe voo-dray ahsh-tay
aspirin	des aspirines/ des aspros	deyz ahs-peer-een/ deyz ahs-proh
gift	un cadeau	uh kah-doe
map of the city	un plan de ville	uh plahn de veel
newspaper	un journal	uh zhoor-nahl
phone card	une carte téléphonique	uh cart tay-lay-fone-eek
postcard	une carte postale	ewn cart pos-tahl
road map	une carte routière	ewn cart roo-tee-air
stamp	un timbre	uh tam-bruh

Numbers & Ordinals

ENGLISH	FRENCH	PRONUNCIATION
zero	zéro	zare-oh
one	un	oon
two	deux	duh
three	trois	twah
four	quatre	kaht-ruh
five	cinq	sank
six	six	seess
seven	sept	set
eight	huit	wheat
nine	neuf	noof
twenty	vingt	vehn

ENGLISH	FRENCH	PRONUNCIATION
forty	quarante	ka-*rahnt*
fifty	cinquante	sang-*kahnt*
one hundred	cent	sahn
one thousand	mille	meel

The Calendar

ENGLISH	FRENCH	PRONUNCIATION
Sunday	dimanche	dee-*mahnsh*
Monday	lundi	luhn-*dee*
Tuesday	mardi	mahr-*dee*
Wednesday	mercredi	mair-kruh-*dee*
Thursday	jeudi	jheu-*dee*
Friday	vendredi	vawn-druh-*dee*
Saturday	samedi	sahm-*dee*

Food & Menu

ENGLISH	FRENCH	PRONUNCIATION
I would like to eat	Je voudrais manger	jhe voo-*dray* mahn-*jhay*
Please give me	Donnez-moi, s'il vous plaît	doe-nay-*mwah*, seel-voo-*play*
a bottle of	une bouteille de	ewn boo-*tay* duh
a cup of	une tasse de	ewn tass duh
a glass of	un verre de	uh vair duh
a plate of	une assiette	ewn ass-ee-*et*
breakfast	de le petit-déjeuner	duh luh puh-*tee* day-zhuh-*nay*
a cocktail	un apéritif	uh ah-pay-ree-*teef*
the check/bill	l'addition/la note	la-dee-see-*ohn*/la noat
dinner	le dîner	luh dee-*nay*
a knife	un couteau	uh koo-*toe*
a napkin	une serviette	ewn sair-vee-*et*
a spoon	une cuillère	ewn kwee-*air*
a fork	une fourchette	ewn four-shet
Cheers!	A votre santé!	ah vo-truh sahn-*tay*!
fixed-price menu	un menu	uh may-*new*
Is the tip/service included?	Est-ce que le service est compris?	ess-ke luh ser-*vees* eh com-*pree*?
Waiter!/Waitress!	Monsieur!/Mademoiselle!	muh-*syuhl*/ mad-mwa-*zel*
wine list	une carte des vins	ewn cart day *van*
appetizer	une entrée	ewn en-*tray*
main course	un plat principal	uh plah pran-see-*pahl*
tip included	service compris	sehr-*vees* cohm-*pree*
wide-ranging sampling of the chef's best efforts	menu dégustation	may-*new* day-gus-ta-see-*on*

Index

See also Accommodations and Restaurant indexes, below.

Photo **Credits**

The new way to
get AROUND town.

Make the most of your stay. Go Day by Day!

The all-new Day by Day series shows you the best places to visit and the best way to see them.

- Full-color throughout, with hundreds of photos and maps
- Packed with 1–to–3–day itineraries, neighborhood walks, and thematic tours
- Museums, literary haunts, offbeat places, and more
- Star-rated hotel and restaurant listings
- Sturdy foldout map in reclosable plastic wallet
- Foldout front covers with at-a-glance maps and info

The best trips start here. **Frommer's®**

Explore over 3,500 destinations.

TOKYO — 7766 miles

LONDON — 3818 miles

TORONTO — 4682 miles

SYDNEY — 5087 miles

NEW YORK — 4947 miles

LOS ANGELES — 2556 miles

HONG KONG — 5638 miles

Frommers.com makes it easy.

Find a destination. ✓ Book a trip. ✓ Get hot travel deals.
Buy a guidebook. ✓ Enter to win vacations. ✓ Listen to podcasts.
Check out the latest travel news. ✓ Share trip photos and memories.
And much more.

Frommers.com